ONE LAST SWIM

RL Monsheimer

Books Academy LLC
5900 Balcones Drive Suite 100
Austin, Texas 78731
Hotline: (254) 800-1183

Ordering Information:
Quantity sales. Special discounts are available on quantity purchases by corporations, associations, and others. For details, contact the publisher at the address above.

Printed in the United States of America.

ISBN-13: Softcover   978-1-964929-07-1
           eBook   978-1-964929-08-8

Library of Congress Control Number: 2024913334

Table of Contents

CHAPTER ONE

Who I am.

My name is John Peters, I am a senior swimmer for Alderson-Broadus College in West Virginia, I will graduate shortly this year. I know my fiancé Julia will be making a big team party as I get ready for the Academic Athlete award that if not for her, I know I would never have won. So every athlete has a beginning and then eventually and end, I am writing this story because, my career is near an end, just found out from my coach, that while I thought he might not take me to conference one of our swimmers is injured so I get to compete for one last time.

The meet has a weird order, I am going to swim 100 fly on Thursday, 200 fly on Friday, and hardest event on Saturday. The ugly 400 IM. I hope I can finish somewhere in the top 16 in each event I have done that a couple of times in my career, and what the heck hopefully my final swim Saturday will let me score. Julia encouraged me to write this story so when we are older, we will have something to remember for our kids. Only one group knows that I proposed to Julia just before Valentine's Day, I proposed to her, and she accepted but since she is a year behind me, we were not going to get married until the summer. Our world is changing as Julia is graduating in 7 semesters to graduate with me, and at the same time, we are going to be parents for the first time later this year after graduation.

So who is John Peters?

John Peters was born in August 1986, to parents Mark and Sharon. My parents met while both of them were attending college near each other in Catonsville, MD. My dad at the time was attending Catonsville Community College, while my mom was an honor student at UMBC. I have a sister Angela, who was born in 1987, right before my dad lost his job at B. Green and Company when they shut down. I have a really odd family life as my dad was Roman Catholic and my Mom was very conservative Jewish upbringing, so we got lots of holidays as kids. My parents compromised on religion and Dad converted to Judaism in order to get married and we now practice Reform Judaism, not nearly as religious as my grandfather David, who is still a practicing rabbi. I was Bar Mitzvahs when I was 13, which made my Grandfather happy, but that year really pissed off my swim coach, losing 2 afternoons per week.

I grew up in Maryland near Baltimore a city called Arbutus. Arbutus is a small town near Route 1 and about 2 miles outside the city. Typical factory town with small houses, most people work for one of the breweries, B. Green and Company, or a few other blue collar companies. If you look today the craft brewery in the area. From what I understand the area was populated because the railroads used to have a station there where trains from DC and Baltimore met to go west to the coal mines of West Virginia.

We have a typical small town main street, with a grocery store, 7-11, an old movie theatre, a couple restaurants, hardware store and a few other things like a bakery and a florist. My favorite place to go is Paul's Restaurant inexpensive food and you get to hear all the gossip of the local town. A lot of people meet there and you can see local politicians pictures and sometimes on Saturdays you see them meeting in person. In fact, if the stories are true, my parents met at Paul's. I always wondered why my family doing well why they chose to stay here as opposed to Pikesville, where a lot of my Mom's family lives. Maybe because she was the only one that married outside of the Conservative Jewish faith, she decided she did not want to have to hear it every day.

I grew up and went to Arbutus Elementary school and Arbutus Middle School, my parents did not have enough money for private school and my mother prevailed that I was not allowed to attend a Catholic private school. I went to Lansdowne High School where I would like to say I was a great student but that would be a stretch, I was basically a B student, truthfully I would rather have been in the pool than going to school. I went to Baltimore Hebrew Congregation, the oldest synagogue in the Baltimore area.

As far as swimming, my main swim team was the NBAC, North Baltimore Aquatic Club, a club famous for a swimmer named Michael Phelps, who won more gold medals than any other athlete. I remember seeing him in the elite practices. I was not as gifted as Michael Phelps but really good enough to get a partial scholarship at AB. My summer swim team was Five Oaks Swim Club, where I was definitely one of the better swimmers even got to a few local all-star events, and I have the medals somewhere in my parents' house. I'm really not sure where the swimming came from, because my Dad played baseball and even played collegiately at Towson University, before he had to withdraw to help support my grandmother and attended Catonsville Community College. I was told he was a gifted second baseman, and possible had a chance at the minors. So I guess somehow I got my desire to compete from Dad and still not sure who introduced me to swimming.

For those that did not know, the DC Area and Baltimore areas have had a lot of history with athletes in swimming going to the Olympics, getting major college scholarships, and a few like me still getting a partial scholarship to smaller colleges. Recent Maryland Olympic swimmers include Michael like I said earlier, and over in the DC area Katie Ledecky, and Jack Conger. I think the DC area started this tradition with Melissa Belotte, who won a gold medal in the Munich Olympics, where another Jewish swimmer, Mark Spitz was the star of the games. Those were the games where the Israeli athletes were murdered by terrorists. Did I mention that I am Jewish just like Mark Spitz.

Well now you know the basics about me, again this writing is really not a book but something that I can remember for my children so they can know what it was like for this half-Jewish boy to go to school, compete and date the woman of his dreams. Julia as I said before is my light and without her, I have no idea of how I could have completed my college experience.

CHAPTER TWO

The Courtship of Mom and Dad

My mom was born in Baltimore and spent most of her life in Pikesville, MD. For those that don't know much about Pikesville, it was the suburb of Baltimore that many Jewish families lived. She was born to Rabbi and Mrs. (Bella) Goldbaum, at University of Maryland medical center June 1966. Honestly, I am not that good with dates, always forget mom and dad's birthdays. My sister Angela always reminds me about 3 days before, so I get a present for them. Sharon Goldbaum had fairly curly dark blond hair, not very unusual for Polish children. She was the second of four children, with an older sister and 2 younger brothers.

Sharon was a very good student and was a merit scholar in graduating from Pikesville High School. I understand that she had a near 4.0 average and had taken a couple of classes at junior college before she graduated. I know that she was Bat Mitzvahs because Grandpa says she was, and mom never talks about her training as a kid. I also know that mom was offered a lot of scholarships at prestigious schools like Cornell, but grandpa said that no Jewish Girl should live away from home, so she registered at UMBC, the Baltimore County version of the University of Maryland. I know that she graduated, Summa Cum Laude, with a degree in English and a minor in teaching. She was also really good at math and chemistry but decided to teach in the Baltimore County area mostly private schools.

Ok, so you are wondering if my mom was an athlete, well the answer is she was a book worm, and I doubt she ever did much other than some ballet as a small child. I have pictures of this tiny girl in her costume, funny pictures.

So, you can understand my mom, she is about 5'2" and maybe 120 pounds, even now that she is now in her late 40's. She now runs every day, and I think she plays tennis a couple times a week up in Pikesville, area.

My Dad (Mark Peters, nicknamed MP) was born in May 1965 to Brian and Melissa Peters. Both of my Grand Parents were Roman Catholics growing up and met and fell in love during High School. They met when both of them went to the St Augustine School in Elkridge, MD and stayed in Elkridge the rest of their lives. St Augustine was founded in 1857, a small but really cool looking school. My Dad just like his parents graduated from the same High school and played baseball for them as I stated before. He was recruited by Towson State College, now known as Towson State University, and while some of the sports at Towson are division 1, it is really low division 1. Dad was a decent but not outstanding student, but I did hear he got some awards for his community service while in high school. Dad went to Elkridge Elementary school, walked every day he says. He went to another unique name school for Junior High school, Elkridge Landing, which is now called a middle school. I guess his parents were keen on his high school being a Catholic experience so that is why he went to the Catholic High School.

Dad learned how to play baseball at the local CYO leagues which took him all the way to High school. I know he won several championships and as I stated earlier, he was a really good second baseman not great on power but at 5' 10" he is not a big athlete, just like a lot of Hispanic infielders though a stick enough to get on base does not clear the bases. I understand for the time he was somewhat of a workout freak, so he was strong despite only weighing 165 pounds. I was told he would workout lifting and such at least an hour a day. So that is why many of our friends say I got my sports ability from him, I guess the patience he had as a ball player did not rub off on me, I like the action of swimming, boom and go.

My Dad has a younger brother by 2 years, Uncle Roger, a great guy moved to Orlando, Florida and works for Disney in management, has three kids and is definitely a devout Catholic. He is on the Board of Directors of his church in Orlando. Uncle Roger got his degree in Marketing management at Loyola. I guess I got my idea of getting a business degree from Uncle Roger, but not much else as Dad and he fought over dad's conversion to Judaism, and they spoke rarely after that. I bet Uncle Roger would laugh that I am engaged to a nice Catholic girl talk about full circle.

My parents told me the story about how they met so many times, that I think I can share with everyone the story of how they met. My Mom was a junior at UMBC, and her friend Judy, went to lunch at Paul's restaurant in nearby Arbutus on a Thursday afternoon.

She said she knew it was Thursday, because if it had been Friday, she would have been rushing to get through the day to get home by dark for the Sabbath meal and services. I call her Aunt Judy, since she used to come over so much when we were kids, she was single, and got married when she was like 38, to a nice real estate lawyer. Aunt Judy is pretty outgoing, I still think it is her that actually got my parents together.

She has 2 small children, having given birth right before her 40th birthday to twins 1 boy and 1 girl.

My Dad was a sophomore at Catonsville Community College at the time, he had finished his first year at Towson, and with my grandpa passing away was working part- time at the A&P, (Super Fresh), supermarket in Elkridge, and taking 3 classes per semester at Catonsville. For some reason that Thursday, he was there with his friend Jerry Gross, who I think knew Judy, from the same social circles. I get the feeling they either dated at one point or something else because I have asked the question, and both have changed the subject. Jerry and Judy may have dated but from what I have heard from both my dad and mom they never talked much together, and Jerry met a nice Russian immigrant and has two children living in Columbia, MD. Jerry is a realtor covers Baltimore and Howard counties and apparently makes a lot of money. At least that is what Mom says.

Paul's Restaurant, Arbutus, MD March, Hi Judy, let's get a table in the front of the restaurant, I like to watch the people go by. No problem, Sharon, I can't believe I actually got you out to lunch. Well, you know how it is, between the weekends at home and the classes and clubs at UMBC, I just don't have a lot of time to spend. Sharon, I see you have everything but time for a relationship. Sure Judy, just what I need a guy to distract me from school.

Good afternoon, Mark, let's make sure we get a table at Paul's before they are all taken. Sure Jerry, but remember I have to get back to class I need to improve my grade in calculus and need as much time as possible to study. Jerry asked Mark where he wanted to sit, and he said somewhere near the front, the back gets noisy, and some people still smoke back there. I see a table near a couple of girls, and I think I know one of them Jerry said. My dad apparently came back, is that a good thing or a bad thing and apparently it was a little of both.

Hi Judy, how are you doing, Jerry supposedly said. Judy said I am doing fine and don't ask me out on a date. Judy I am already dating someone else and is it ok if we sit next to your table or will I bring down your mood. Judy said it was ok, and besides not that many small tables left in the front of the building.

My dad said I guess you two know each other but I am Mark Peters, and your friend is who. My mom then turned around and introduced herself as Sharon Goldbaum. My dad was immediately stricken with my mom the instant she turned around, with her dark blond curls, green eyes, dimple and a trim figure. Judy said Mark don't I know you from the area, and Mark said you probably do I have done a lot of volunteer work with the firefighters in the area doing collections of money for muscular dystrophy every summer, but I was a baseball player and we played in a lot of fields in the area.

My Aunt Judy said they must have been immediately attracted to each other as they turned chairs to each other and proceeded to have what was the first date with both Jerry and I with them.

So here I am going to just say Mark and Sharon, because easier than saying Mom and Dad as they were just Mark and Sharon at that time.

Sharon asked Mark where he was going to school, and he said he was at Towson last year but was at Catonsville Community College this year to help out my mother.

Sharon asked why, well because my dad passed away at the brewery last year and money is tight even though they paid his life insurance it is enough for mom for about a year so I am working at A&P part-time and getting 3 classes in if I can get past Calculus, it is really kicking my butt. I played baseball at Towson and was like the first guy off the bench, but I don't have the time now to play. I do get to work out some at the gym. Unless I can figure out this calculus class my education may come to an end, I am getting a C- and mid-terms are next week, and just need to get a B in this class somehow.

Mark wanted to ask many questions of Sharon, and funny thing all he asked was how Judy and she knew each other. Well, you would have thought he had asked for a dissertation. Judy and I have been friends since grade school, and we went to the same Sunday school for years and the same high school. Judy decided to go to college close by, my decision to go to UMBC was my parents' idea, they did not want their daughter to be out of town away from religious upbringing. I really wanted to go to Ivy League and was accepted to Cornell but either money or parental decisions stopped that. The good thing is because I had really good grades, I was offered an academic scholarship at UMBC. I will have to take some classes at UM either College Park or downtown because UMBC does not have the chemistry classes I want. I wish my parents had let me go away to college, but they are really strict about what Jewish girls can do. Sharon asked what my major was, and I said at this point business marketing but needed calculus as my math course as it was required if I wanted to do my minor of biology.

My Aunt Judy said, they barely got to order anything for lunch as Mark and Sharon kept talking for what must have been an hour.

Mark asked if he knew anyone that could tutor him in Calculus as he really needed some help, and Sharon apparently jumped at the opportunity and said that she could help him. Mark said I can't pay what some of the tutors are asking, they want like $50, an hour, any way you can help me out, money is tight at home, about half of what I earn goes to my family for food and the rest pays for school. I am working at a grocery store because as an employee we get discounts on food purchased at the store and that stretches our money. We are trying to stretch the insurance from work to get three years instead of one and the 25,000 of other life insurance was used for a funeral and a plot. That left us with about 20,000, which we then paid off the mortgage of the house. Sharon said this is what I will charge, either I can charge you like $15, per hour or you can use it to take me out to a movie during the next week. With that discussion the dating apparently of my 2 parents started.

Thinking back on it now, I now see why I was attracted to Julia, both of the Peter's men needed a strong partner to get us through academically. Just like Julia, we had an instant attraction, while mom is a dark blond, Julia is definitely the Sicilian with a permanent suntan, very dark hair and eyes, that can pierce your soul. Mom looked like her Polish heritage, blonde with hazel eyes, that my dad said instantly he was attracted to her despite wearing glasses.

Judy said to Sharon, I thought you told me you did not have time for any romance. What do you think you just had at the restaurant, and Sharon simply said I was having fun? Fun for you, but I had to talk to Jerry, and we really don't like each other. Sharon when are you going on your first date? I am meeting Mark Sunday afternoon after he finishes work at the school library, he says he knows where it is. By the way it is not a date, I am just going to be tutoring him in Calculus.

Judy could not stop laughing, $15, per hour, or a movie? I heard that, you and I know that you are going to a movie with that boy. By the way I think he was cute also, but he is like 5"10 and you are like 5'1", isn't he a little tall for you.

I think he is about the right height for kissing me. Now who's time is it to giggle.

Judy just started giggling, so my uptight academic friend is going on her first date, by the way you know he is Catholic right. How are the Rabbi and your mother going to react when they find out you are dating a catholic boy?

Sharon said didn't think about that, can you keep this quiet at this point I have no idea if we will really date much or is this just a way to go to a movie.

Judy said to Sharon, I saw you two talking, this is not a causal thing you are smitten by Mark, and you have to admit it.

You may be right, he is a very attractive guy and how he is helping his family is way beyond belief, quitting his school and losing a scholarship so he can make sure his family is taken care of, this is more than just a silly 20-year-old. Plus I like his athletic build.

Tutoring may have a completely different meaning with you two.

Oh, stop now, you would have me married and you just said he is Catholic, and my parents are ultra-conservative it will never go anywhere.

Judy just started laughing, just make me your Maid of Honor. (From the pictures of the wedding Judy was there as Maid of Honor, but Jerry could not be best man because Judy and he still did not get along, Jerry was an usher he did not have to proceed with Judy)

So that is apparently how Mark and Sharon Peters met. (My parents)

I forgot to say that Catonsville Community College is a 2-year college, Mark transferred from Catonsville after 1 full year and went to nearby UMBC where Sharon was a student already. He took summer classes and was able to catch-up on the lost time he had when he supported his mother.

The next story I will talk about my parents is dating and the wedding. My dad did the ultimate by converting to Judaism, so that he could be married, but that was almost 3 years later, and I am getting way ahead of myself.

A lot of what I am going to say comes from Aunt Judy, as Mom and Dad don't like to talk about the details of how they met, dated, and then got married. I guess that is not the thing that parents talk much about with the kids, especially things like intimate relationships.

On the Sunday afternoon that my parents first met, at the library now known as the Albin O Kuhn Library, Mark came with his calculus book and notes. I know they studied until 5 PM because Aunt Judy said they stayed until the library closed. Sharon who was very good at the subject was as interested in the subject as she was in the boy and suggested that they continue to study for an hour more at Paul's restaurant, since it was affordable and nearby. Aunt Judy told me that the dinner studying for an hour lasted until the restaurant closed at 9:PM, thus I am not sure that you count the studying of calculus or studying each other as a first date. They were together for like 7 hours so I guess you could count it as both. I think Mark suggested that they go to Hannah and Her Sisters as the compensation for the tutoring, but Sharon suggested Star Trek IV, so Star Trek was the movie they went to for their first date. Even then Sharon could be quite convincing on what she wanted to do, I swear she would have probably really wanted to see the other picture first, but she had her mind set on something that Mark might like to see. Star Trek IV was the first date my parents agreed to go on the following Thursday evening. (Mark got an 82 on his test that he took Tuesday, I guess the 7 hours of studying something helped him)

Since Sharon worked 2 hours at the library and some more at the restaurant, she said you owe me both the ticket to the movie and a drink, can we get popcorn to share.

Mark said I think I can spring for the extra's, just won't be able to get any candy. Sharon said something like, aren't I enough candy for you, that is still a joke they say to each other. Mark just said more like a hot pepper, but I will take you as candy. I am told my mother has very sharp elbows that she hit Mark in the ribs with them and almost spilled 2 soda's. The details for this first date all come from talks between Aunt Judy and my mother, so it may be a bit shaded. Mark was very stiff with Sharon, and finally she said to him aren't you going to put your arm around me, and Mark said I was not sure that I should make a move on my tutor. Sharon said if you don't put your arm around me, then you won't get any more tutoring. At that point they apparently had the first kiss. Aunt Judy says Sharon does not remember the end of the movie, and maybe that is why she actually watches the movie now until the end. I know that the two of them simply walked out of the movie theatre in Arbutus, and when Mark walked Sharon to her car, a very passionate kissed was initiated and stayed in front of Sharon's, six- year-old Citation. (One of worst cars ever made in the USA)

Three days later, Sharon and Mark were again at the library both studying their own subjects, and this time the whole-time holding hands. Sharon simply said maybe we can go on a bike ride this week, how about meeting at the Fort Smallwood Park, and we can ride there and maybe do a picnic. Mark said I don't have a bike rack, so can you meet me at my house in Elkridge and we can pack my bike. Sharon said no problem but remember this is not a date and I am not sure I want to meet your mother at this point.

Mark responded, why are we taking food to this park, and the very quick-witted Sharon said, because I will be hungry and thirsty after we bike. From what I hear the picnic had very little food and very much passion, enough that they continued later that day at Mark's family house in Elkridge, fortunately my grandmother did not get there until later.

My parents may have never dated again had my grandmother known what had gone on under her roof.

For the next 2 years apparently Mark and Sharon were secretly dating and keeping it from Sharon's parents by library dates on Sunday, and outdoor dates when both were free of schoolwork. Of course, many Thursday afternoons were spent at Paul's restaurant in Arbutus, sometimes with both Aunt Judy in attendance, and sometimes with Jerry and his new girlfriend Annie.

By the end of May 2 years later, it had become obvious that the 2 love birds were graduating and were going to need to fully come public. Graduation comes, Sharon Magna Cum Laude, and Mark, after transferring to UMBC, graduated the same month by taking additional courses over the summer at Catonsville Community College and at UMBC the last summer. Mark had somehow managed to pull his grades up to be Cum Laude, which he credited to the library dates they had for the last 2 years.

While Mark's family had met Sharon and really had taken a shine to her and as a couple, Sharon's parents not only had never met Mark, but they were totally clueless that Sharon had been dating. At least that is what Sharon thought. Right after graduation Mark decided that it was time that the two of them should take the relationship to a new level, and that had to be a very scary moment for Sharon. The Jewish families in Baltimore, tend to date and marry within the community, so with

Mark being Roman Catholic, I guarantee that this was not going to be an easy decision for Mark and Sharon to take on. I know that Mark asked Sharon to marry her on memorial weekend, they had gone biking, when Mark sat down at the old fort walls at Fort Smallwood and got on one knee and proposed to Sharon. The people around them, started to applaud. Mark's mother had given him her engagement ring for the occasion until they could afford a ring of their own. Sharon started crying and said maybe, we need to do this in front of my parents they don't even know that we are dating, they think I am tutoring you. Mark started to laugh, you must be a good tutor, 2 plus times a week every week for 2 years. Sharon just said and without me are you sure you would have graduated? Now comes the hard part for both of us, I am sure Rabbi has a guy already in mind for me from Pikesville, so this is going to be a very hard on both of us, the screaming will begin and end.

Mark said to Sharon, I have never been a good catholic boy, so as part of this proposal what would happen if I promised to convert to Judaism. Sharon started crying again, kissed Mark, and said you are the perfect guy, I am so sure that this will make a difference but let's wait a week and let my parents know that we started to date before you formally ask for my hand in marriage.

Sunday dinner, Pikesville, MD, home of Rabbi and Mrs. Goldbaum. Mom and Dad, I would like to introduce Mark Peters to the 2 of you. I wanted to bring him here as we have been dating for a while and thought it would be nice for all of us to meet. Mark recently graduated with a business marketing degree at UMBC, and we met while studying at the library.

Mrs. Goldbaum then took Sharon to another room, so finally I get to meet the boy you have been dating. Mom what makes you think I have been dating him for very long. Darling, I know you and when you introduced the boy you lit up like a roman candle. So why have you been hiding him from us? Mom, he is not Jewish, and I know that the Rabbi will go crazy as his little girl is dating a "Goy" he will go crazy. Yes Sharon, I see that he is a Goy, and you are in love with him. Mom, I am deeply in love with Mark, he has helped support his mother after his dad died, got his degree while working at A&P and graduated Cum Laude. He is currently working at B Green and Company, as a manager in the marketing department. I know Rabbi knows some of the owners of the company, isn't he friends with the Cardin Family? Your dad knows the family including the congressman, are you sure you really want to be with this boy. Never mind, I see it in your face you and he are way beyond dating.

Rabbi, thanks for having me over for dinner. Mark, you are here invited by my daughter, and I am very surprised that my daughter was brave enough to bring someone over and then tell me that you had been dating. Are you 2 very serious, because I was really going to introduce Sharon to a local boy that just came back from graduating from Harvard, Irving Sigman. I suspect that my daughter and you have been dating for a lot longer than Sharon let on. I want to know some things about you as she is my youngest daughter.

I just recently graduated in marketing from UMBC, Cum Laude. My parents met in the area and lived in Elkridge, and I still live with my mother and when my brother comes home from college he comes over. I work at B Green and Company, and work for Bernard Green in the marketing department learning how the grocery business is done. My father used to work for the Schlitz brewery but passed away of a heart attack at work, I had been working at A&P while I was in college to help support my motherr and my younger brother.

What college does your brother go to. Roger just finished his sophomore year at Loyola of Baltimore. Really so you are catholic. Yes, sir I was born catholic. So why are you dating my daughter, you know we are Conservative Jewish. Yes, sir I understand we are different religions and I think Sharon probably can answer the last question better than me. Just so you know her friend Judy told me that Sharon had been going out with a "Goy", but I can't believe that she would bring you to our house.

Well sir, I thought it was time that we got together and yes, we have been dating for a while. If not for Sharon, I would not have been able to graduate college as she helped me get through Calculus and a couple of other courses because she is very good at them.

Well now that we have all met is there something that the two of you want to tell us said Mrs. Goldbaum. Right there and then, Mark got down on his knee and asked Sharon to marry him once again in front of her parents. Sharon knew that her father would go nuts about this, so she responded I cannot marry you because you are catholic, and you know my father is a Rabbi. As on clue, Mark simply said, if it means being with you, I will convert to Judaism. With that said, Sharon said, Oh Mark yes, I want to marry you and gave him a kiss.

Rabbi Goldbaum simply said if you love my daughter, then I will not stand in your way, and you know that will take a year to happen. I understand sir, I have begun learning from Rabbi Levi, in Columbia, MD. I started this a week ago, and yes, I was circumcised when I was a newborn. Rabbi Levy has already inspected to make sure.

If you convert to Judaism, I will give you my blessing, and understand only if you complete the entire requirements. He then hugged Mark.

Sharon and Mark then embraced and said thank you mom and dad, we are really in love. Rabbi Goldbaum then went to the couple and said "L'chaim" With that my parents were formally engaged, and the ring my grandmother gave them never was returned, my grandmother refused to have it back.

My Parent's Wedding – December 8th.

My parents were married on a Saturday the 8th of December. Just over 6 months from when they were engaged. Many of Mark's family did not want to come because it was a Jewish wedding, and he has converted in rapid time. They still managed to get over 50 of them to the wedding. His brother Roger was the Best Man, Jerry was one of the ushers, and another friend George Rather was the other usher. The wedding was at 7 PM because it had to be at least an hour after Sabbath ended at sundown. Sharon had Judy as her Maid of Honor, her older sister Bella, was part of the party as was a mutual friend, Judy Lipshitz, (no kidding that is the real last name). I understand that before she got married, she did change her name to Lips. Sharon's side of the family had 70 people and my grandfather both gave Sharon away and was the Rabbi that married them. Rabbi Levi, from Columbia, did a section at Mark's request but no priest like we will have at our wedding.

The ceremony lasted until 8 PM, with the traditional stepping on the glass. It was actually a light bulb to make enough noise so that people could hear it. The reception was at the Martin's Caterers which is only about 5 miles from the synagogue. Starting with drinks at 8:30 PM, dinner was served just before 9:30 PM, and with a DJ they came to the first dance with the song "Let's Stay Together" by Al Green.

I have to ask Julia what she wants to do as our first song. I wonder if she will be able to dance as she will be like entering her fourth month of being pregnant, although she really does not show yet, other than her boobs look fantastic.

My parents spent their wedding night at a hotel near BWI airport, and then flew to a hotel in Miami for a week. The Fontainebleau is a famous hotel on the beach, apparently Rabbi Goldbaum, had connections and was able to get the hotel to give them a honeymoon suite at a single price. When they got back from the honeymoon, they knew I had been conceived interesting that I was born in August which really means that I think mom was pregnant at the wedding.

So now you know the history of how my family was formed, I did forget to tell you I have 2 siblings, my sister Angela was born October 14 months after me, and then my younger brother James was born another 2 years later. Three kids in like 4 years, my mother chose to stay home with us until my younger brother was 8 years old, and then she taught at a private school in the area. James got to go there for free which is one of the reasons he is a lot smarter than me. He was awarded an academic scholarship offer at Lehigh, in PA he apparently loves engineering, so he attends the school which takes my parents about three hours to see him. James also plays baseball for the University. My sister decided to go to University of MD, College Park, and will be a doctor eventually. She will be a pediatrician someday, and at 5'4" and blond like my mother is having no problems getting dates.

My dad was lucky after B. Green and Company closed or sold the wholesale division, he was able to get a job with the State of Md and is now a director in the state department of Health and Human Resources. Between what he makes and what Mom makes they have been able to afford 3 children in college with expenses.

So, you know how the family Peters got started, typical Baltimore family in an area with both Catholic and Jewish areas intermixed throughout. Both religions are very family oriented, so I guess if you take the religion out of it, they have a lot more in common than they would like to admit.

CHAPTER THREE

The Early Years

I write this piece of the story to let people know the next piece of the puzzle from my parents dating. I grew up in Arbutus area of Baltimore County, we had a small house that we rented through my kindergarten years. With 3 children at home and mom not working, it was all we could afford. I remember it was an older house, it had a chain link fence, kind of rusty so we were told not to climb it, we always wanted a dog there, but mom said she had enough children to handle and did not need a dog also. I was born in August, and I guess my mom was not thrilled with me being the youngest kid in my class, so she held me out until I was 6 years old. I was always near the oldest in my class, weird because this caused me to be always a year in school behind some of the other kids in my age group swimming.

In 1996, I started at Arbutus elementary school, to say the least I was not a great student, while I entered school reading due to the pre-school my mom took me too, I still did not have that much zeal for reading or writing. I discovered in first grade that I was pretty good at math. The following summer, I had my first swim lessons with Mikaela Blount, a swimming instructor who had spent the first 10 years of her life in Russia. I would like to say I picked up the swimming really fast, but I barely got through. I learned how to do freestyle and backstroke, which are two of the fundamental strokes in swimming, most people learn the two-armed strokes later, (breaststroke and butterfly), the 2-arm swim events are much harder and slower to coordinate. While I may have picked up swimming rather slowly, I am somewhat strong for my age even slow I was able to do 10 lengths a day when many others could barely do 4. But enough about swimming, this is to provide an overall world of the really young years from 0 to 10 years old.

I mostly received B's on my report cards the first few years, always said "he could do better if he chose to concentrate", I guess I was more interested in other things, but the truth is once I thought I knew something I simply quit listening to whoever was teaching the subject. I always was good at gym on things that were running or jumping, never as good at catching a football. I could hit a baseball fairly well got to play T-ball as a 6- year-old with dad as the coach. I never was very good at English, grammar was not my best subject, got through it but not easily.

Because money is tight with one person working and three kids, we did not join the synagogue until I was getting ready to start Sunday school. While I waited until I was 6 to start kindergarten, my mother enrolled me as a first grader in Sunday School, kindergart6en in regular schools. One reason very few of my friends from regular school ever saw me at Sunday school, they were usually a grade behind. We went to the creatively name Baltimore Hebrew Congregation not far from our house, but as a reform Jewish community most drove to the Synagogue. Because my mother was the daughter of a Rabbi, we went to a lot of Friday night services, which was great because we got food at the end of the service and then we did not get home until beyond my normal bedtime, so a double treat. Also, we were one of the few young families at services, we were spoiled by other grandparents in attendance.

I always had good relations with the little girls in my class, I am slightly above average height, and, in those days, I had dirty blond hair similar to my mother, and then hazel/blue eyes depending on what time of the day you saw me. I also asked the girls anytime I was having trouble reading something or pronouncing something in Hebrew. The little girls liked me asking them and it made my life so much easier, so they simply made me friendly with the little girls in my class. Because I was not afraid to talk to the girls, I got invited to a lot of the birthday parties, it also caused a bit of teasing by some of the boys I knew because they rarely got invited.

In 1997, I joined my first summer swim team at Five Oaks Swim Team, because we were young and did not have much money at the time, they let us join the first year as a summer only member which meant, you did not have to pay a capital fee that year.

Mikaela was the swim coach that year, and as an 8 and under, very few swam the 2- arm events. Mikaela must have viewed something in my strength, so she insisted that I learn how to do butterfly. By the end of the summer season, I was in the top three in butterfly. That meant my poor mom had to wait until the meet was mostly over until I got to swim. As a 6-year-old, I made one third place finish in the last meet, and my mom sealed the ribbon in plastic and gave it to my grandparents. After that ribbon, my parents agreed to join the club and committed to the $500, capital fee but were able to get this done at 167, per year for three years.

The next 2 years school was again fairly easy or easy because I did whatever effort it took to get B's, never really worked hard enough to get anything else. My only difficulty came because I was a year ahead in Sunday School, I had to get assistance all the time because my reading was a year behind, Miriam Levi, was my savior here, she would help me understand the words. Miriam was a very smart and very eastern European looking girl with very dark hair, green eyes and light skin, she was the envy of most of the other girls in our class, but she always helped me out. We became friends and when she graduated high school a year-ahead of me, I went to her graduation party, and my friend gave me the most passionate kiss I had ever received. She then said, "I think you will do well without me next year, don't forget me I will write you each week". I guess college went well, I never received a single letter but still remember that kiss. I better not let Julia know this.

Now back to swimming, I never really understood the backstroke, but made a few of our Saturday meets swimming freestyle and butterfly. I finally figured out how to do the breaststroke kick, which is most difficult piece to understand in swimming and in the final meet I got a third-place finish in it. My mother learned her lesson though, she would drop me off for warm-ups for the meets and then come back for the second half of the meets and leave my 2 younger siblings to watch my dad play baseball.

Meanwhile I actually won my first event in the 8 and under 25 fly on the third meet of the season, our best swimmer was out on vacation. My mother was out there yelling, go JP all the way until we started. Truthfully, it was very embarrassing, as she could be heard over every other parent. Who would know that a mother that short could be that loud, I guess she wanted to be heard.

One year later I was again swimming for the summer swim team and now an 8-year-old, I was able to make three swim events every week, swimming the freestyle, breaststroke and butterfly. Freestyle was my weakest event, I think I may have scored once the whole season, while I could usually finish top three in breaststroke. The fly was the interesting event, I won 4 times out of five and trailed only 2 swimmers the whole season. I got to swim the divisional which is like the conference meet in college, limited to the top 2 swimmers in each event, I got to swim breaststroke and butterfly. In breast, I did not finish in the top 10, but I won my very first medal in the fly, by finishing a close second to the guy that beat me earlier in the season.

My sister Angela was now on the team, she had learned to swim the previous summer and was having fun learning to be on a team. My mother loved it as she now could go to the pool and have the 2 children there and when my youngest brother was not with my dad at baseball games, he could come for the afternoon. It was really great for my mom that for the first time, we all were potty trained so she had a lot less work and could enjoy the pool.

Like most summer teams, Five Oaks had a swim team banquet with awards and trophies for rewards, the first 2-years I received a little trophy everyone that swam got but not this year. After dinner was served, Brian Hassett, a parent that was president of the pool, announced the most improved swimmer awards before the outstanding athletes. To my surprise, they called my mother Sharon to the front of the picnic area. Sharon, I want to let you provide the trophy to the most improved male swimmer this year, JP, come on up and receive your award for the

Most Improved Male Swimmer this year. Mom was tearing up as she gave me the trophy with my name on it. Brian then talked about my improvement from barely making any events, to placing second in the division meet. Finally, he said Sharon, I hope you are not doing anything next weekend because JP, is seeded 5th in the 8 and under 25 fly at the Baltimore County Championship meet. After the applause, my mom got on a phone and called dad to clear the weekend. I understand he was not thrilled because that meant the next Saturday not only was he coaching but had to bring both Angela and James with him to the games.

One week later, I finished fourth in the County, my father Mark did not come as I said he was coaching baseball teams. In the crowd, a young lady came to my mother and said, you may want to think of a winter swim team for your son, he may be a really good swimmer. The card was from NBAC, the greatest winter swim club in our area and maybe due to Michael Phelps one of the most well-known. I did not realize until later that his family was from West Virginia, why this is important you will see later but needless to say without that connection I would never have met Julia.

NBAC, had a tryout and the coaches were not very impressed with my swims in the first three strokes. Unlike most first-time try-outs, I was only 8 and most were 9 or 10. The coaches then got to see me swim the fly, and one of them said, do we take a chance to let him swim here, he swims one event well and as soon as the others get his strength, they will surpass him. A week later I was sent a letter saying that I was invited to the developmental team Sunday nights, and 2 workouts during the week. The developmental team is really not a team but more of an expanded swim lesson, I did not make the main junior team this was just an opportunity to swim all winter for the first time. I never competed in any meets that winter as this was not team orientation just a way to develop strokes. This was the first time I was up for something and did not get it. My parents liked the fact that this was a lot less cost and something that with my dad now working in management at the state we could now afford. At least, I got to play T- ball in the spring, I was pretty good at hitting, my fielding was not what my dad wanted. This way he got to have me play and James with us learning also. Mom and Angela would spend time together without the guys.

In September, the Peters family moved to a new house about 6 blocks from where we had lived in Arbutus, Mom was doing a little teaching at the Sunday School, so we were able to save on tuition. Our new house was a typical 4-bedroom house in the area, with my sister getting one bedroom, my brother and I sharing the second largest bedroom, my parents the master bedroom, and then a Jewish studies room. That room was filled with books and had a spot for the children to read, what I called that room later was the prison camp, it was where they made us study for our Hebrew. Also, since I was not getting the grades that Angela received often was my punishment room for additional studying while others were out doing fun stuff.

9 and 10:

With my season over and starting to swim at NBAC I figured this would be my year. Boy was I wrong, the difference between a 9-year-old and a ten-year old physically is a lot, and not only that but freestyle is now 2 lengths, a fifty-meter swim. My first year, I literally only got to swim butterfly, I was our second swimmer and placed in every meet in the top three. I again tried out for NBAC main swim team only to get the same letter as the year before, only good enough for the developmental team.

I was now in third grade and still not a great student, my parents were like how you expect to go to college if you only get B's. I had no real idea of what that meant but now I guess that meant you succeed only by going to college.   I was like, what is college and why are you so upset with straight B's. My report card said, John gets the idea of what we are doing and then ignores me and looks out the window. My mother asked me why it was this way, I simply said I get bored waiting for the others to get what we are doing, and I just don't want to listen anymore. My mother then said, if you are that smart why aren't you getting A's. My dad calmed her down saying I was not much better and see how your tutoring helped me. Our son takes after me, I guess and with that the ugly confrontation ended, dad was always easier on me with my schoolwork than mom.

Sunday school now had an extra day on Tuesday's I started Hebrew school. Lucky for me, Miriam was in class, and truthfully, she made life really easy as every time I did not get something, she would call me afterwards and explain it to me. I really miss her now that she has gone to Georgetown a year ahead of me in college. All three of us were now in Sunday school, my dad often would drive us and eat bagels and coffee with the men in the library. Well, that was in the winter, as soon as March came around, he was busy coaching his spring teams. Mom stayed late after finishing teaching the fourth- grade class. Angela would come home with my mom in those days.

My second season with the developmental team was going much better than the first. I was able to swim a new event called the 100 IM. For some reason it was my best event, trouble was I was 10 and this was restricted to 12 and under, so did well in practice not so much in the meets. I got to swim in something called "B Meets", that is for swimmers that are not fast enough to race the top swimmers, like being a AAA ball player is what my dad says. I know I won a couple of 50 Fly events in 12 and under and placed a couple times in the 12 and under 100 IM. I got one top three in breaststroke in the 50.

My dad had me playing little league baseball, I really did not like it, but I guess as the coach he would have had a hard time explaining why his son did not play. I would like to lie and say I did well, truthfully if I played more than one inning a game it was because someone was out on vacation or sick. Good hitter terrible at fielding, outfield is boring and apparently, I lost attention while waiting for action. James though would practice with the team, and took to it right away, the clone of my dad. Even looked like a picture of him as a boy.

The summer I was 10 years old, I was again the top fly swimmer for my team, and now was the second best 12 and under 100 IM, because I was only 10 I could only swim 3 events, so I often swam freestyle. I won every meet in the fly and placed top three in every meet at 100 IM. Freestyle still was just good enough to score occasionally.

I won my first gold medal in the division meet, but only placed top 7 in the county championships. I qualified as the 16th and last swimmer to make the all-stars in the 100 IM. I only swam the fly, my parents thought I was too young to swim the 100 IM. My younger sister started to be in the meets this year and unlike me was good at backstroke and I think won an event as an old 8 and under. My younger brother was definitely the better baseball player and he and dad were at T-ball, so my dad never saw me swim the entire season until all-stars. He said he was disappointed that I had done better 2 years ago. Wow, still top 7 in the county and not even out of developmental team, most of the people I was swimming against were swimming 5 days a week.

This is about all I remember from the early years; I was never a really good student; apparently too lazy I was told. I truthfully just was not interested. My parents were pretty strict so very little free time, if we had time, they would send us to prison to read about Jewish heritage or practice Hebrew. My swimming, well ok, for some but nothing outstanding. The enthusiasm from 8 and under was lost as I guess I did not develop as well as others thought I would.

The Middle Years – Ages 11 through 14

After the conclusion of the summer season, I had to go through another tryout for the main NBAC swim team and of August. I thought for sure I was doing another year in development, but a coach Brian Cale, who had swum at Davidson at college took an interest in me. Brian looked at both my backstroke and breaststroke and said to my dad, we fix those 2 strokes, and he will be good at the 100 IM as a 12 and under. My dad said, but we are supposed to go to Ocean City, MD for vacation the next 2 weeks. Brian offered to let me live with him in his apartment for the next 2 weeks so he could figure out why my 2 strokes never developed. A price was negotiated and while I was thrilled to have coaching, the loss of 2 weeks at the beach really sucked. What I did not know was that my time away from the pool would be limited all the way until college.

The family would get vacations, but I was often stuck at practice or meets.

Brian looked at me and said, you are physically stronger than most 10-year old, that is why you are able to do the butterfly so well. We need to completely look at your backstroke and your breaststroke, and afterwards, I think we can fix your IM, so you will be a top 5 all-star. Like any other child told he could be a top athlete I ate it up totally.

Brian's apartment was a small 1 bedroom close to Towson area of Baltimore, I got to sleep and watch TV from his sofa, well now thinking about it, had to have been a love seat because I could barely fit in it at night.

Every morning, go to pool to practice with his swimmers, then he set-up a VCR with swim instructions or heats of swimmers.

First thing he said, I don't mind your arms for the breast, we are going to change your kick to what the Spaniards do, and then we have to do the timing of coming out of the pool, some people call it the pop. I had none of the pop before the first week, and after more swimming than I had ever done before, somehow, I managed to get the timing of the new kick and the pop. Both double arm strokes done, now to work on the one arm strokes.

Brian looked at my backstroke and immediately said, good thing about your backstroke is I can change it all, it looks terrible. First, the kick, I was doing something that looked more like a trudgen stroke upside down. That stroke has your legs all over the place like a scissor, while it is legal it is not effective. Monday practice, 500 yards on nothing but kicking, then back to video's looking at just the kick, then back to the pool with the afternoon practice all kicking for me. By Wednesday, I no longer wanted to do the other kick.

Wednesday afternoon, Brian looked at my arms, and said nothing here I want to keep. After putting both my legs in innertubes he said I want you to extend your arms as far as they go and hit your ears on each stroke. I swear I almost drown as every time I tried it, I got messed up and had to stop and bounce off the bottom of the pool. By Friday, I could get a length without having to bounce off the bottom of the pool. On Saturday, we put it all together, and Brian stated it is not pretty, but now you won't lose as much time as you did before, and you can be ready to finish them off in the second half of the race.

Sunday came and my parents picked me up, they were all tanned and looked relaxed, I was exhausted and simply went home and slept the rest of the afternoon. My mom asked my dad when I woke up, was it really worth having him miss vacation, look at how tired he is. I said Mom, I will be an all-star next year just you wait and see.

Monday morning was another trial at NBAC, and while my freestyle was ok, I was close to the top trying out in fly. I was able to get through backstroke in the middle of the pack, which was way better than before and in breaststroke, I was top 6 so still not sure I could make it. The next race was the 100 IM, a requirement for the 11 and 12 swimmers trying to make the club. I guess between Brian's instructions and all the recent swimming with Brian, I somehow managed to finish second of everyone trying out.

Friday, we received the letter, I was invited to swim the main swim team at NBAC, four practices a week. Dad also convinced my mom that I should swim with our summer team on Sunday nights so I would workout 5 days a week. With that letter my vacations were eliminated, no summer camps either. Some of my friends got to have fun in the summer, but I think my dad saw athletics was going to be my way to get to college from that point. Always about the cost of college, something I really had no idea of what he was talking about.

In order to stay on the NBAC team, you had to commit to one swim meet per month, so that now meant, I would probably miss one Sunday school class per month. My mom got the notes from the teacher, and then Miriam on Thursdays would then help me during the week to catch-up. Because I had Hebrew school right after school one day each week, I had to do go straight from school to Hebrew school, and then catch the last half of the practice, so by the time I got home, I was exhausted.

11-12 swimming – Well now that I had improved my other 2 strokes, I learned that while I was only really good at butterfly, the IM was a possible great race where I had to incorporate all of the events in one race. The event is longer than any other, my strength also played into this race as a possibility. During the winter I was swimming in my first "B" meet, and won the 100 IM for the 11-12, and literally was just 3 months older than 11, so I was now able to swim the A meets. In the winter they swim 2 lengths for fly, so now I was able to swim 2 events at A meets so my parents were happy that I could go to only the A meets instead of every weekend being one or the other.

Brian Cale was the first assistant on the deck with our junior practices, so I got to see him, and he gave me encouragement. I remember that I used to be in the end lanes for most of the freestyle and backstroke, and then they would move me to the primary lanes for the fly and IM, which pissed off some of the supposedly high-level guys as I was able to keep up with them.

With the winter prowess, you would have thought I would have been the top of my summer team, and still the best swimmer, was Kirk Schmidt. Kirk, was routinely a top 5 swimmer, very unlikely that me being one year younger could do much, but as the number 2 100 IM, and number 2 flyer, I got in to the meets every week. The 100 IM for 12 and under is the first event of the meet, so my mother, would drop me off knowing she would come back and see my fly later in the day. Kirk and I were a really strong team in the 2 events I got to swim, he won every week, and all but 1 week I was second with him. When it came to our divisional, we finished 1 and 3 in both events, I got bronze medals for both events. I got invited to the championships in both events, finishing 9th in the 50 fly, and 14th in the IM. I thought nothing could be better than swimming all summer, and then getting a week at the Delaware shore, this year Bethany Beach. Brian had other thoughts; he convinced my parents that he could work with me on my weak strokes to improve my positioning. So away went my beach week, my parents said goodbye and I got to live on the couch again.

I forgot that my dad was coaching again and then going to baseball with my younger brother James He never saw me swim a single meet that summer. My sister did get in to the meets in 9 and 10 , and even made it to the division meet not doing well but enjoying being a key member of our team.

My mom was not thrilled with my academic progress and almost ended my swimming right there because I got a C in English, and if it had not been for Miriam, I would have been in trouble. Miriam said Well, for a little money she would tutor me in English after reviewing Hebrew work. I was thinking, really, your only 1 grade ahead of me, but truthfully, she was really a good teacher and an extremely attractive girl. My mother somehow agreed to this, and the deal was done, Miriam became my 2-course tutor.

Did I mention that Miriam was also not bad on the eyes? My dad never really said much as long as I was able to get decent grades and maintain a moderate level of success in sports. He was busy with T-ball and baseball with James, as I said was a lot better player than me, and quite frankly I was glad not to add that with my busy schedule.

I forgot to mention this was my last year at Arbutus Elementary, I was so glad to be done with one classroom most of the day, so boring.

The next year was going to be very difficult, I had to do Sunday school, and 2 days of Hebrew school getting ready for my Bar Mitzvah training, swim at least 4 times per week, and still maintain school. As I turned 12, I also began to go to middle school. I went to say hello to Miriam at school one day, and found out something really quickly, 7th grade girls do not talk to 6th grade boys at school. Oh well, I would still see her for Hebrew support and once and a while other subject because while others were home on the weekends, I had to travel for swim meets at least once a month, and sometimes that meant that my mom was with me, or sometimes Angela and I would both swim.

After having success at the summer pool, the expectations for me as a 12-year-old for the summer team was immense but we also went up a division. They had the 2-best swimmers in the league in the 100 IM in my age group, so I still got third in my divisional, and managed to get second in the fly, and even qualified for the division as the second swimmer from our team, I did nothing to show I could do anything with that opportunity finishing 10th out of 12 swimmers.

At the championships, I was able to move to 4th in the 100 IM, not bad, and stayed in the top 6 of the fly, but other swimmers were coming in stronger and I was not longer really ahead of them. Angela qualified for the backstroke in her first time at championships, but only managed to finish 11th, next to last but I think she was just happy to have made it. My mother was there at the meet, and even both of my grandmothers came to see us swim. Again, James and dad were away at baseball and never came to a single swim meet. I could start to see the divide the smart women, and the baseball men, I was not neither so I really did not have a parent that was in my corner.

13 -14 – The lost years.

I could tell you that my ability in the summer swim meets got better with my practice, but I would be not telling you the truth. I am a consistent swimmer and not a sprinter, so during the winter I could score in things like the 100 fly, the 200, IM, I simply did not have top end speed like the sprinters. Winters I could make the A meets in those 2 events, and funny thing I was now developing a really consistent breaststroke, I tried the 200 for the first time and made the finals in a Richmond, VA 50-meter pool, I think they call it Briarwood Invitational. I had never been to an indoor meet with a 50-meter pool, our competitions, use to go the other way, 25-yards or meters. I saw the pool and it was really intimidating, It is so long it looks like you can barely see they other end, and you get a lot less turns, so it favors people that are consistent more to my liking. I also made the finals in the 100 fly, the first time I ever had gone that far in one race. Neither of my parents came to the meet, Angela was studying for her Bat Mitzvah, and since it was March, dad was doing his baseball teams.

I made the all-stars in fly and the 100 IM when I was 14, but did not score above eighth in either event, the guys had caught-up to me in height and surpassed me. They had the sprinter in them, I just did not have that gear. Coach Brian kept reminding me that I was destined for the more difficult events, he said anyone can sprint, but sprinters can't do what I could in swimming IM's fly and distance freestyle. That did help as I have AA times in at least three events now. I was now getting some attention as the odd young kid that did the hard events and was not as good as a sprinter.

The one thing that was great was that I got my Bar Mitzvah completed. The party was fantastic, and I know that it cost my parents a lot of money, and interestingly both the Catholic and Jewish sides of the family actually came we must have had 125 members here. I guarantee my Hebrew was not great but got through the piece I was required to read, and my grandfather was also on the bema, to help me. I wondered how he got out of being with his congregation, but he did have a younger Rabbi at his congregation that took over for him occasionally. While I invited Miriam, I was surprised that she was willing to come as she had finished her Bat Mitzvah almost 6 months before me.

I will admit I had a crush on Miriam, and as soon as we did the service, she reached out to me and gave me a kiss on the lips and a hug congratulating me. I instantly fell in love, well I thought it was love. I also realized that with this done, Miriam would no longer be my tutor except if I was falling down in a subject. I thought about messing up just so she would have to come over my house every week. Miriam said to me, you did it, and I am proud of you. With that event, my Sunday School and Hebrew learning ended, but Miriam and I talked to each other every week. I was much better academically in middle school than I was at elementary school, that was a mistake otherwise I could have been with Miriam more.

This concluded the early years of swimming. I actually got to go with my family when they went to Ocean City that year, my first year at the beach with the family. The girls on the beach looked really nice, and the skeeball got most of my money at the arcades. Then there were the thoughts of Miriam, what she would look like in a bathing suit, or even less. My brother and dad rarely saw me swim, as they pursued baseball, and I had given that sport up a while ago, just not enough time. Swimming is an evil sport, you just simply can't take time off to do other sports, you just fall behind, so baseball was done. My sister was a good but not as serious as a swimmer as I was but during the summer, we both swam so mom was able to enjoy the pool and played cards in the afternoon.

I forgot to tell you that I had progressed to the second-tier practice at NBAC. My results in events a lot of others did not want to swim, kept me up there. Brian reminded me that most of Michael Phelps wins were in events that required endurance as much as speed, you have the endurance someday you may get that fast speed. (I was no Michael Phelps) Either way, nothing I was good at was what they swam in the summer. I was finally finished with my Jewish education, and then there was the older woman, that I dreamt about most nights, and who called me every week.

My Dad's family had finally reconciled with the fact that he had converted, and it appeared the hatchet was buried at my Bar Mitzvah. Uncle Roger even came to the event after swearing he would never talk to my father after he converted. His hug to me was the first time I had met him in a very long time, and no he does not look like my dad, only figured it when my grandmother introduced him as my uncle. I had put my hand out to greet him and he hugged me and said, I am so sorry I missed you growing up, I am sorry I let my argument with your dad keep me away from you and the other kids. He then went on to say, you look like a cross between my mother and your grandfather. I saw the 2 grown men hug and cry at the event, and I know that they talk to each other now at least once a week now.

I did my part of the Bar Mitzvah very well, at least in my opinion. The party cost a small fortune and was held at Martin's. Miriam had agreed to come to the event. She said she was so proud of me and that while she would not need to be my tutor, she wanted to still call me to see how I was doing, again she was a year ahead of me in school.

James did not attend the party; he was away at a baseball tournament that a neighbor took him to. My mother and father had argued a lot about that but in the end my dad had prevailed, baseball over anything else according to him. Several swimmers came to the event, as did Coach Brian. As you will see throughout, James and I may stay together in a room, but at the very least we don't like each other. He is the clone of my dad, and I am the son that chose another path. The event had a DJ, and my sister wanted to get me to dance and finally pulled me on the floor, while she was 12 you would have thought the way she was managing me that she was older than me. When they got a slow dance, somehow, she made it that I was with my tutor for the event, Miriam with heels was like 4 inches taller than me, and while we were swaying, I could only think of what it would be like if we actually dated, but she was so popular in high school, and a grade ahead of me. I guess I was just going to be lucky to be among her friends.

The next step towards the end of my swimming career started out very sadly and ended with me coming to Alderson Broadus, but that is the next stage of the story.

CHAPTER FOUR

High School Years

With Middle school ending at Arbutus Middle School, I knew my world was going to change. Lansdowne High School was like 3 times larger than my middle school, and now I was going to be at NBAC every afternoon and would not do the Five Oaks swim practices on Sundays at Catonsville Community College.

Right before the start of the year, Angela had a Bat Mitzvah during the last week of August, just as students were returning. The event was smaller than mine, I guess the time of the year a lot of families were out of the area, so we had about 75 people.

Miriam sent her regrets, she was away with her family, they were going to Disneyland in California. Angela though was a champ at the torah section she had performed, and even impressed our grandfather. He said if she wanted to, she was good enough she could have studied to be a Rabbi. After the ceremony was over, I told her how proud I was of her and she just gave me a hug and said sorry that your tutor could not make it, I know you and her have a special relationship. Neither my dad or James made it to the event, they were away at a tournament. My dad had argued with my mom to try to change the date, but there were no open slots when they decided to try so the compromise was that the 2 of them would try to get to the afternoon reception. They never made it, supposedly the game went into extra innings.

Did I tell you Miriam had spent the summer at Camp Louise, in the mountains of Maryland, it is located right on the border of Pennsylvania, it is alleged that there are a few secret government places around it. Well, we wrote letter to each other as no phones allowed at the camp, I guess they want the kids to stay away from them for a while. She wrote to me how it had been as a freshman, and that at first, she had been picked on and then the guys were always trying to get her on a date, but her parents said no dating until she was 16.

I guess here is where I should talk about the argument my parents had for funding swimming for Angela and me. Dad said swimming was so much more expensive than baseball and maybe he should try to have me play baseball instead, it would save like $5000, per year. He also argued that there is no money in swimming, so why are we supporting it we could use the money elsewhere. Finally, dad did not like it that on many nights he would have to come home and wait for mom to make dinner, meaning we would not eat until after 8PM. The yelling was so loud that we heard them arguing from our bedroom. James said see I knew you should have stayed playing baseball, you are the reason that our parents are fighting. When it was all said and done, my mom said look if you need me to ask my parents to pay for a part of this no problem, and after that swimming was paid half by my grandparents and half by my parents. My grandfather said, I knew he was always a cheap son-of-a-bitch, that was the only time I ever heard the Rabbi cuss. After that we had a little peace in the family around swimming, dad could not argue, because the Rabbi contributed like $250, every month, so his argument was stifled.

This was the second time that I would not be in the same school as my sister, who was 1 grade behind me. She would have to mentor our younger brother who was in his first year at Arbutus. With all the kids now out of elementary school, our mother began teaching at a private school. We did not know that while we were at school the last couple years, she had earned her Maryland teaching certificate. This would be the first time that all of us would have to get ourselves organized in the morning, including getting money or lunch ready, breakfast and making sure that James actually brushed his teeth, man he had bad breath when he didn't. (We did not want him to be on the bad side of everyone in his classes, so we made sure by doing a breath test every morning). My dad received a promotion to an associate director of the State of MD agency he worked in at Baltimore. This means for the first time, we were not watching every penny we spent as a family, which was good because NBAC is not cheap, (odd situation for my dad to say above and whine now that we were not having financial problems, but that was my dad, truthfully, he just did not understand a non-professional sport) again neither is the travelling that James does with our dad for baseball. My poor sister, my mother insisted on going with me to meets in the region so often times Angela was the only one in the house. Angela was at practice before me at NBAC, not having graduated to the later practice time. My mom got some relief when a couple of families starting carpooling together to reduce the time, they had to go to the pool plus it saved money. Well, Angela did have company when we she was not in the meets, the Golden Retriever we adopted from a neighbor who had become ill and could not keep up with the dog. We adopted our 4-year-old named Brutus, funny name for such a wimpy dog. The kids all promised to help keep the dog, and I bet we did little more than the morning stuff, mom appeared to let him out in the evening, and he was always within 5 feet of her whenever she was home. Well, we also had enough money and not enough time that we had a cleaning service come to the house every other week. That is the latest on most of our family, except my grandmother, Mom's mom had a stroke, some call an aneurism, she is now living at a nursing home, she cannot speak yet, and has just started to walk again with a walker. She understands everything we say, and she is starting to learn to mouth words again. The hope is she will be back home within the next 3 months, as Grandfather Rabbi, still has a lot of work to do with his synagogue.

We are going to put a ramp to the house they live in so they can get in and out with the least amount of effort.

The bad thing about being a freshman and also 15, is 2-fold. Freshmen are the lowest of the low in high school and are treated that way in all ways including trying to ask anyone out. At 15, you are also the youngest age of the 15-18 swimming, so expectations are you are either still so great that you still dominate, or you struggle with taller older swimmers. I am unfortunately one of the second group. The IM is now always the 200 IM, the fly is always 4 lengths, and now we get our first distance exposure in freestyle, 500 in high school meets and the 1650 in US Swimming events.

To my surprise, I am the number 1 flyer at Lansdowne high school, and never before was ever good at anything in freestyle, well you know what strength is better than pure speed in the 500 freestyles, so in high school my second event is usually the 500 freestyles. I don't even get to swim the 200 IM, but it was odd thing because, Lansdowne had a lot of swimmers that could do well in the 200 IM, so as a freshman, they would not let me swim it. Nobody wants to swim the distance events or fly, so that is basically the events I get to swim that year.

I would like to say I was an instant hit, but many guys are like three years older than me as I said earlier. In the fly, I was usually good enough to ward off the second swimmer from the other team and finish second, in the 500 freestyle, I won one meet but most of the time, I was third or second. I also got to swim the 400-medley relay, as the fastest in the fly leg most of the year. (I need to tell you about what happened at the championship, it really sucked)

Our 400-medley relay was seeded third, and we had three seniors and me swimming the event. Our coach decided to let me swim the trials in the morning with the team and we were able to finish as the number 2 seed for the evening. For the finals, our coach Fran decided that she wanted to give all four seniors a gift and she came to me and said I am pulling you from the finals tonight so all four seniors can swim together. The result, my replacement was three seconds slower than me, and they ended up fourth and with me I think we could have challenged for winning. Hey, in my mind that is what I think would have happened.

High school swimming is fun, but truthfully the majority of swimming is done with the US Swimming team events at NBAC. I got my first experience at the 200 fly, and I can tell you one thing, it really is a hard event, I went out way too fast and died the second half of the race. Note to self, learn to chill the first 100 to survive the second half. I had the 200 IM, where I was getting better, but as a 15-year-old mostly B times, not until April of my Freshman year do I get an A time.

I guess I should explain that US swimming has categories of times for events. B times are pretty much the lower tier, A times get you in to the better levels and the AA times or better are for national caliber swimmers. You see I struggled with getting with the better swimmers.

I say that but on my second time swimming the 200 fly, I got my first A time as a 15-18 year old. A day later in a distance meet I swam the 400 IM at my coach's insistence and low and behold, I had my first AA time, neither my coach nor I could believe that I was now rated in the top 200 in this event. It was an amazingly horrible event; I cannot believe the pain it creates different breathing pattern in every hundred. Truthfully, not that many swimmers want to do this event, it sucks the life out of you.

Miriam called me every week, and you would have thought the way we talked that we had been born to the same family. As much as we talked every week, never at High School, as I said earlier, I was a year behind her. I have been told in West Virginia women and men are rarely friends, but I really thought she was a great friend I could ask her anything. I think she always wanted to find out if I was dating anyone, but with swimming practice and swim meets for high school and US Swimming on weekends, I had no time, plus as a 15-year-old who wants to be driven by their parents. I asked her several times about her dating and said her parents still did not allow one on one dates, but she had several friends that were guys at the large friends' events she went to.

School itself was not really an issue, I could get my B's and keep my mother from asking too many questions, and truthfully, I had no real interest in all the AP stuff that others wanted to do. I heard if you did an AP your life was hell with homework, I had no more time to play.

The summer team was not that great for me either as 15-year-old I was able to get in to the fly and the 100 IM, but not much else. Swam the 100 IM at divisional but did not qualify for championships, just like many swimmers my age the older guys really had an advantage. After swim season ended, I turned 16, but with my schedule with school and swimming, I knew I would not be able to get my license, plus it was expensive for the insurance, my dad reminded how much everything cost. With my brother doing well in baseball, Dad and he were away in tournaments most weekends, but this year in Ocean City, they met with us on Sunday night and stayed with us until Friday.

I was hanging out at the beach with my brother one evening and a group of girls came by, and we started talking. One girl must have taken a liking to me, because we talked for a couple hours before, we both had to go back to our respective families. (Tammi Glenn). Well next day I see Tammi at the beach, and she comes over to me and says, I guess I should give you, my number. I guess I am not that swift, I asked her why I would need that number and all she responded because I want to hang out with you tonight.

Tammi, was entering high school the next month at BCC high school in Bethesda, MD. Her parents apparently had a lot of money, because she had a credit card of her own and had more cash than I think I had ever viewed. Well, we hung out not only on Monday, but Tuesday, Wednesday, Thursday and Friday, with my brother and her friends. On Saturday, I called her can we hang out tonight, and she said sure, but my friends left this morning, it will have to be just you and me. Again, I was not that swift, and realized later that meant my first ever date.

We were walking on the boardwalk, when she grabbed my hand and looked straight at me and asked do you want to kiss me? I simply leaned over and awkwardly kissed her on the lips, well she was much better at it then me, and we lipped locked for what seemed like a minute. She held my hand and we walked to the beach together.

Tammi, said let's sit down and near the boardwalk, well we were basically under the boardwalk when she initiated another kiss. It was late, and we saw nobody else at the beach, and the next thing I knew we were kissing, she knocked me down and was lying on top of me. We were very passionately kissing and started what others call petting, and then she undid her top and asked me to kiss her again. The next thing I knew we both had out clothes off and I will not go into more details, but I became an adult that night. I called her Sunday, the phone rang and rang, and then nothing. I went over to the house and noticed no cars there and then a cleaning crew came over. They said the family had checked out earlier that morning and had gone home. I did not have her home phone number in Bethesda, and my summer of love was over. I tried to look her up and call her, but I never heard from her again. I never talked to Miriam about this one, she had been at Camp Louise as a Counselor in training most of the summer.

The next 2-years went by similar to my freshman year, I was good enough to get B's in school, I took high level classes but no AP courses. My mother did not bother me about school because I think she realized it was school or swimming and I truly preferred swimming.

My high school career had plateaued, I was the top flyer only, won about half the time but our team was not that strong, we had very few winter swimmers. I did not place in the State championships in the top 20, and it looked like my swimming career was likely over after my high school.

And then, it happened, I was at a USA swimming long-course event my junior year in March and placed in the top 6 in the 400 IM, top 12 in the 200 fly, and top 12 in an event you have never heard me talk about the 200 breaststroke on Saturday. On Sunday I made the top 6 again in another event you have not heard me talk about, the 1650 freestyle. With these results, Coach Brian at NBAC said to me, don't even bother swimming your senior season at Lansdowne, they are for sprinters, and you are not one of them, you are an oddity a long-distance and endurance swimmer. We may need you to get exposure in these events if you are going to swim division 1. I simply laughed, I had no letters from any school, and nobody had heard of me in my mind. I know that numerous guys from NBAC get college scholarships, even Michael had swum one year at that level. For me, I saw no way, but Coach Brian had ideas.

The following week on my weekly call with Miriam she was crying, she had been dating another senior David Horowitz, and he had called her the night before and after a year of dating said he wanted to break-up because he did not want to have a long-distance relationship when they went to college. He was planning on attending UCLA, and she was staying on the east coast. After she stopped crying, she said and what really pisses her off is that Senior Prom is three weeks away and now she was going to either skip it or go by herself. I can tell you I said something I probably thought was insane, I simply said Miriam, we have been friends for so long, if you don't mind going with a junior, I would love to go with you to Prom. The phone went silent for what seemed like five minutes, I am sure it was really shorter.

John, you are one of my best friends, and this would not be a date because we have been friends for so long, and I know everything about you. The girl I knew everything about and had been friends with forever just kept on talking and talking almost like she was extremely nervous. I then asked her again Miriam, would you like to go to your senior prom with me?

Finally, she said you are the only person I would like to go with. (Really, you have been dating someone for a year, and only this year will you even talk to me at Lansdowne) Because even then I did not drive, Miriam said I will pick you up in my car let's figure out the details over the next week, I will send you an e-mail with the date and times of the dance.

I told my mother and then my coach that I needed the first weekend in May off from any swim meets, and in unison they both asked why is that, John? I am going to the senior prom at Lansdowne with my best friend Miriam. My mother said of all the people I would thought you would never have gone out with is Miriam. I asked her why, and she said I thought the two of you were like brother and sister. Mom, she has just broken-up with her boyfriend before the prom, and I offered to go with her as a friend and she agreed so I am going to have some fun. By the way, I need dancing lessons from you and Angela. I don't understand people sometimes, I got a hug from my mom, and coach said, no problem with that week off it is not a really good meet for you anyway, mostly sprints.

Later that night I had to ask my mother, ok, what do I need to do for a prom. Well normally, we would expect that you will need to get a tuxedo, and that means real shoes and not flip flops or a bathing suit. Next, we are going to order a corsage for Miriam, and we will give you one that goes on her arm, so you won't have to worry about awkward pinning. Finally, I am calling Miriam's parents so they can come over our house and take pictures of the both of you. I am thinking we should get limo or something like that.

I finally had to stop her from going on and on, Mom we are just friends and Miriam is driving to the school and I don't drink so I think we are good on that. Angela, who was hoping her boyfriend would ask her to the prom also, just asked me how the heck did you get one of the most popular girls in school to agree to go with you to the prom. With that, she gave me a kiss on the cheek and said the two of you have always been good friends, you better behave.

My mother tried to horn in again and said Well Angela if you are going shouldn't we get a limo for the 2 couples. Angela gave her a look of total disgust, leave it alone mom, Miriam and John are friends only, give it a rest. That was the last time the three of us talked about it before the prom. My dad and brother had no interest in what was going on with that side of the family, they had baseball together and nothing else really mattered with the rest of the family. While I love my dad, with me being in a sport that he never understood, we really had very little to talk about, so we coexisted in the house, no conversations just head nodding.

Like many schools, Lansdowne had high school prom on a Friday night. Ours was the first Friday in May. I laugh because many of the students that took AP courses were totally burned out. They were ready to do anything but school. Miriam had worked with the ladies of the Peters house and scheduled everything out. She was coming at 6 PM, for 15 minutes of pictures and then dinner was scheduled downtown with other graduates 7 PM. We would leave for the dance at 8 PM and be at the dance no later than 8:45 PM. The dance went until 11:30, and at 12:00 we had an after-party at a local Holiday Inn. We had tickets to the after-party, but no I had not acquired a hotel room.

Lansdowne students had been banned from getting them, we were expected to leave sometime around 5 AM, and return to our homes to sleep. The party is a way to get people not to got to drinking parties and frankly it is actually not bad. Games and prizes through the night and of course the idea is that we are not in hotel rooms.

Miriam, like a clock arrived in her parents Cadillac at 5:59, PM. Her parents were 5 minutes behind her in the jeep her mom likes to drive. I need to stop and describe how incredible Miriam looked. Miriam with her very dark hair and green eyes, already is incredibly beautiful. She was wearing a peach-colored dress that swept around her torso, the dress had a slit on the side mid-thigh opening and ended at her ankles. The high heel shoes made her go from 5'4" to almost my height at about 5'10". Truthfully with her make-up on she looked like an eastern European model. To say she took my breath away would be an understatement. The man who marries her is going to be challenged, with her looks and smarts, every man in the room will be looking at her.

For me, I had been convinced not to get a powder blue tuxedo, the women got of the Peter's family chose for me to wear a charcoal gray tuxedo, with a grey stripped cummerbund. With my black hard shoes, I was nearly 6" tall. Truthfully though next to Miriam, I looked just what I was a fish out of water.

For 15 minutes the two families took pictures of us and finally, Miriam told her parents we had to go. We had an interesting challenge, normally if the guy is driving, he opens the door for his date then walks around to drive. Miriam says to me, you want me to open the door for you. This was a joke apparently as she said get in the car fish man.

Miriam had planned with 2 other couples to get a reservation at a Russian restaurant. Pikesville area of Baltimore has a large amount of former Russian immigrants, so we went to a restaurant called "Bravo", that the couples had chosen. We were given a very nice table near the back. No alcohol for us, but we had a dinner served in 4 courses plus an easy dessert, all took about 1 hour. I had cash out for our share of the dinner when the waiter said, the meal has already been paid for. I still gave him a twenty- dollar bill for the excellent service they had given us. The waiter then took pictures of all of us together and said Miriam this is for your parents. I knew they were well connected I just did not know how well connected.

Miriam and I were outside the restaurant when she leaned over to me and said, thank you for coming to my rescue. Miriam, I know over the years you have been there for me academically and spiritually, so tonight it is a little payback. She just said you have no idea, and truthfully, I did not.

The school gym had been turned in to a wonderful party atmosphere, Miriam of course was in her glory and when we arrived, it was like a celebrity had just entered. Of course, they looked at me as the dumb schmuck that had been recruited to be her date. Miriam introduced me to a few people as a long-time friend who was on the swim team. We danced at least 5 songs before a slow dance was initiated. Miriam and I were at the table, and she got up and said let's go I want to do this dance. The Peter's women had trained me enough to not look like a fish out of water, of course that is what I was, and with my hand on her hip and the other in her hand we danced for what seemed like eternity. After a couple of minutes, she leaned over and kissed me, I think every man in the room was jealous. For me, my fantasy of the incredible Miriam was realized, and the rest of the dance was nothing more than a dream.

At roughly 11:15, we were back in her car getting ready to go to the Holiday Inn, she then leaned over from the driver seat and kissed me again, this time, she opened her lips and forced her tongue between my lips. I was a little surprised by this sudden show of emotions, we were supposedly going as just friends to this evening. I had this funny feeling that this evening was going to be much different than originally thought. Since the party was much more informal than the dance, Miriam pulled another dress from the trunk and said she was going to change, and she would meet me at the front entrance in 15 minutes. I swear she must have waited somewhere, but in exactly 15 minutes, she came in a burgundy dress with much shorter shoes, I guess the tall ones were killing her and truthfully, she still looked gorgeous.

I know that we participated in many games and Miriam even won a gift certificate at IHOP. At about 5:AM, Miriam said it's time to get out of here. I said sure and then she said, are you up to sleeping here this morning, I am really tired and don't want to drive anywhere else.

I thought we were prohibited from getting a room from the hotel, and apparently the well-connected Miriam already had a suite key. I told her I did not have a change of clothes, and she told me that the suite had robes that I could wear. I probably should have insisted that we go home, but I had dreamt of Miriam for many years and the reality of her beauty was breathtaking. 5 minutes later, Miriam came out of the bathroom and had a very beautiful nightgown on, and I noticed that she had very little else on. I went to the bathroom myself, hung up my tuxedo and then put on the robe. I was very tired and thought I was going to go sleep. As I went to lie down, Miriam came to me and gave me a very passionate kiss, and again slipped her tongue between my lips, this time I also responded. Miriam turned her back to me and the nightgown came off and then she turned to me and said we will remember this morning the rest of our lives. She then came back to bed, untied my robe and pulled it off. Our kissing was insanely passionate, and then it got really passionate for both of us. Miriam said to me don't worry John, I am on the pill, and you are the one I chose to be my first true love.

An hour later, we both fell asleep, having consummated our friendship in a very different way than I had imagined. (Julia, I had not met you yet, so don't get really pissed at me for this)

Miriam and I never talked at school or did anything that would have indicated we had been intimate. We talked on the phone every week just like we had for years. Our family was invited to her graduation party and that was the last time I ever got to see Miriam again. She was a counselor at Camp Louise over the summer and then went away to college the following August. Our weekly calls ended that summer, and I will never forget the incredibly beautiful Miriam and all the time together. I think our talks made it easier for me to talk to women than most men, I simply had been trained to talk to them by Miriam. I have a feeling that my sister knew about the planned events that night, she simply smiled at me and said did you and Miriam have a good time, and just started laughing?

Well back to swimming, I was doing a lot of practice with the distance swimmers to increase my ability to control breathing over a longer period of time. I was going through practice one afternoon and swimming fly when I hooked shoulder with another swimmer going the other way in the next lane. The pain was incredible and went to emergency room immediately after practice. After 4 hours of waiting, the doctor looked at the X-rays, nothing looks broken, and you need to go see an Orthopedics' man.

It took a lot of doing but our NBAC coach got me in touch with a really well know doctor, Dr. Ormond, and we went through an MRI immediately. What was discovered was rotator cuff was swollen but not torn, it appeared I had some fibrous tears throughout my right shoulder and that I needed to be out of the water for the next 2 months. While everyone else was practicing with our summer team, all I got to do was kick a couple thousand yards each day. So absolutely no swim team for the summer, neither the summer swim team nor USA swimming at NBAC.

My sister was on the summer swim team so my mom and her went to the meets, they asked me to come along even though I was out injured. I think the real reason they wanted me there was that after my time with Miriam, I fully discovered girls and with all those girls in bathing suits at the pool, I felt like I had a feast to look at and play with. I think the ladies of the family were worried that something would happen at the house with nobody home. As usual, my dad and brother were away at a baseball tournament, so making the excuse for me to be at the pool Saturday morning kept the house clear of any potential temptations.

I should mention here that I had received my life guarding certificate, and was able to work part-time at our local pool as the extra guard when someone was out so for the first time, I earned money almost every week.

For those that know about college recruiting know that the summer of your junior year is when a lot of coaches contact you and your age group coaches. Because of my injury, nobody came calling so while I may get back to AA times, I knew my swimming was likely over at the end of my senior year.

As my upcoming senior came to a start, I took my SAT exam after reviewing all summer. I did well enough, getting a 1990, in all three sections of the exam. My math score was 700, and my English was 650, so the core was mid 1300's, not good enough for elite schools but good enough for any second-tier school and good enough to get in to UMBC, which is where my mother wanted me to go. My Dad said, hey we can save money if you go to Catonsville Community College and live at home. Truthfully, I had no interest in staying home and looked at West Virginia University, Shepherd University, and then some in VA, PA, and MD. None of these schools were interested at me as a swimmer, injured swimmers are not on the radar screen. In addition, because of title IX, not that many swimming scholarships anyway. A lot of the division 1 scholarships go to foreign students older and more experienced than many American seniors.

Then again, I need to start the recruiting conversation to the next section, the reality was that if you had the twists and turns of my senior year, you would never been able to predict it.

CHAPTER FIVE

Does Anyone Want Me:

As I stated earlier my shoulder was injured in June just as I was completing my junior year of high school. All summer was kicking and waiting for my shoulder to recover and in September came the second MRI. The doctor had told me not to be surprised if it had not healed and plan to do surgery, so it was great reluctance that I went back for my MRI. I thought it was the end and then came the news from the doctor in his office in Baltimore. John, you can start exercising that shoulder again, but here is the problem you have, the muscle density is so diminished that you can't go back to the pool until you get a lot of strength back. You need to regain muscle density or you will be injured again as soon as you start swimming fly again.

With that pronouncement the fall season was over, 10 weeks of rehab and weightlifting to get the shoulder back. Most people are recruited during this time period, and I was totally on the sideline. Coach Brian at NBAC created this really odd program for me to supplement the three times a week weightlifting, a practice so odd that nobody thought it was even possible.

The practice was so bazaar, that all the other coaches said it made no sense to them.

To keep the arm from getting sore again it was the following practice:

Warm-up was 200 with the kick board

Next 10 x 100 free, but like nothing I had ever done. Alternate kicking and right arm only for the first 100. Second one was same thing with the left arm.

Another 200 with the kick board

6 x 100 backstroke, just like the free style, left arm first 100 and then right are the second.

Another 200 with the kickboard

6 X100 Fly – a double armed stroke, but not for me dolphin kick and alternate 3 right arm strokes and then 3 left arm strokes

Another 200 with the kickboard

6 X100 breaststroke, and again one arm only same pattern as fly 3 right arms and then 3 left arms.

Another 200 with the kickboard

200 cool down, so a total of 4000 yards Tuesday, Thursday, Saturday or Sunday, every week. The bad part of this was because of the oddity, the coaches all agreed I could not do this with the team, so at 7:30, when everyone else went home, I got to start my practice by myself, the same rehab training every time.

Monday, Wednesday and Friday were reserved for 60 minutes of weightlifting workouts, so boring, all rehab exercises at first. Then by October double arm weightlifting for the first time. By November, the strength was insane with working out every day in the pool or weightlifting or even stretching exercises. Angela said I looked like I had bulked out like I was ready for wrestling season and not swimming.

All by myself, nobody watching, nobody giving me hope of returning to the pool with any speed or strength. It was absolutely the worst, no friends just the endless rehab exercises.

While this was happening, I took the ACT which is required for other schools, mostly in the south and averaged my low score as expected was 26 in English, which is still the 80%, but remarkably I was 31's in Math and Science. I also had a 27 in Reading so overall score was like a 29 composite, good enough that I started receiving brochures from all sorts of schools. I really liked some of the nice schools in VA but with the costs I knew it would be very difficult without a huge student loan as my dad was not going to spend much money on me. I really like the University of Richmond, but that was way beyond what my family could afford, I even thought about Duquesne in Pittsburgh, or the University of Pittsburgh. My school counselor said I want you to apply for these 2 schools right off, UMBC and West Virginia University, both are available to you and are affordable.

The only swim school that I received anything from was a small division 3 school in Southeast Virginia, Christopher Newport University, they even invited me to have a visit with them.

My dad was still thinking that the only school he wanted to pay for was Catonsville Community College for my first 2 years. He did not want to waste money he said for someone that had never been academically inclined. He told me had you been as good as your sister I would be willing to take a chance, but you have averaged B's your entire career and not very good at studying. In fact, I think if it was not for Miriam, you probably would never have done that well. My sister started laughing hysterically, you have no idea how much she helped John out. I told her to shut up, and the look we had at each other was pure hatred.

Miriam was gone, I tried calling her but as I said before she had moved on to college, and I only got a call back saying she was busy and would call me back sometime soon. That call never happened, and even when she came home for the holidays, she was busy with her friends, so I was sure that it was over. There were a lot of Freshmen and Sophomores who were looking to go out with a senior. After finally getting my driver's license the first week of October, I could play the senior card with car and dating. I really played that card well for all of the fall, nothing else to do on the weekends. I think I had a different girl out for six straight weeks, a little dumbstruck with seniors they were anxious to play around, and I have to admit I liked the attention and took full advantage. One such girl was Lucy Schmidt, a cute sophomore that was on the high school swim team. When I say cute, she had light brown hair, blue eyes and a shapely athletic build that had just turned 16. While not as gorgeous as Miriam, she was still turning heads at high school.

On our date, Lucy saw my shoulder in my polo shirt, and asked why I had quit swimming, I told her I had been injured and that I was in a rehab and not cleared for competition. She then had me pull my shirt off, not what you think, and then made me look in the mirror. Lucy said, I have seen other swimmers, and very few have that much shoulder and arm strength. Why don't you try to go to the high school practice? I thought about it and realized I had not signed up for the team and they were probably full anyway. I just shook my head; I think I will have to have a private meeting with Coach Fran to see if that is even possible. Lucy said I will give coach a call in the morning, I want to see you in your swimsuit. A kiss later and the date was basically over, well over for what I will reveal. As I said previously, she was very athletic build.

Monday Morning: 2 days after date with Lucy.

Good morning, Coach Fran. Can I talk to you this morning? John, sure, how is your shoulder doing.

That is what I wanted to talk to you about, I have been in rehab for the last 10 weeks, practicing with a special practice and weightlifting. What is the possibility of practicing with the team this week?

John, do you want to practice, or would you like to join the team?

Truthfully, I am nervous to do both, I have not had a regular practice in nearly 5 months and would like to test the shoulder without the pressure of NBAC until the first of the year. Is there room on the roster to add me for the season, and in practice?

John, we only have 16 boys on the team this year, your sister and Lucy called me this weekend to ask if you could join our team. Truthfully, I was surprised to hear from them and not you but understand you did not want to take up a slot and not be able to perform. So here is what I can do, practice the week before Thanksgiving with us, and we will have a time trial the Monday afterwards for just you and see if you have anything left to contribute. If you have any speed, then we will talk about putting you on the roster and potentially swimming you in some dual meets. The only thing you have to do is get full clearance from your doctor, I am not going to be responsible for injuring you for the rest of your life. It must be in writing for the athletic director.

Coach Fran, I agree to terms, and thank you. Doctor Visit Friday afternoon: Dr Ormond office:

John I am looking at your shoulder range of motion and it is fully available. I am now going to do some resistance exercises to see how much pain I create. The exam took about 3 minutes and I guess he was looking for me to wince. John, I see no material pain.

Dr. Ormond then measured the muscle size and took a few minutes write his notes in his computer.

John, after reviewing everything you must have taken your rehab very seriously, your muscles are now fully regenerated, and you appear to have absolute full range of motion. I am printing out for you the approved release for you to continue swimming.

I could not wait to thank Dr Ormond, and I gave him a hug and thanked him.

When I got home, my sister and Lucy were waiting for me, and they could tell by my smile that the news was positive. Lucy said so now I get to see you in your bathing suit, at that my sister looked at me and with malice in her voice just yelled "again".

I am assuming that she meant another girl was dating me. That is at least what the PG version I want to reveal here meant. I love my sister, and truthfully though I already have one mother, does she think I need another. Sometimes I think she forgets that I am older than her, because I swear, she acts like I am the little brother.

Thanksgiving Week:

With an annoying get up my sister Angela, woke me-up at 5:30. Hurry-up we need to be at CCC at 6:00. (CCC is Catonsville Community College). After eating a protein bar and water, I grabbed my swim bag with all my stuff in it. After leaving later than Angela wanted, we got to the pool at 5:55, after a quick change I get to the pool deck for a competitive practice for the first time in 5 months.

Coach Fran then stopped me and made an announcement to the team. We have a swimmer here trying out today in John Peters. My sister started laughing. For those that don't know John, he has been a good swimmer for us and has been out with a shoulder injury for the last 5 months. John will start practice with the guys in lane 1, and then we will see if he gets to join our team after our two practices this week.

Lane 1 are the slow swimmers and novices. I know that the high school practice is not that serious, but I was lapping these guys all morning. (Lapping is when the person you are pursuing is so far behind you that you literally are on the same spot only, they are 2 lengths behind you) 30 minutes in to my first workout, I hear John please take your stuff to lane 2 to finish practice.

Wednesday before Thanksgiving:

I hear Angela yell, it's 5:30 get your ass up for practice or Lucy won't get to see your bony ass this morning. Ok, Angela, I have my gym bag packed can you get me a bottle of water and a protein bar. On the way to the pool, Angela said you better treat Lucy nicely, I know what happened with you and Miriam last year, and Lucy is a sweet and innocent girl who is infatuated with you and may do something that she is not ready to do. I simply said, yes Mother Peters, I will treat her nicely. Angela just said, that does not mean nicely in bed, that means you will treat her nice and if something happens, she will tell you, not the other way around. With that conversation my fooling around the rest of the year was concluded, the girls swim team has decided that I can only date Lucy and have to be really nice to her or life was going to be horrible. Nothing like the entire women's team making sure you knew your place. Truthfully, Lucy was cute, and really easy on the eye but never will be Miriam. Miriam was a Porsche, Lucy is like a really nice Jeep, looks fairly good and you take her everywhere. Miriam was that 1 in a million, I had opened up to her for years, and then gone. Lucy was here and very friendly and I had to remember she was only just now turning 16.

Practice went well, I swam for 45 minutes in lane 2, and then I hear, John Peters move over to lane 3.

Coach Fran said we are doing 5 50-meter sprints. John, you are swimming fly and I expect you to stay with these guys swimming free. I am amazed the first time I let go and all five swims I swam and stayed with the guys swimming the easier freestyle.

Thanksgiving dinner:

Mom and Angela had been in the kitchen cooking all day, my dad's mom, Grandmother Peters, was joining us for dinner and my job was fairly easy. Coach Brian said he wanted to come by later but would see me at the pool Friday morning instead of my usual practice time.

I think my grandmother was a plant, so she said to me, John have you started swimming again, I like watching you swim that butterfly thing. My parents in unison said John is just doing rehab, he has not been cleared to do anything yet.

Angela starts laughing, Mom and Dad, I think you may be a week behind. John has been cleared by Dr Ormand to swim and has 2 practices under his belt this week with our high school team.

My mother was furious with both of us, and I could see it. Why have you 2 been keeping this from us.

My comment was pretty easy, Mom I frankly am not sure that I will be able to swim again, and this was just high school practice.

Angela just said to my mom, he let it rip yesterday for the first time, boy is John fast. John was kicking everyone's ass yesterday in the sprints, and you know he never was a sprinter before.

My Dad looked up at her and his question was so John was swimming freestyle with the guys. Nope, he was swimming fly while they swam freestyle and he was leading the sprints by the last one, they literally can't keep up with him.

So that is why coach Brian is coming over here later, I am asking to swim at NBAC, and he wants to figure out where do we put you after being out for 5 months. I think the idea is to put me with the fast juniors the 14 and under and see if I can keep up.

With that the cat was out of the bag, and my 5 months of hell was over. The problem was that no college coaches had seen me swim, I had no times to offer recently so the likelihood of swimming past the next 3 months was at best limited.

Coach Brian came over to the house and said everything is ready for you to swim with the team again. For the first month you swim 3 days per week with the junior team, and then 2 days per week with the outside lanes of main practice. If you deviate anything from what we say, you are considered to be off the team. This is a one-time offer to see if you can come back, we are not going to get you injured and be harmed the rest of your life.

First High school meet back:

Lansdowne was playing a school in Howard County as our first meet of the year. River Hill high school is an affluent area of Clarksville, MD, they had half of the team as winter swimmers, so a good start to the season for a team like us learning to play with a lot of younger guys.

Coach Fran posted the line-up for the meet, when I looked, I was only in 1 event, the 200-medley relay. I went to her and asked why, and she simply said you are on limitations according to the NBAC coaches. Either accept it or you are off both teams. We are not ruining your shoulder you have a lifetime to go through.

Medley relay is first event, we had a freshman swimmer Joseph Pearl doing backstroke, and sophomore Brett Katz, doing breast, then me and then another senior Bob Fiend, the freestyle. Our backstroke caused us to be behind by a body length, and by the time breaststroke was completed I entered the water 1 ½ body lengths behind. That poor freshman from River Hill, by the time I got to the turn I was behind by only a body length and at the finish I not only caught the kid, and at the end but ahead by ½ body length.

Bob finished the event by barely holding off the swimmer from River Hill, and we won the relay event.

My sister and Coach Fran came over to me, how fast did you think you went, I just put my hands out and said I have no idea. Coach Fran said the fastest 50 fly I have ever seen at our school. I will call you coach at NBAC later today and let him know that you looked good. So, coach, can I swim the 100 fly then?

All I heard was you are done for the day, and you know better than to ask. Damn.

The team went on to win the women's event and lost the men. We really had no depth, and I was restricted to one relay event.

Monday After high school meet:

Coach Brian, I am here for the 4:15 practice with the junior kids. I understand John, can you do 15 minutes with the senior team. Angela will be pissed if I don't pick her up, but she will have to live with it. Practice ended at 5:15, and then I had to wait until the senior's finished warm-up.

John who do you want for your 100-fly time trial, I think Brad Shultz would be good he is a pretty fast swimmer. You don't want to swim against Michael, in your time trial. No coach I would prefer not to swim against an Olympic gold medalist in my time trial.

I would like to say that Brad as a 15-year-old was someone I should swim against, so they gave me another National caliber swimmer to play with along with Brad. I did not know who he was but was told he was top six in the country and placed fifth in the recent Olympic trials. He was visiting the area and the coaches had agreed to let him practice with us for the week. The three of us got on the blocks and I put on my goggles for my first 100 fly race in so long I could not remember. Take you mark, and go:

For the first 50 yards, I was only a ½ body length behind, and at the end the near Olympian finished 3 seconds ahead of me and I was 2 seconds ahead of Brad. Coach Brian is beaming, and says welcome to the senior team, this was your tryout. If your shoulder starts to hurt, I will throw you off the team immediately. You are restricted to 1 arm butterfly in practice, live with it until we tell you otherwise. If you deviate from anything we tell you to do, you are off the team, and the same for Lansdowne.

As the high school season went, I was allowed to swim only 2 events per meet, usually the medley relay and the 500 freestyle or the 100 fly. I never once got to swim the 200 IM.

In the final home meet, I was the last senior that went through the door for senior day. I continued to swim the medley relay and then this time I was allowed to swim the 500 freestyle and the 100 fly. I was a winner in all three and reported that to coach Brian at NBAC.

Four days before Baltimore County High School championships.

Lucy and Angela came to me and asked what events I was swimming this weekend. I looked at them and had no idea. It is posted and I think you are going to be surprised.

You are swimming the 200 IM, you will be swimming it with a no time so you are the lowest ranked swimmer in the meet. You are also registered to swim the 100 fly, and you are swimming the 50 freestyle again with no time you are seeded last. I went to Coach Fran and asked her about it, don't look at me this is the decision of NBAC.

Lucy asked what the heck was going on, and all I could say was NBAC made this decision, I have no idea why or what they are doing. This is my last swim meet as a high school swimmer, and I have no future after that. Lucy gave me a kiss on the cheek, and whispered you still have no idea. After holding hands with her, she said everyone is in your corner so let's see if you are ready.

Baltimore County Championship:

Lucy and Angela left for the women's room, and I left for the men's locker room, found one locker left at UMBC and was ready to go.

The 200 IM was my first event and with my no time, I was the absolutely slowest seed of the slow heats. With Lucy and Angela clapping, I saw my name on the heat sheet and proceeded to lane 1 of the slowest heat they had. A little over 2 minutes after the race started, I had finished with a time that was fast beating my heat by 1 full length of the pool, Coach Brian is in the stands, oh crap, why did we wait this long. After all the heats were over, I had finished sixth overall, and qualified for the MD State meet. The 50 free was not as good, still not a great sprinter so I had no idea why they had me swim this race, but I did manage to finish 12th overall. The last event I got to swim was the 100 fly, and I was in the fast heat, seeded 6th. I would like to say that I won the event, but after taking the lead going in to the 50, 2 swimmers came from behind to beat me by less than a second. Coach Brian starts laughing, so 7 months after your injury you are now faster than you have ever been. Your 100 fly and 200 IM are now top 100 in the country. We have a lot of work to do and very little time to do it, trust me in what will come next.

Coach I am going to ask what this means, I am applying to colleges at the end of the month, and nobody is recruiting me, I am damaged goods, and you know it. We will see here is your meet schedule for the next 4 weeks.

Md State high school swim meet, swimming 200 IM and 100 fly.

Senior meet 2 weeks later at University of MD you will be swimming the 100 fly, 200 fly, and 200 IM.

Long-Course meet, we are going to have you swim the 400 IM and the 100 Fly. Ok, I get the meets and all but what good is going to be nobody has money left.

Division 1 schools may be done but division 2 has economic money, academic money and sometimes a few athletic bucks to go around. I think we will have some interest. If worst comes to worst, you can swim at Catonsville Community College until we get scholarship offers for the next year.

Lucy and Angela are waiting for me, what the hell was that all about. All I could say was that Coach Brian thinks some colleges may be interested in me. Lucy gave me a hug, I told you that you were better than you think.

During the week I put in applications to CCC, WVU in Morgantown, and UMBC. I would find out later that all three had accepted me, my dad would be thrilled if I went to CCC. Cost is low and I don't think he thinks I can finish college.

Md State Championship one week later:

Montgomery County is the dominant swimming in the state, Baltimore swimmers are lucky to be in any of the finals. With my first swim in the Baltimore County meet I am seeded 18th overall in the 200 IM, and 8th overall in the 100 fly. This meet has trials in the morning and finals in the afternoon. Lucy and Angela were swimming but neither made the top 12, so they were done early in the day.

With both of them done, I had the 200 IM left in the trials. My fly was the same as it was the week before, and finished 7th, first lane in the consolations. The 200 IM was fast and I was not sure how fast until they announced the results, when it was all over I was announced as lane 6, of the finals.

Coach Brian came over to me and after I got my sweats on and introduced 2 coaches, the first was with Duquesne University, and the coach of Alderson Broadus. Ok, I knew one was in Pittsburgh and one was someplace in West Virginia.

Coach Edwards introduced himself, I am creating a new legacy at Alderson Broadus and want to know if you are interested in swimming beyond high school. I said yes, and how did you hear of me, and he smiles, let's just say someone that went to the Olympics has a mother that grew up in West Virginia. She said that we have a poor swimmer, that is swimming great and not a single team in the country is recruiting him. Let's see what you do tonight in your 2 races.

Duquesne coach said to me right now I have all my scholarship money tied up, but I have a possible person that will turn down his scholarship, I will get in touch with you, damn you really improved the last 2 weeks. I wish we had you in our radar earlier.

On the way home Lucy sat in the front seat with Angela sitting in the back. Both of them went on and on about what was happening and how are we going to tell your parents. I swore the two of them to secrecy, nothing is being offered and it really is too late for me to get a scholarship. Lucy leaned over to me and again said you still have no idea of what is going on and that is so cute. I got the feeling that a great joke was being played on me and I was the only one that did not understand the joke.

Finals Md State Meet:

As I said earlier, the 4A/3A swimming championships is dominated by Montgomery County teams, great teams with long history.

First up 200 IM, in the outside lane, I was seeded as the 6th and last swimmer in the finals. At the end of the fly leg, I could see that I was ahead of lane 5, and at the end of backstroke we were even. My breaststroke leg kept me just ahead of lane 5 and after free I touched him out by 0.5 seconds. I looked up and had ended up 4th overall. I was the first finisher from the Baltimore area.

30 minutes later the 100 fly consolations, and coach Brian had asked me to try something different. He asked me to do a consistent but not outstanding first 50 and then come back the next 50. I did what the coach asked and was only fourth at the 50, then started moving up through the second 50 and was just touched out by a swimmer in

lane 2 from Montgomery County. So that was the last swim of my high school career, I had just established two Lansdowne records when I was very questionable during the entire season. Our medley relay without me finished 7th overall, coach Fran was told not to put me in that event.

I get home and Angela and mom are waiting for me. I asked what was up and they just started laughing. You think today was your last team swim right, and I nodded yes, all done. My mother just shook her head, you have no idea do you. No mom I have no idea what's going on. Between your 4th place finish and 8th place tonight, you must have impressed some coaches. We have coaches calling form PA, VA, WV, division 1,2, and 3 schools want to know who this top 100 guy is that nobody has ever heard of.

The coaches from Edinboro, Clarion, and Slippery Rock called tonight. We heard from Alderson Broadus, Shepherd, and Christopher Newport University. The Duquesne coach said he has no money but if you enroll, he will get you some work study money and possible some other ways to reduce your tuition. All I could say is you noticed nobody offered a scholarship, all of the money is gone so I will probably have to go to CCC and swim a year and hope somebody remembers me.

Senior Meet, UM at College Park.

This is a "AA/AAA meet", and because my times are from high school and have no official times to play with my coaches appealed with US Swimming to put my times from high school and it was granted.

I am the lowest seed in the 200 fly because I had no official time other than a practice time at NBAC. USA swimming allowed me in and again at the slowest time possible so first heat. I was very worried about this event, and really should not have been, the swim went well with me winning the heat by 15 seconds. After watching everyone from the regional meet I finished 10th overall, not bad for my first swim in a year.

The 100 fly was not much different, ended up 12th overall, still using the strategy coach had asked me to use.

The swim of the day was the 200 IM, with the seed from the last week, I ended up sixth overall.

I called Lucy from my cell phone, and she asked me why have you not been answering your phone. Lucy, you know I put the phone in the car and stow it so nobody will steal it in the car while I swim. Well John, you need to call your home apparently, you have coaches calling from Ohio University and someone from Akron. John, you understand that you are going to swim collegiately right. Lucy, all I have heard is that if I am lucky, I am going to have to go to JUCO for a year and then hope they recruit me again next year.

When I get home, my dad is at the door, looks like you need to go to CCC for a year at least, all these coaches are calling and saying we have our money spent for this year, but we want to monitor John's progress and be ready to recruit him as a deferred freshman. I really don't want to go to CCC, and really don't want to live at home for a year when all my friends are going away to college. Son, I think that is nuts, where you going to get the money to go anywhere else, we have 2 more kids to put through college and James's travel is very expensive in elite baseball. My dad revealed his favorite was James with that statement, and guess what older son, you need to stay in your place while the 2 favored children get money for college.

Long-Course meet. The meet is at the same pool in College Park, but this time, the pool is configured as an 8 lane 50-meter pool. Coach Brian is there as an assistant and Lucy said she wanted to come sees my races. She must have the patience of Job because swim meets can be as boring as hell. I am swimming an event I have never swum in my life, (400 IM) and they gave me an estimated time for my seed, which leaves me seeded in the back of the next to the fastest heat. I noticed that only 4 heats of this event and 8 at least for all the others. My swim was consistent but not as spectacular as I would have hoped, but I did manage to make 6th overall, which was not bad. I have to admit that was the most horrible event I ever swam; it took 10 minutes in the pool to get my heart to calm down.

I had to wait 2 hours before my next event, at least I got to sit in the stands and hold hands with Lucy. I had to admit she was growing on me, my sister liked her and apparently the whole Lansdowne swim team had made sure that is the only girl I could see this year. Truthfully, it was funny we had done nothing but hold hands and kissed, very little extra activity, and that was fine with both of us, and at least I thought it was.

The 100 fly went alright, although I did not make my seed time and ended up 12th overall.

After the 100 fly Coach Brian came over to me. I think you will need to make a choice do you want a year at JUCO or go to college next year. I looked at him and said nobody has made me an offer. He just said not officially, the coach from Alderson Broadus wants to come to your house tomorrow and asked if I can be there when he discusses your next step. I believe John, you are going to get a scholarship offer and you can take it or play one year at CCC and do this recruiting all over again.

On the way home, Lucy came over to me and said can we park somewhere? I said sure, and what does she want to discuss. When I stopped at a parking lot of an old Kmart that was closed, she leaned over and kissed me. I know you won't be here next year and that we will probably not continue our relationship when you go to college next year now that someone wants to offer you money. She then came closer to me and proceeded to give me the most passionate kiss she had ever given me. My parents are not home until 11 tonight, how about we stop at my house I want to give you something to remember me by when you are away at college.

When we get to her house, she went to the kitchen and got us some soda's. I was sitting on the love seat in the living room. Lucy came over to me and sat down on my lap and gave me a kiss. She then whispered the gift I want to give you is for you to be my first, and then proceeded to give me a long and passionate kiss. Within 5 minutes we were on the larger couch and going at it, with virtually no clothes on. I would like to say that it was me that initiated things, but it was Lucy. The one thing she said is I am going to give you something to make sure I don't get pregnant, and with that we made love for what seemed like an hour and at 9:00, I looked over her shoulder and said don't you think my family will want me home. Lucy said, Angela has made it possible for you to be home by 11:00 tonight without questions. Lucy started kissing me again and her athleticism was apparent as we finished at 10:00, and we both took a quick shower before we drove over to my parents' house. We got home by 11:00, and Angela just looked at the two of us and smiled.

My mother said about time you got home from the meet; we have a request for a Coach Edwards to come by the house at noon tomorrow. He said he is from Alderson Broadus and wants to talk to all of us and your NBAC coach.

Mom, I met him last week, some school in rural West Virginia, nice place apparently but very remote.

Sunday morning noon:

Welcome to our house Coach Brian, is the AB coach with you? He is finishing a call and will be here in a minute.

Coach Edwards introduced himself to my parents and talked about his college in the mountains of West Virginia, and simply said, I know you probably think West Virginia is the oddest place to go to swim when you are here in the midst of the best swimming in the USA. Well, I am trying to upgrade our team, and recruiting from all over the east coast for those swimmers that others may have overlooked or have potential to improve. We have a major sprinter from Pittsburgh already committed and I need a distance swimmer, IM swimmer and flier. I see you as at least one of those pieces and God knows that nobody else has money this late even for a miracle swimmer the last few weeks is going to offer what I think we can offer.

Coach Brian stopped him at that point and said let me see what it is you are asking because we think if John goes to CCC for one year division 1 schools are going to come looking.

Coach Edwards then proceeded to drop off the written offer in a package for Coach Brian and my family to review.

Well, here is what I am offering John to make sure he wants to come to AB. I am offering a 50% athletic scholarship that is a series of one-year offers, the school based on your ACT is willing to give you what amounts to 25% more for academic aide. I am also looking to get you into work study to have money to spend each month. Your cost of going to college will be the same if you go to CCC or go to AB.

My dad was more impressed than Coach Brian or myself, you could see the dollar signs in his eyes.

Coach Brian just said, let's discuss this and we will call you Monday night which way we are going. We all agreed that Monday night we would let AB know.

Monday night, NBAC office. Coach Brian, my parents, Angela and Lucy in attendance. Coach Fran came by at the last minute. Coach Edwards, we have you on the phone with a group of people that are friends and family of John Peters.

This is John speaking, after consideration I want you to know I have just signed my National Letter of Intent to commit to Alderson Broadus. I have the fax with the offers from your school that I will be signing tonight. With that offer, I just extended my swimming career for 4 more years. Even my dad was impressed and that rarely happened in my life. Lucy, Angela and I were in a group hug, and then I received a major hug from Coach Brian, and he called out to Coach Stephens, we have one more college swimmer from our team. Coach Stephens just said, great who is it. John Peters just signed his letter of intent. Everyone was laughing, you mean the kid that we had limits on for 8 months, and he said yes. I guess that crazy rehab worked.

That was April, 2 months after most of everyone had signed. I called the Duquesne coach and he said damn, I wish I had been able to help you.

I went to the senior prom with Lucy and the after prom with her. I will say other than a lot of hand holding nothing more went on, I think we both knew it was going to be over after the school year ended. We had taken lots of pictures at her parents' house. Lucy looked very nice in a yellow prom dress, and I gave her a corsage for her arm. We changed at the after-prom again at the Holiday Inn, and she looked very comfortable in her jeans and polo shirt. I had been nominated by the girl's swim team for prom king, I did not win that honor. Lucy was quieter than normal as we left early in the morning.

When I drove her home she said to me, John I will always think of you but time we go our separate ways, I don't want to be waiting by the phone every night hoping you will call. She then kissed me again, and if you and I finish college and you are still available, I am coming after you. I guess I should shield Julia from Lucy, otherwise it could be very interesting.

I got home and Angela was waiting for me, she had just gotten home ten minutes before me. Angela, did you know we were breaking up tonight. She nodded yes, I knew, and it is the best for both of you. You need a fresh start away from Lucy, Miriam's memory and away from Dad. It is time for you to create your own legacy and with that a hug from my sister and tears in my eyes. I have mom and James has dad, you have been on your own for so long, time to get away and create your own life. Angela was crying and we were exhausted, and both went to bed.

Graduation was in June, unlike many I had no party, my parents said they were saving up for college, but the reality was I was not anyone's favorite and by the time they thought about anything it was too late to do anything meaningful. I never saw Lucy again and you already know what happened to Miriam. Grandmother Peters gave me a check for $500, and in the envelope was a hand printed note.

Dear John, you and your dad will never like each other, because the both of you are exactly alike, independent and people like you. I know you and your parents have not had a lot of good days, I am here for you as always and expect you to call me from college. I gave my grandmother a hug.

My grandfather, the Rabbi, sent over a $25. Check and it simply said congratulations, please come back to Baltimore, they don't have Jewish families in West Virginia. I just had to laugh at his request. My grandmother had never recovered from her injury and had passed away in March, at a nursing home. I think my grandfather was as much relieved as he was devastated, she had been in a nursing home for over a year, when they simply called and said she passed during the night.

The next morning, my dad was waiting for me as I went down to breakfast. John, I need to talk to you about your remaining balance for college. Look, I don't think you are dedicated enough in your classes for me to throw away money for your college experience. I know that you are getting ¾ of your college money from the University, and that leaves me with $5000, plus expenses that needs to be covered. I have decided that based on your past history, I am not going to give you the money. I established a student loan for you, that you can draw from for school expenses. If you graduate, then maybe I will help you pay the loan off. In addition, since you will be spending most of your time with the team and using the cafeteria, I know we had agreed to give you $250, per month, but I think that is way too much, so we will send you a check for $100, each month for you to use. Between the $100, and the work you have during the summer you should be fine, and we won't hurt our family finances before the other children start college.

Dad, why have you decided to renege on what you committed to when I got the scholarship?

Truthfully John, you assumed we would cover the costs, and I never said I would. I had to put myself through college so you should also. It will mean a lot more to you if you do it on your own.

Dad, you and I know the real truth, you have never supported me in any way either academically or athletically. It would have been nice for you to tell me I am now borrowing $20,000, for college. Does mom even know what is going on?

She understands my position, and has decided that she will not fight it, and that maybe after you graduate, we might help you. As far as supporting you, I did every month by sending a check to NBAC, and your grades were nothing special like Angela or James, so look at it this way it is a way for you to prove yourself.

I reminded him that Grandpa had paid for half of the money for the swimming, so he was overstating the support.

Nothing else for me to say, everything Angela had said was true, my dad and my mom were not to be trusted. They had given up on me and now that I was 18, I had pretty much been cut loose. With that I realized 2 months to go to get out of this caustic relationship.

I did not swim for the local summer team, many college swimmers did what I did just swam with the US Swimming team and to be ready for college. My mother worked the swim meets, as a timer, and Angela did well and made her first county championships.

I just worked as the pool as a lifeguard, and stayed away from all the girls, I had already been burned twice and enough for now.

My summer was mostly a regiment of going to NBAC in the morning for work-out, getting a ride home, breakfast, and then bicycle to work. I was a lifeguard most days from noon to 9 PM, except for Sunday and Monday days off. I spent as little time as possible at home, but with my dad either going with his teams or with James's travel squad, I had my room mostly to myself anyway. While I will admit seeing so many girls in bathing suits was tempting, I did not go out on a single date all summer. I needed the money now to be able to survive my freshman year. A lot of book costs that I need to cover.

Truthfully, my dad and James were away most of the summer, I don't think he and I spoke more than 3 times the whole summer. I think he was relieved that he would not have to ever talk to me anyway. He was neither proud of anything I had done or cared anything about me or what I needed. Angela told me before I left that dad was really embarrassed that he had no relationship with his eldest son. I laughed, because if he had wanted some relationship, you would have thought he would have driven with Mom and me to AB, but alas another tournament for him that weekend. Maybe he would have actually gone to a swim meet over the last five years, but obviously I was the family embarrassment to him.

James blamed me for not having a relationship with dad. If you had just stayed playing baseball, you would have had a great relationship with dad. I simply said, you were so much better that I had to find another sport. With that he shook his head, such a drama queen, dad and I can see it. Why didn't you choose a man's sport like I did.

I was ready to go elsewhere, nobody in my family would miss me much. The night before Mom and I were going to drive to AB, Angela said she is joining us, so mom has someone to drive home with. Before I went to bed, she said I am going to miss you nobody to talk to about swimming, and mom is trying to be brave, she is going to miss you even though she and I are tighter. Dad and James are away so much that she feels she is on her own. Angela was the only one I would miss from the family; the way it was I was surprised mom even agreed to drive me. Until a week ago I had assumed that I would be taking a Greyhound bus, to the school. When I was on the phone with Greyhound, she said hang-up the phone I am going to take you to Alderson Broadus.

I never heard from Lucy after the break-up. Angela said she had cried the day after prom and called her sobbing. I felt like I just abandoned John when I was really just doing what was going to happen anyway. She asked was she insane for breaking up with your brother just because he was going away to college. Angela just told her let John be on his way to college he needs some time away from Baltimore, you did the right decision, knowing he needs to find his own path. He has nothing here and I really doubt he will be coming back; I am also afraid that the family has cut him off and I won't see my big brother again. You have no idea how bad it is for John here now; he needs to get away and create his new life. He puts on this tough exterior, but it is killing him that our parents have basically cut him out now, like they only have 2 children. I love my brother and don't know how he can strand being here, he never eats with anyone in the family, barely talks to anyone, gets home from work, and most nights he is on his own for making any kind of dinner. One day he was getting breakfast, and the confrontation with dad was so weird, so yes you did the right thing for John, he needs a clean break from everyone here. We have so broken his heart and he is so stoic, that he just takes it. He never smiles anymore, just exists here.

In late August, with several hundred freshmen coming in, I was done with my Baltimore home and ready to go to freshman orientation at AB.

Goodbye Baltimore, time for the hills of West Virginia.

CHAPTER SIX

Hello New World

F reshman orientation at Alderson Broadus was Monday through Wednesday, the upperclassmen, then come in for school on Thursday and Friday, then everyone is off for a three-day weekend. Most go back home, but for me I did not have a car, and what was I going back to, Dad would be away for a Labor Day tournament with James. My sister and mother would probably go to Ocean City, they had a condo from a friend that told them they could use it that weekend.

The Journey:

Saturday morning before Freshman orientation:

To get from Baltimore to Philippi, WV, takes about 4 ½ hours to drive. We leave bright and early with me driving the first 3 hours, going through Frederick, MD, to Hagerstown, and then Cumberland, MD. Over the mountains, and then we stopped for gas and change of drivers in Morgantown, WV. Change of driver to Angela, for an hour on I-79, before we changed drivers again, with mom, driving the last leg to the college. My dad and brother did not even bother to change weekend plans to see me off. Why was I not surprised? I realized I was going further west than I had even been before, the farthest I had ever been before was like, Harrisburg, PA.

The college had signs out welcoming the freshman class. I had to check in and sign forms, so I could get a room that night. When I get to the registrar, they asked my name, and I told them. The older woman came out and said wait a minute, you will have the athletic department coming for you. They have your room assignment. A girl with a thick southern accent came over and said, are you the Peters? Yes, I am John Peters, and she said follow her car we are going over to the dorms, your room is already assigned.

My room was on the first floor of an old building, each room had 2 people, and when I looked inside nobody had checked in. The girl said her name was Sally Lambert, she was a senior major in physical education teaching. My sister said, don't get any ideas John, and I just started laughing, look at her hand she has an engagement ring on.

When we finally got to the room, it was assigned to 2 freshman swimmers, Paul Cunningham, Pittsburgh, PA, and then John Peters, Arbutus, MD. Sally said we like to keep the swimmers together, they tend to get in trouble otherwise, I had no idea what that meant, an inside joke, I guess.

We unloaded the car and put everything in the dorm room, my mom insisted on bringing out the clean sheets and making the bed. With that mom said I would like to stay and see the campus, but it is getting late, and we have reservations to stay at the Fairfield Inn, in Cumberland tonight. Supposedly the downtown area has decent restaurants, and the State of Maryland has invested in the downtown, but we don't want to get there too late. Standing outside the car my mother hugged me, and was absolutely bawling, she said you better be good, I love you. I just wish we had been there for you more.

Angela just said to me, I want to see you so make sure you come home for Thanksgiving. I'm going to miss swimming without my big brother, it will never be the same again. Mom, whispers in my ear, don't get any of these girls pregnant, you are on your own up here with the temptations. I just laugh, mom I will have no time, swimming and school will keep me busy. With that both of them went in the car, leaving all my remnants of Baltimore with them, all except my Raven's poster.

5PM, I had set-up my side of the room claiming the side away from the window, so I could sleep in the morning. In walks, this really tall skinny dude, and introduces himself as Paul Cunningham, I am a sprinter and 100 Flyer.

I introduced myself to Paul and his family and told him I am here supposedly to swim fly and maybe IM. I'm from Baltimore area so sorry about the raven's poster, but I needed something from home.

Paul just smiles, so you are the last-minute miracle swimmer I am hearing about. Did you really get to the top 100 of the country with a no time listed? Yes, and apparently, I have an Olympic swimmer's mom that helped me get recruited here.

You have met Michael Phelps, and I had to admit I had talked to him, and he actually was a real nice guy.

You won't mind my poster of the Penguins Stanley Cup then? I laughed, I never followed hockey, we don't have a team just baseball and football.

For our kids, Paul and I stayed roommates for all four years, 2 years in the dorm and then an apartment.

The rest of the night was easy, a cafeteria run and then to the room to get it set-up. I tried to call Angela and it went to voice mail, later she called back and said that they were eating and did not want to take the call in a restaurant.

Just like any freshman, Paul and I had to go through orientation, and get our classes, unlike others being athletes had a privilege, our schedules were waiting for us, and we did not have to fight for classes. A tour of the school and we were free for the day. We talked about our families, he was from a big family with six kids, I told him about my family, and said that I was the child that they wanted to throw away, not smart like my sister and not a baseball player like my brother.

AB is an interesting school, at that time there is like 2 women to every guy and so it was like a feast for the eyes. The words that Sally had said got me a little worried about the swimmer reputation because when I was outside the women's dorm, when Paul said we were swimmers, all the girls could say was we know about you guys. I truthfully had no idea of what that meant.

Classes started Thursday and with me having 17, credit hours easy class was Accounting 101, but calculus, was going to be tough 4 credit card, 1 credit art appreciation class, English, and speech were the main courses, and economics 101, was the odd class on Tuesday evenings.

We were not allowed to practice as a team until a certain date in October according to NCAA regulations, Paul and I would do the posted workout very easy about 3K, yards a day and weightlifting 3 days a week until December.

My classes were hard, and I know that I would end up with slightly below a 2.5, GPA at mid-term, with a C in calculus I was doing well enough in the other classes to bring it to about a 2.5. I chose not to have my parents get my grades. That allowed me the luxury of not having to listen to them whine about what I was doing.

The team was fun like high school swimming on steroids. Because I was the great unknown, I never got to swim with the same group twice. As October ended and hard practice began, the practices went to about 5000 yards in the afternoon, and then we had to do 2 mandatories out of 4 morning workouts. I chose Monday and Thursday; Paul of course woke me up on Tuesday and Wednesday for his mandatory and went with me for an extra practice on Thursday. The skinny swimmers still were weightlifting into November, but I was done, coaches said too big already, we are cutting yours out. Paul was not happy as I got to watch him lift and do nothing but bicycle.

I had an odd encounter with Coach Edwards that took me off-guard. I asked him for a day off from swimming. He asked what I needed it for, I said I wanted to go up to Clarksburg with a couple of other Jewish students for Yom Kippur services. He looked up at me, if this was for a test, I could make an exception, but I can't have you taking time off for your religion. I was like my professors are ok with this, and he simply said I am not your professors, you are part of a team and if your religion takes you away for this practice what are we going to do for Friday night meets. I was perplexed and let Paul know what he said. Paul also agreed

71

that this was odd behavior. Reluctantly I had to eat right before practice to have enough energy to swim, I practiced but wow not the reaction I would have thought, simply the holiest day of the year I needed off. This odd behavior was just the first comment from Coach Edwards like this.

Our first meet was going to be the weekend after Thanksgiving, and I was thinking about that and really was wondering what to do, they really closed the school down so had to figure what to do.

I had a conversation with Kevin Durkin, a soccer player from Baltimore, he asked do you need a ride to Baltimore for Thanksgiving break, I looked at him I truthfully have not discussed it with my family at this point. Maybe I will let you know.

On my weekly call 10 days before the school would close for the Holiday, I called up my mom and asked her, if I get a ride will it be ok for me to come home for Thanksgiving.

She said it was ok by her, but the house would look differently than when I left. I decided to get a ride back with Kevin, we left at 7:00 in the morning and he dropped me off in Arbutus just about 11:30.

The Confrontation:

I could not find my key, so I had to knock on the door, mom came to the door and asked who it was. It is your son back from college, remember me, John. She opened up the door and gave me a hug and said welcome home. I grabbed my duffle bag, and was getting ready to take it upstairs, when my mother said, we set you up in the basement. I was like what, she said since you were not here, we decided to set up your stuff in the basement and let each kid have their own room. (I was like wow; they really could not wait to get me out of here) Mom, who decided this, and she said well you father figured you weren't here, and James and he were looking at game films and hitting videos, in the love seat in the upstairs bedroom. (Why did I come home, just the same as before)

Angela came home, and threw her arms around me, have you grown you look taller and bigger. "Angela, yes, I am now just under 6 feet now, and gained 10 pounds with all the weightlifting. Just to let you know, I have been very good, I don't think I have gone out on a date more than twice the whole semester. No time, and quite frankly, I have been burned enough the last couple of years."

"Angela burst out I am early admission to UM College Park, going to be a science major (Biology and Chemistry)."

Angela took me to the corner and told me that dad was coming home, and that mom and he said that he needs to clear the air with you. I was like, "great, just what I want to hear, the old man and I have nothing in common, barely speak, and why would I want to talk to him."

After dinner, my dad said he wanted to speak to me and then proceeded to take me to the study and closed the doors.

"John, your mother has asked me to speak with you to apologize for the last couple of years, she thinks that I spent too much time with James and my baseball teams, and that we need to fix this situation."

"Mark let's understand the situation, in all my years of swimming you showed up to maybe 3 swim meets in total. You spent every weekend you could with the teams or your James tournaments, but never spent any time with me. When I was injured all, you could talk about was me going to CCC, because I was not a good enough student for you to spend money on. You did not even really want me to go to college, so why should I accept your apology. It did not take long this afternoon when you moved my stuff to the basement so you could spend more time with James and make me even more unwelcome here. There are 2 types of abuse, there is physical abuse and then there is mental abuse. You are the second, you never gave a damn about me once I quit baseball, you know it and I know it. The only reason you are trying to do anything is because mom asked you to. The only thing I remember from you for the last 7 years was a check each month to NBAC and that was only for half of it. I get that you and James have a common bond in baseball, you just forgot you had another son, and frankly I called you Mark because I don't have a dad. Coach Brian was more of a father than you were, and Grandpa knows more about me than you do. The only reason I came home was for mom and Angela and the fact that the school closed the dorms for the weekend, and I don't have enough money for a motel for the weekend."

"First of all, you will address me as dad and not Mark, I am still your father. I had to do coaching, so we had enough money to go on vacations each year, pay the bills and pay for you expensive swimming. I guess I should have found a way to go to the swim meets and I know nothing about swimming so what would I do there. As far as putting your stuff downstairs it made sense for you to have space for yourself when you are here. I thought you would be pleased with it; you did not have to share space with your brother."

"I will call you dad if you insist, but the move downstairs was only for 1 reason so that you could be closer to your only son. I am not your son; you just donated the sperm for me to be born. As far as being pleased about it, let's see you never told me or asked me about this, I have no shower just a toilet and sink here, I think they call that prison dad. You have the smart one in Angela, and your clone in James, I was just the other child that you never gave a crap about, never encouraged, almost never spent any time with me, so what am I supposed to do forgive you, for what?"

Mark responded, "you are right I have made mistakes, and probably should have spent more time with you and even encouraged you, but again I knew nothing about swimming, your mom and Angela seemed to be your go to people. I did the best I could by supporting the family financially and you have never missed a meal. So, for your mother's sake can we at least get along."

"Dad, I am not really interested in the apologies and as far as I am concerned Grandpa said he is paying my way at school, you would only pay $100, per month because you did not think I was ever going to graduate. With the money I made this summer I can almost make it with the work study money."

"John what can I do to help make this situation better for us. Your mother thinks that we need to find a common ground because she cries every time your name is mentioned."

Mark left the room and all I could hear is a grown man crying and I have lost my son.

I decided to leave the house immediately, took my jacket and walked all the way to downtown Arbutus. Angela came with the car about an hour later, she was really freaked out. Thank God, "I found you, mom is worried that you are trying to go back to school tonight. I have never heard our father cry and after you and he were in the den, he came out sobbing and I think he still is."

I am sorry about making the old man cry, but you know what it was time for it, he had it coming, and even you told me to leave and not come back because neither of my parents cared much about me. I just wish I had never come back.

Angela put her arms around me and said "I think they are trying to make it better for you."

Arbutus Home:

I returned home with Angela at almost midnight, my mother was at the kitchen table. You could see the tears in her eyes, I never knew how much you and your father were so far apart.

"Well, this is what's going to happen, your dad is coming down here in 10 minutes, he and James moved the love seat to the basement and your bed to upstairs. It took us an hour to break it down and get it upstairs. I threatened him that we will get divorced if he does not find a way to patch it up with you between now and winter break. He has made mistakes and so have you, you really hurt him by telling him he was not your father, that Coach Brian was more of a father than he was."

I grabbed my duffle bag and took it upstairs to see my bed, nothing else went upstairs no dresser or whatever. James looked at me and said your such a drama queen, we thought you would like it downstairs. James, did you even think to ask me, I might have been ok, but when I show up and my stuff is in the basement, what would you think. I guess we did not think about asking you, I was really excited when dad suggested it.

Yes, that is because you 2 spend lots of time together, me nothing. I have nothing in common with him and he has never supported me, and you aren't much better.

I was able to get some sleep and knew my grandparents were coming over for Thanksgiving dinner and Uncle Roger was in town checking on Grandma, his wife and kids were coming up Friday.

I was studying Calculus when my mother came up to see me, you are having trouble with the subject. Not really trouble, just not going to get anything better than a "C" I think. Mom laughed same problem as your dad, and she sat down and helped me study for my next test.

My grandfather came over to me and said I need to tell you, your dad just handed me a check for $2500, and said it is my obligation to pay for my son and not yours. I don't know what went on last night, but I have never had your father so quiet. I told him that basically he was not my father that you and Coach Brian were my father, he never cared about me or supported me. My grandfather hugged me and said he is trying to make up for it now, I just don't know if you have it in your heart to forgive him.

The rest of the dinner went by quietly on my part, I sat next to my grandfather who kept putting his arm around me. I asked if I could come by for Friday night services, he looked at me and said I would love it. I explained, I need to see some Jewish people no synagogues in West Virginia, I miss seeing the people.

On Saturday I went with my mother to the local Walmart, I needed some items for the upcoming winter, and I did not have the money to buy it. She asked me how much money I had left from the summer life guarding job. Let's see, I have $500, left and need about $200., per month for dinners, entertainment supplies and snacks. The problem mom is that we get done with swim practice right before the cafeteria closes and very little I want to eat left, so about three days a week I have to go out and get something else and with no transportation, I have to walk about a mile each way to find anything other than fast food. Plus, no Sunday night dinner in the cafeteria, so that is where my savings are going.

I did not tell you, because you know the answer, dad was not going to support me, he said he would then renege on what he promised, and grandpa paid my last quarter of my tuition and food. I bought my own books out of my work money so trying to find a way to get through the year since work study gives me about $75, per month.

She leaned over and kissed me and said, "that is ending tonight." I will make sure you have money in your account tonight and if you were in so much distress why didn't you say something. Mom, I am the child, what was I supposed to say, my father turned his back on me. I did not want to be a burden and did not want you and dad to fight, I already knew I was on my own, I was trying to figure out between grandpa's assistance how to get money enough to get through.

My mother simply said, "I am fixing this you better come home again and see us. I will take control of the situation, and with Angela getting academic money, we should have some money for you. We are not poor, I don't understand why you father refused to give you money, we have money in an account that has to be spent on education, I guess he thought if he got tough on you, that would make you study more. I see now that was a total mistake, instead he looked like an ogre. That part will end."

My mother and Father had a discussion as soon as we got home, I had no idea but she did most of the talking and he did most of the listening.

I wanted to go to Arbutus, so walked over and back. My father was at the house when I got back, and I was not looking forward to speaking to him. Dad, I need to give a call to Kevin to make sure when he wants to go back to AB. I have tests to study for and need to get back because I have a make-up practice at 6 PM.

"Son, I don't think you will need to call Kevin, I talked to your mom, and I did not know you were walking every week to the grocery store and to go to dinner. I had a friend who has a used car business in town, please look at the driveway, nice car for James, I think. No John, this is for you, I can't imagine with the weather getting cold up there in the mountains that you had no transportation at all. I got an 8-year-old Chevrolet Malibu that was painted dark green so ugly but at least it was transportation. No more walking to the grocery store. I'm so sorry the way things have worked out, I'm proud that you got a scholarship, and the way you recovered from the major injury. I thought it would have been better if you had stayed home for another year, I realize now that you had nothing to stay for, every weekend your father and brother just abandoned you. I had no idea that you only had your grandfather and coach to talk to. He leaned over hugged me and said, here is my cell phone number, no matter where you are I expect a call every week."

That was the first time my father had given me his cell number because he had never called me in the three months at college nor had he been on any of the weekly calls with my mom and Angela.

"I really want to be a part of your life, obviously I have failed at that until now."

Early Sunday morning, I was ready to go in the car, Angela, mom and dad came to say good-bye, James never said a word to me, I think he was pissed because he probably thought he was getting the car. I will tell you James never spoke to me at winter break, or when I came home for Spring break. I think the car idea was originally intended for him, and he blamed me for not getting it. My dresser was back in the bedroom when I got back for both breaks. Typical James, he was the spoiled youngest child.

The next Sunday, I got a call from both my mom and dad, it was the first time I had a conversation with my dad over 2 minutes since I was 12.

Back to AB Swimming:

We had a relay meet the next weekend in Youngstown, Ohio, a really sucky town but with a nice pool. I got to swim the 400-fly relay, and the 2000-yard free relay, but nothing in the IM, we had a lot of upper classmen that swam those events, so coach was trying to figure in where to place me. Funny thing is I could beat all of them and had done so at time trials. Our team did well finish in the top 6 of 12 teams. Paul's relay of the 4 X 100 free finished second to a division 1 team. My relays were not so lucky finishing near last in the distance freestyle and 10th in the fly relay.

We had one dual meet against Frostburg at home, so was able to study before finals week. At Frostburg, coach let me swim the 500 free and then the 200 fly, nothing else. I finished third in the free and second in the fly. Our team went on to win by 30 points.

Paul and I were kind of now in a routine, and people thought we were monks while others went out to party on the weekends, we were primarily three-fold, practice, class and studying was like 90% of our waking times. No time or interest in the ladies. Paul was pretty dominant and was the top free sprinter we had and swam both relays.

My finals went better than I expected with calling to mom for coaching in Calculus, I somehow managed to get a 2.75, GPA. I told everyone, that I had a 2.0, nobody needed to know that my mother helped me pass the subject.

We were a big team and Coach Edwards had posted for a team manager, the week of finals I look up and a very attractive girl who I knew was introduced as our new team manager. Her name was Joanna Harrison, from Charleston, WV, she was just like Paul and I a freshman. Paul said this is going to be hard to travel with a girl that attractive, I said just think of her as your sister, and call her the lovely brunette, that may help you keep from getting in trouble.

Good afternoon, my name is Joanna, I am not your girlfriend, or a squeeze, I am the team manager, I will be the person, that will do the things like logistics for meets and making sure we have enough seats and buses. If anyone thinks I am your gal pal, or someone to say nasty things about, I have it on authority to kick your butt, and Coach Edwards has my back.

Paul who was never afraid to say anything, team think of Joanna as your sister. Treat her like your sister and none of us will be in trouble, unless you are really into incest. Think of her as a sister and none of us will get in to trouble and maybe she will introduce us to her sorority sisters.

I decided to leave for home early, while everyone else in the Peters family was having Christmas dinner at Grandmother Peter's, I was the only one from our household at grandmothers and have a dinner with her. The rest of the family decided to be Jewish and not go.   I took on the well-cooked dinner.

My parents provided me the first nice gift I had in so long I could not remember, mom and Angela had gone to the outlet mall and got me a great winter coat and gloves, plus a wool cap. I got everyone something from the AB school store, for the parents' sweatshirts that said proud parent of Alderson Broadus Student, for the siblings' sweatpants with Alderson Broadus on it.

I went to Friday night services to see my grandfather lead the congregation, he introduced me to a girl named Tomi Greene, she was a senior at private school, and we were pretty friendly that night and she handed me her telephone number. We went out for New Year's Eve that the synagogue had for young adults, and while I had a good time with Tomi, we agreed to write each other, no real spark, just a friendly kiss on the cheek and allowed both of us to have something to do on New Year's Eve. I think both of us wrote 1 letter and then it ended. I may have to blame Julia for that one.

I had to leave the 2nd of January, to be back in school, the coach had made sure our dorms would be available for us, limited food until the school came back 2 weeks later. My mother gave me a care package of Jewish foods like bagels, lox, and some other stuff I could not get in West Virginia. A half pound of chopped liver and corned beef ended the care package. My dad made a point to say he was paying our portion of the bill for the second semester, and he gave me a hug. I got a hug so hard from Angela, that I thought she would kill me, and of course James was nowhere to be found, as always, the baby brother from hell.

Back at school I had to wait a couple of hours before Paul was getting back from Pittsburgh. We had the bulk of our season over the next 5 weeks, then conference the third week of February. I primarily filled in the 200 fly, and the 500 free every meet, occasionally I got to swim the 1650, when the team did a distance meet. We did that against Davis and Elkins, coach asked for a volunteer to swim the 400, IM, nobody had their hand up so the next thing I know, I got to swim the event I had only swum once.

I am getting ahead of myself. During this time, Joanna needed some help moving things so she called up and asked if Paul and I would help her. I asked her what happened to her roommate, she told me she had transferred and that a first-semester freshman was joining from the Clarksburg area. The next day, Paul and I went over to the lovely brunette's apartment to help her move the things and her new roommate was just getting in.

I don't know what was in the room that day, she turned around and said she was a pre- law and science major, had graduated a semester early. I said Well pre-law and science major what is your name, and when she turned around fully, she said her name was Julia Ferrara, and with that turn around, I knew my life was never going to be the same. I tried to tell her my name, and nothing came out. Joanna stepped in and said that is John Peters the other is Paul Cunningham.

Julia has dark hair not much different than Miriam, but she looks eternally tanned, bedroom dark eyes, a dimple on her right side, and while not a model like Miriam, she was and is extremely attractive.

Joanna said normally John is quiet, Paul is our new star sprinter and well nobody knows what John is. From what we hear, he got a scholarship with the aid of an Olympians mother, but that is probably just a good story.

Julia was inquisitive, Joanna what is the mystery about John?

Paul jumped in, he had a miracle swim his last event in high school and made the top 100 of the country. Then he swam a major meet with a no time entry and proceeded to again make the top 100 in the country. So far all we know is that he is a business major, lives near Baltimore, has a really odd family relationship, and lies about failing classes. Yes, by the way he swims the events that nobody with common sense wants to.

Julia, put her hand out and said nice to meet you, John Peters. We shook hands and I know this may be silly, but I felt a chill all the way up and down my body. Something inside me said you need to know more about this girl. I barely was able to now say to her nice to meet you, Julia.

We loaded up the stuff and went to practice. Paul looked at me, did you see a ghost or something, I thought I was going to have to rescue you, did her roommate take you off guard or what?

All I could say, there is something about her that is different Paul clapped me on the back, so the monk, may be attracted to girls after all? Let's get to practice and you can think about her during the long workout, it will make it go faster.

This is all hear say from Joanna, so you will have to take it as she tells it.

Joanna got back from the pool and Julia was still there. Julia, what the heck was that about, you had John Peters totally tongue tied.

I don't know, but when we shook hands, I got goose bumps up and down. I find him attractive, but he is very reserved, I doubt he would ever have the courage to actually talk to me and ask me out.

Julia, I don't know what is going on, I know that the entire girls swim team likes to talk to him, and not a single one has had a date with him. John is kind of a mystery with the girls here at AB. He's like 6' tall, wide shoulders, hazel eyes, and light brown hair with blonde highlights. I know the other swimmers go to the parties and go wild, but not John. Paul says he has been burned by a couple of girls, so he is very reluctant to start anything new. I can tell you there are quite a few that would like to know him, and for some reason you had him tongue tied, nobody else has had that kind of effect on him. I do want you to know one thing, John is Jewish, and you are catholic, so maybe it's the religion thing that prevents him from dating anyone up here.

I don't know Joanna, but he is cute, I have dated before, but something about him made me uneasy tonight. It was like, he could see me and knew everything about me.

Julia, that is called infatuation, I think you have a thing for the swim team Jewish monk. Nobody has penetrated that guy, but boy did you get him off his game. I have never known him to be sarcastic, it was instant. Paul said he has a picture of one girl that he keeps in the dorm, and apparently, she was drop dead gorgeous and smart. I think that girl was the one that broke his heart. So be very careful with that one, who knows what drives him. I do know that he was reluctant to go home, for Thanksgiving, and now he gets calls like every day from his sister, and parents, so maybe he is just homesick.

The dorm Paul and John's room.

Spill it John, what the heck was that with Joanna's new roommate. I have dated like 6 girls here; you have never gone out with anyone here.

I have no idea as soon as we shook hands, something was strange. I think I need an excuse to go there again. What can I ask the lovely brunette, so that I have to come by again?

I am sure we can find something. John, I think we can put that picture of your Miriam away now, you may have a new lady to put up here. She is attractive though, not the looker of Miriam, but I get that she has something that is driving you nuts.

Paul, I need to talk to that one again, her name is Julia right.

We were busy with swim meets, class and studying for the next few weeks. I swam my first 400 IM and came close to breaking the varsity record of one of our seniors, so I am expecting that I will swim that event at our conference, but coach has me in events that I guess he was hoping for points, 100 fly, 200 fly, and 1650 freestyle. Only one of these were my best events, but as a freshman you really can't complain, it does not do any good.

Right before conference I found an excuse to come over to the apartment of the lovely brunette and her roommate. Joanna had to go and get something leaving the two of us at the apartment alone.

Julia, was the one that talked first, and while I know she was saying some words, for some reason I could not hear them. She asked if I was paying attention, I just leaned over and said can I kiss you.

Julia stepped back, and laughed, so you too. I leaned over and we kissed for the first time. By the time Joanna, came back she caught us holding hands on the couch.

The lovely brunette said, ah ha, so John Peters, will we be seeing you a lot over here then?

Both Julia and I just smiled. I asked please don't tell the swim team about this, I don't want to be the center of jokes.

Your secret is good with me, but how long do you think the two of you can hide this.

Julia saw I was worried, well we could just call you coming over as tutoring, I think we both have the same biology class anyway, I can help you in the class.

With that the Julia and John times began. I did get an "A" in Biology, and not the dirty way, we were both naïve and didn't do anything more than kissing, hand holding, and studying. The team had no idea. Because I was studying every night with Julia, it did one thing, I was getting good grades for the first time. My mid-terms said 3.25, all B's and an A in Biology. Something about being with Julia caused me to focus on school.

At the conference I swam fairly well, placing 10th in the 200 fly, just missed scoring in the 100 fly, and finished 16th in the 1650 freestyle, AB finished fourth overall. Paul made the finals in all of his events and the 400 free relay he was the star of our team; I was currently just a cog in the wheel.

I did not qualify for nationals, so while Paul and a couple of the others went to nationals I returned home for a week in Baltimore. I wanted my dad to see my grades, so I took my mid-terms with me, and he was impressed something must have changed. My sister pulled me aside and asked who she was that had turned my head.

I tried to deny it, and she looked at me, I have not seen you like this since your Miriam, and you went to prom. I came clean, nothing serious but I am dating my tutor, a girl from Clarksburg area, her name is Julia Ferrara.

Whatever it is, you may need to keep the smile down, or our parents will know you are dating a nice Italian girl. That won't' go over well with them.

By the way Angela, she is Sicilian and not Italian, and no she is not a member of the mafia nor are her family. Nobody on the team knows we are dating, so how did you figure it out.

I am your sister; I know you better than anyone else does.

I left a week later; James was out of town at a tournament, so I did not see him until the last day I was there. We never spoke even at Passover Seder, still pissed he did not get the car.

For the next few weeks back at AB, we had limited swim practices expected, not allowed to be coached. Julia and I continued to study, and only the lovely brunette and Paul knew we saw each other almost every night. My grades ended up a 3.5, for the semester, amazing what happens when you have incentive to study.

School ended and I had a lifeguard job at an apartment complex in Howard County for the summer. Julia was going to work at a fabric store in the Clarksburg, WV area, so we had to communicate when we could by phone. With a handshake Paul and I agreed to be back together in the dorm the following year.

That was the end of my freshman year, swimming was ok, and I guess grades were better than expected overall just above a 3.0, which impressed my parents. I found my most serious girlfriend, and really, we had no sexual activity at all. Joanna said we were such a cute naïve couple.

Sophomore Year:

The summer was so rough, the head guard at a swim club, long hours and extremely friendly girls that did everything but throw parts of bathing suits at you. They also averaged 14 years-old, enough of a pain in the ass that you really got tired of them. When I was not working, I got to swim with NBAC seniors, practices were so much harder than at AB. I also, missed not seeing Julia all summer, I wondered if we could make it and I had to be careful not to call so my parents would not get a bill. I just told them that I had a weekly call to my tutor. Somehow my mother and Angela saw right through that excuse.

I helped Angela move into Montgomery Hall at the University of MD a week before I was ready to go back to AB. I told her that I was proud of her, and she better find a way to stay in touch. With my mom and dad in the car behind us, we all hugged her and said our goodbyes.

Angela said I want to meet the girl that stole your heart. Do you even think of Miriam or Lucy anymore? You may try to fool the men in the house, but we know, tutoring was how mom and dad met, you should have come up with a better one than that. Please send me a picture soon of the two of you, I don't care what others say, she really has brought out the big brother I always dreamed of having, confident. I will see you Thanksgiving I will come home and you better.

One week later I packed up my bags and was on my way to AB. After not speaking to me for almost a year, my younger brother said good luck in school. My parents gave me $200, in cash, hugged me and then said I would like to talk to your tutor sometime, the athletic department gave you. Sure, if she has time. (I had not intent for this to ever happen)

With my dad not in hearing distance, mom said, you and I know she is much more than a tutor to you. I don't know what you 2 are doing but keep up the grades, you did so much better the second semester.

It did not take me long to drop off my stuff and then drive over to the apartment of Julia and Joanna. I knocked on the door and after a minute, Joanna came out and said your tutor is not here yet, she will be here later tonight. She told me to tell you she can't wait for classes to begin so that you 2 can study together. I think that means she misses you and wants to see you as soon as she gets in. When can I let the team know that you are off the market?

I simply said I never knew I was on the market and at that Joanna, the lovely brunette, just smiled God you are so naïve, swimmers are coveted here by the girls especially the swimmers from out of the state.

One day later classes began, I had 17 credit hours and nothing real difficult except English, Accounting looked ok, marketing was going to be easy, and 2 credits for varsity swimming was sweet. A couple of history classes and this looked like something I could do. Julia was in my English class, so the one hard class I had my tutor.

Back for a second year was Thai Cung, a sprinter, Paul our top sprinter, and Brad Fox one of our divers and me. Two of the others simply chose not to come back or went elsewhere. We had one new breaststroker and a guy named Jeff Kissinger was going to lead the IM's, coach also recruited a top distance swimmer, so I had no idea of what I was going to swim this year.

I had a closed-door meeting with Coach Edwards, it did not go as well as I expected. He told me that while I had done ok last year, he really did not get from me what he thought when he recruited me. I had to recruit a new IM swimmer to replace you. I recruited a new distance swimmer so you will be our third choice for distance and third for the IM, maybe we can use you in the 200 fly as lead, but you are going to have to prove yourself this year.

Coach, you really never gave me much of a chance last year, never swam the 200 IM and I beat all of them all the time.

Then the truth came out, I had no idea that when we recruited you that you were devoutly Jewish. I think you had it too easy growing up, and I was pressured in to keeping you around. My past tells me that Jewish athletes never achieve potential, so truthfully, I really did not want to risk our team results on someone who I did not think I can trust.

When I got back to my room and told Paul, he just said what kind of crap was this, he told you all year that he did not trust freshmen, now we know he just is a bigot. I feel for you because I know that you can beat them if you have a chance.

The rest of the fall season went as expected with team doing better this year, and me staying away from coach as much as possible. I beat the prized IM'er in time trials but yet he would not swim me. I mostly swam the 200 fly mostly because nobody else was any good at it. In the October relay meet, they did not even swim me in the 400-fly relay, just the 800-medley relay and the 2000 freestyle relay. I just kept beating these guys every week in practice, but coach was never going to let me have the IM, he decided being Christian was his choice of swimmer.

Fortunately for me, I could go to see Julia at night, and the crap from the team went away, my grades with studying with her as much as possible, I had a 3.5 again at mid- term, primarily because coach had given me a B in varsity swimming, you could not reason with the man.

Julia and Joanna asked me whether I had thought about going to homecoming this year. I really had been without thought about it at all, well, the women said, how about you and Paul getting dressed up and being our dates for the dance. I was like, are you sure about this, Julia and I have never been seen together outside of this room, not sure about this.

Isn't this a high school thing, and the next thing I knew 2 women had given me a look that told me not to say anything else.

Julia spoke up my sorority sisters insist that we go, and it's time that my imaginary boyfriend comes out of the dark. Joanna needs a date, so I thought Paul would be good.

I guess your mind is made up so sure we can go, I will need to get a suit and as far as Paul is concerned Joanna, didn't you say we had to treat you as our sister, I don't see Paul as a guy that would take his sister to a dance. Do you want me to ask him and in unison the 2 girls said tonight swimmer boy, do it tonight?

With that conversation we had agreed to go to a dance that I really had no intention of going to. I did get a suit, and Paul had his sent from Pittsburgh.

Joanna looked absolutely gorgeous when she answered the door with her blue dress. Julia looked like heaven to me in her dark pink long dress and matching shoes. Her hair was done extravagantly done, I later learned she had spent 2 hours at the hairdresser.

Paul and I both had grey suits, and even Paul was slow to talk to the girls after looking at the beautiful women we were escorting.

I felt very odd when we got to the dance, not thinking this was a big deal, but apparently many in the Greek areas were dressed up. I felt uncomfortable that Julia kept introducing me to so many people she knew from sorority. I asked her what this is all about and I got a look that I should never have asked.

Since you won't take me out for a real date and everybody thinks you are a figment of my imagination, I just had to make sure everyone knows who you are and that you are taken.

Really, so you would like to go on real dates now, and the answer was, why do you think we are coming out here tonight. One of us had to finally push the envelope.

I would like to tell you what happened after we got back to her apartment, I can tell you that she said she had been patient with me since I had been burned by others and that she wanted to let me know that she was not going to run off. She grabbed me by the hand and took me back to her bedroom, where she said, now let's get this straight I love you and want a full relationship. 2 hours later I came out to get something to drink, and was surprised that Joanna was not back yet, so well at least that was something I avoided.

At that point, we just jumped the relationship to another level. I even held her hand out in public. Joanna was so funny about it, thank

God you 2 came out of the closet, I can finally quit the conversation with the women's swim team from asking me when they can ask you out. Who would have me Joanna, I am only a second-tier swimmer, and she said I don't think they cared about that, and gave me a hug? I am so glad that it is my roommate that made you happy again, I never see you smile unless you are with her.

I wanted to ask about her evening with Paul, but let it go and never asked Paul, some things you just don't want to know.

November came and practices became the same, practice 8 times a week, swim one event right before we went home for Thanksgiving break. Before I left, Julia wanted to drive home she wanted me to help her pick-up a trunk she wanted. Well, it was an interesting visit, I guess I passed the inquisition, because Julia's dad just said you better treat Julia with respect. My response was I always treat my tutor well sir, nice try son we know you are dating; Julia does not hide things from her parents. After that trip, I spent many a quick trip to her home, and even a Sunday dinner with relatives.

Another trip to Baltimore for Thanksgiving, and things were different, Angela came home a few hours before me, and was getting settled in when I showed up, she had been doing laundry before that. Angela saw me and threw her hands around me, big brother, you never sent me the picture I asked for. I then presented her with the Homecoming picture of us together and said this is yours for the keeping apparently my tutor had several copies made.

Angela smiled and said to me I have never seen you this happy, you chose well for yourself. Are you sure I chose her, or she chose me, I think the latter may be closer to the truth?

We had a large gathering, and my dad toasted the two college children that had come home. My younger brother still had almost no words for me, but I spent most of my time with Angela and my parents. I spent little time in the bedroom and back to school for the main part of swim team and finals.

We had one swim meet this time against Fairmont State, a small team with 2 stars, we had enough people to take them on. I finished second in the 200 fly and swam nothing else. Paul was upset, and Thai finished third, so we did not lose many points. Brad did well in diving winning by a very wide margin.

With swimming over for the semester concentrated on finishing school, I actually got a 3.7 GPA when Coach Edwards relented at the push of our team captain gave me an "A" In varsity swimming.

For the first time, we had a swimmer's holiday party, it was going to be a buffet but reality it was going to be a beer party. Joanna asked me to invite Julia to go and I said if you think it is a good idea sure. Great because I can finally brag about you and my roommate and finally put to bed the Jewish Monk theory.

When we entered the room, hand in hand, a buzz could be heard. Frances Gearhardt was there, a very good athlete, wow now we know where you have been keeping yourself. Jewish Monk be damned, the both of you are so happy with each other, all the girls know you are absolutely taken. Julia, take care of him, the monk only smiles when you are with him. Paul had a little too much to drink, so Joanna agreed to take him to our dorm room. She never came back, and I assumed she went home. Julia would tell me later, he was not really drunk and wanted time with the lovely brunette as I called her.

Back to Baltimore for a week before practice began. Angela came home a day after I got home. I went to Synagogue again to see grandpa do this thing as he was set to retire after Passover. I stayed home for NYE, really did not want to go anywhere, and at midnight, the phone rang, Angela answered it and then yelled" John your tutor wants to wish you a Happy New Year". I thought I would kill her as she spoke to Julia for about 5 minutes before handing me the phone. Angela was trying to hear what we said to each other, and afterwards, interesting conversation with your tutor, so obvious sir, you got to learn to hide it from us better.

Angela could always read me well, I just told her that I was deeply in love with Julia, but the religion thing was going to be tough, and Angela reminded me that just like our parents, are you living your life or repeating them.

The season was pretty much the same except for the meet against Asheville, where they swam distance events. I got to swim the 100 fly, but they had three lanes for the 400 IM, coach threw me in to the outside lane, I guess nobody else wanted to swim it. While Jeff won the event, I finished second three seconds behind and gaining the whole freestyle leg. Our team won the meet.

On to the conference meet again I swim the 100 and 200 fly, and the 1650 freestyle. As you can see, I still was not invited to swim the event I was recruited for, either IM. I finished last in the consolation in the 100 fly, just missed the finals of the 200 fly, finishing first in the consolations. The 1650 freestyle I finished 15th this year, a little improvement and just about the same time. My 200 fly was a National B time qualifying for Nationals. Only qualifying in one event, Coach Edwards says he will not take me to nationals, Paul and three others went this time. Jeff was our first Honorable mention All-American finishing 16th in the 200 IM.

I went home for spring break, and while it was pleasant everyone was busy and truthfully, I was missing Julia. I drove over to see Angela, at MD. We went to the dairy and had ice cream, she introduced me to Kurt Furberg, who she had started dating a month ago, he was a senior and about to go to med school. The conversation had not gone very far until the subject of Julia was discussed.

Angela saw in my face that I missed her, you are so taken my brother. All I could respond with is you trained me well, I guess.

She just smiled, of course I did. Didn't I set you up in high school also after Miriam.

With swimming officially over for the year, the only thing left was Julia's formal and finals. She was lovely in a red formal dress and her mothers' pearls. I had to rent a tuxedo; it was very obvious that her sisters in the sorority approved of us as a couple. Not a single snide comment, and Julia made sure to get me on the dance floor with my arm around her. I think she was very much making sure that everyone saw us together.

Joanna had convinced Paul to come with her as her date, they looked good together, but not once did they hold hands or kiss, so I assumed that Paul was Joanna's safe date. As you will find out later, I was so wrong.

My grades were fantastic 4 A's and a B, a 3.8 GPA. So much better to take classes you want instead of mandatory. It did not hurt that I had a great study partner, who I was going to miss with her in Clarksburg and me in Arbutus.

Sophomore year ended 2 weeks later, back to home and the pool for the season, this time as the assistant pool manager and assistant swim coach. My phone bill would have been high, but we now had unlimited long distance when the family got FIOS service at the house. Julia was working at a summer day camp, she said she wanted to have a tan so that when we got back in August, she did not want to look like a ghost next to me. Besides the money was about the same as working inside at a mall.

CHAPTER SEVEN

Injured Again

Back in Arbutus with your love of your life 200 miles away is a tough way to spend the summer. Julia and I called but it was not the same. Life with the family was passable, James was almost nice as he was getting ready for his junior year in high school, he even asked what it was like to get recruited. The answer I gave him was let's see mine was done in 7 days; I hope yours is easier than mine.

You will get letters and information from coaches all over the country, simply acknowledge them as you can't sign a letter of intent until after June anyway. Make sure you acknowledge them because you don't know who knows whom, and decide based on what you want to do, how far you want to travel, and how competitive the program is. James simply said thanks will keep that in mind.

Finally, make sure this is your decision and not what dad tells you, this is your life decision.

Angela stayed in College Park, no longer with Kurt, but was doing a summer intern program that could lead to a top medical school, so money is good and opportunity to see what the field is about. I went to see her every weekend, we usually got ice cream but occasionally we would get pizza at Ledo's, a famous place near the university.

My work was not bad swim practice started at 8:00 and I was finished by 11:00, then 4 days a week I had to come back from 3 to 9 to close the pool. I went to NBAC to practice in the evenings when I could, swam the normal practice on Monday and Friday. Coach Brian was no longer at NBAC, he moved to some place in TN, with a club of his own near Nashville. Before he left, he wished me well, and with his bride and newborn, he finally got to lead a program of his own. The other coaches encouraged me, but I will always thank Coach Brian for being in my corner.

My grandfather was now retired, he would do occasional funerals and weddings over the summer but now, he was retired and looking to move to Berlin, MD. A nice area and a small synagogue there. That is the city where they filmed "Runaway Bride", that is all I know about it.

My parents started to get along together again, dad quit coaching teams and just went to games where James was playing, so he was home about half of the weekends.

As August started, I planned for my first apartment with Paul, we were about a half-mile from Joanna and Julia, so that would make it easier to see Julia. Coach made us get a basic meal plan at the cafeteria, not sure why, but it was based on a number of meals, good for 15 meals a week, so we were able to do cook our own dinners and such. My mother taught me how to make several dinner meals, and she sent me some powdered soups so I could always have a something when I was too tired to cook. She also sent with me a series of Jewish foods including kosher salami, pickles and many other items. I was prepared, plus Julia's mom was going to teach me how to make basic pasta meals so I could eat well. I think it was really so I would make sure that Julia came home for a few weekends.

With everything ready, I now drove my ten-year old car back to Phillipi, to be a freshman counselor, I was told I had to do this as part of my scholarship. Angela came up from College Park to see me off, and said to me something I was fearing, I am coming up in October, so I want to see your tutor.

As long as it is only you fine, no parents please. Angela agreed, but said you know I have to give mom an update, she already suspects something more than you have told her, because you are still with the same girl, you add it up. With a hug from Angela, a handshake from my dad, and tears from mom, I was on my way back to school. I stopped at McDonald's just north of Cumberland and called Julia to let her know I was on my way back. She answered the phone, and when I told her I would be back tonight she said she and Joanna had already set-up her apartment, and there was room for studying. This studying thing is getting to be a joke, but truthfully if it was not for our study dates, I am sure I never would have done this well. The last thing she said, I can't wait to see you please drive carefully, and finally did I tell you I am in love with you lately. I teared up as I started to drive through Frostburg and on my way back to West Virginia.

I got into town at about 4 PM, and for the first time ever Paul had beat me to getting into town. I figured out why, he chose the larger bedroom, he said because I know I will be here all the time, you are out studying a lot. The apartment was furnished, so all we had to do is bring our other stuff with us and A TV set and stereo. I bought the TV at Best Buy in Baltimore, a 23" special, cable came with the apartment. Paul brought his stereo back from home, it was like 6 years old, but good for CD's still.

The apartment came with a functional dining room table, everything else looked like it came from a yard sale, but it was functional and affordable.

The next day all of the returning swimmers had meetings with Coach Edwards, I was next to last with the only Brad Fox, our diver after me. Brad had come out of the closet at the end of the year last year, so I guess coach wanted to deal with his kind first and then the Jewish guy and the multi-cultured gay guy next. When I get into his office at the time scheduled, Coach Edwards was on the phone. He was talking to a pastor from the area. This pastor was well known for still blaming Jewish people for the death of Christ, a pure fundamentalist, and now I knew that Coach Edwards was one of his church elders, a high-level person. Now I knew where his hatred of Jewish people had come from, he practiced it every week. I could not even imagine what it was going to be like for Brad, African American and gay.

Coach Edwards said to me sorry about the interruption that was my pastor on the phone I was talking about church business, you can understand that, wait no you can't you are a Jew from Baltimore, this was about charity work of the church. I forgot that being Jewish you don't do charity work, all about making money. I had no words to say for the bigot I was tied to for the rest of the year. Obviously, he had no clue and I was not going to get in to an argument with him.

Coach Edwards turned back to me and said take a seat need to talk to you about this season. We need you to continue swimming the fly events, but this year we don't have many IM swimmers, so this year in the dual meets you will be our depth person in the 200 IM, and then maybe the 400 IM, when we have it. (Finally, I get to swim my best events). I still am not sure you are dedicated enough to do anything, but I was convinced that you should get the opportunity to prove your scholarship this year. By the way Frank Pompano, (AD) wants to meet with you today, I am assuming he needs you to sign some paperwork.

Not much of an endorsement from the guy that has not done much for me in my career, had to be convinced just to give me an "A" in varsity swimming.

I knocked on the athletics office and told the summer intern that Frank needed to speak with me. After five minutes, he came out and said let's get to my office.

I know that life here in a small town is not always easy. I was asked if I could find you a synagogue for the holidays, I was told that you missed being with your kind. I have talked to some people, and you are going to be invited to the Clarksburg families when the travelling Rabbi, comes around. I will get it cleared that you could go to High Holiday services if you choose to. I am trying to get cleared that you will not have to practice on those 2 days, but you know that your coach does not like to make exceptions. John, I want you to know that there are people here you can trust, not everyone is like Coach Edwards. I will just leave it at that, your friends have been very convincing that we find a way to allow you to practice your heritage. Oh, by the way, I am really impressed on your grade improvement last year, keep this up and you could be in the running for our 4-year academic athlete. I want to hand this to you, this is a certificate for academic all-conference, you may want to get it framed, you had one of the top GPA's for your sophomore year in the conference.

I simply smiled and thanked him. I also told him it was nice that the athletic department was supportive of someone from a different background Frank just said, many of us are welcoming, some still can't handle that the old ways are dead.

Shaking off the events and the whiplash of what had just taken place, I was eager to see Julia, Paul and the lovely brunette. Paul was already at the lady's apartment when I got there. I pulled the certificate out of the brown envelope to let Julia read it.

Julia read out loud John Peters all-conference academic athlete award representing swimming, the top GPA of all men swimmers in the conference. Paul slapped me on the back, I guess Julia's tutoring really has worked.

Joanna, I think I need to thank you also something the AD said, I think you must have been the person to help with getting me a day off for Yom Kippur. Julia, you have always wanted to see my religion, I am going to invite you to the holiest day of the year and guess where, Clarksburg.

Julia said great then we can go over my house to eat, I reminded her that the fast would prevent me from eating until sundown. Julia said Well if you don't mind Italian food, I think my parents could help you with that.

As always, she found a way to make things better. I can't believe how lucky I was to be with her, and her parents had been comfortable that I was Jewish. I simply leaned over and gave her a passionate kiss and told her I love you with the others hearing for the very first time.

The next morning, we began school, 5 classes with 2 in economics, 1 in accounting, and the other 2 in marketing, all fairly easy classes in my major and required classes. This was the first time; I did not have Julia in one of my classes and we discussed it. I was still invited to come over and study, the lovely brunette just asked that I actually do some studying instead of making whoopi with our future lawyer. I had to promise to be a good boy most of the time. Julia just insisted that I better not be a good boy all the time. That night, I was not a good boy, and the future lawyer would agree. I spent the Labor Day weekend with Julia's family, I was restricted to her brother's room at night. There was not going to be any bad boy this weekend, her parents would have made sure of that.

Now that we had our apartment, Paul and I began to split our time cooking our own food and using the cafeteria. It not only saved money, but it also allowed us to have a full dinner without going out, but for some reason he never came over to the girl's apartment when I was studying, and the lovely brunette would often leave quoting not wanting to be around the love birds, it was like being around maple syrup too sweet.

2 weeks later practice began the unofficial season. We added a new backstroke, (Jeremy Lattimner), from Walt Whitman High School in Bethesda, he had done fairly well in the Metro's meet) specialist, but coach did not recruit any more talent, so now I know why I was being elevated. We added 2 additional freestylers one for long distance and one for middle distance, John Franklin, distance and middle-distance Richard Freeman. Both were as good as I had ever done. So no longer wanted to train in the distance lane. Both of the distance swimmers knew each other and had come from an area near Cleveland, Ohio. (Berea, OH)

Time seemed to pass fairly easily, I told Coach Edwards that I was going to miss a Friday workout due to the Yom Kippur Holiday, and his reaction was typical. I always knew I was going to have to make accommodations for you, why is this holiday so important for you. While I wanted to say because it is you prick, I simply said it was the holiest day of the year and my parents had asked me to attend a synagogue that day. I knew it was a lie, and it was easier than telling him it was none of your fucking business you racist. Julia and I went to the very small gathering place, and old warehouse that was set-up as a synagogue. The population from Morgantown to Clarksburg all came together for the event, the rabbi was actually a rabbinical student from Cincinnati. Nice guy about 5 years older than me, and very accepting. We went to the morning service then the concluding service including the Yizkor service, celebrating those that have passed. While Julia did not read Hebrew about ½ of the service was in English, she looked so lovely in a dark blue dress she borrowed from her mother. The rabbi asked which college we were from, and I said AB, wow I did not know they had any Jewish students, I said we have three, and Julia is my girlfriend, and this was her first services. He welcomed her and said we always welcome young couples to our services, please come back.

We went over to her parent's house and spent the night before going back to school. Her mom had a really nice spread, and somehow had decided to get apples and honey, I did not have the heart to tell her that that was the holiday that just ended, I just thanked her for doing this. Her response was amazing.

I don't care which religion you two choose when you get married, I just know that whatever it is you are both amazing and really amazing together. I just realized that she assumed we were going to get married, a few steps ahead of me, but Julia just smiled.

On our way back to school Saturday morning, I had to ask, was that you're doing about getting married or what. Julia started laughing, that was her way of saying she approves of you and so do I. She kissed me on the side of my cheek, and then nestled as close as our seat belts would allow.

Mid-terms and full practice began in October. I was working out with the middle- distance swimmers and backstroke swimmers, no longer doing the distance workout, now I know why Paul felt better than me at night. (so much less swimming laps) I received my first 4.0, and immediately bragged that one to my parents. Mom said your tutor is doing a great job, I guess. The athletic department must be proud of the job she is doing with you. 2 Days later the first of my family arrived by bus to Clarksburg, I picked her up.

The first question I got from Angela was so what is going on this weekend, and when do I get to meet your tutor. I responded homecoming is this weekend, and if you have a nice dress the lovely brunette, would get her a date for the dance later tonight. Angela said you did not tell me to bring a nice dress, just happens that Julia and Angela were both size 4's, so the dark pink dress from last year was made available to her. I did not know it, but Jeff Kissinger had agreed to be my sister's date for the evening. Joanna knew that she had to do something, or I would not be able to go with Julia. Always the resourceful one, she found a way to make it all work out. My sister looked gorgeous, and we met Paul and his date the lovely brunette at the girl's apartment. Jeff came over about 5 minutes later with a suit on, crap we did not know he owned anything but T- shirts and torn jeans. He said I did not even know you had a sister, you are so quiet, and my God she is beautiful. I responded remember she is my sister, if you mess with her, you will have Paul, Joanna and me to respond to. Just kidding, I already have been told to behave, by our team manager. I know better than to piss her off.

Then out from her bedroom, came Julia, wearing a beautiful wine-colored full-length dress, and with 4-inch heels looked everything a goddess would look like. Julia as normal was just the most welcoming person ever, so she introduced herself to both Jeff and my sister Angela.

I was very nervous about my sister and Julia meeting, when they went to the bathroom together so they could help Angela put on make-up I was really anxious.

Angela came out of the bathroom looking very much the same, so I wondered what had happened there. Julia grabbed my hand and then looked at both Angela and me.

Angela looked at the both of us holding hands and said, Julia, you and John look like the perfect couple together. You know I had set him up with at least one girl to make sure he did not get into a lot of trouble. As you can see, he is kind of naïve about his looks, and thinks he is lucky to get a date. After seeing the both of you, I have never seen him so happy, and the glow when you saw him tonight, I know that you two have something special, especially since your relationship is as tutor and student. Neither my mother nor I have bought this story, but we have let John live with it you see my mother used the same story with her parents about dating a catholic boy, she started tutoring and ended up marrying.

I got a kiss from both my sister and Julia, and even the lovely brunette gave me a hug.

Paul and Jeff said, how come the stars of the team don't get this much attention. I put my hands up, don't ask me I'm apparently the naïve one.

The dance went well and both Julia and I had to be on good behavior. Neither of us wanted to be the local gossip subject. Jeff and my sister had a cordial evening, and the third couple appeared to have something more than just a date for tonight, but I was never going to ask Paul or the lovely brunette, because I'm not sure I really wanted to know.

Angela was staying with Paul and I so very little romantic possibility with Julia that night, I will tell you after Angela left, Julia and I had a romantic meeting at her apartment, no studying that evening. The only thing I had to discuss was why I had never told her that my dad had grown up catholic. I reminded her that I had never said much about my father he and I were so different. Unknown to me, Julia and Angela had talked about the relationship between my father and me, and the fact that until college the two of us had almost no relationship. Angela went on to talk about the confrontation we had and how much my grandmother had said we were more alike than different. Only after this conversation did Julia understand why I had kept so much to myself. Julia asked a little about Miriam, and was told that she was my first love, I had been in long conversations with her for years, and that she was incredibly both smart and beautiful, and really never looked at John the same way he had looked at her. She talked about the arrangement that she had made for Lucy my senior year, and that Lucy cut it off so I could go to college and not be looking back. So now almost all of the history was out, and yet Julia was still with me and wanted me.

I drove Angela to the bus station and stayed with her until the bus came. We had a long conversation and she thanked me for the fun time she had. Told me nothing was going to happen between her and Jeff, so don't worry about it, but it was a fun date. I got her a half dozen pepperoni rolls for the road.

I have to report back to mom, and you know she is going to ask. I find Julia a fantastic partner for you, wondering when you are going to come clean. I love you big brother and I am going to tell mom that you are apparently very much and entirely in love with Julia and that the way I saw you two this weekend, I am waiting for when you will tell us you are getting married.

Sis, I love you, and you know whatever you tell our parents is what you are going to tell them. She whispered in my ear, you chose wisely, Miriam was too much of a model and this girl is not only attractive, but she is also smart and totally in love with you. I am so proud of you. See you at Thanksgiving.

With a hug, and a promise to see her next month, my sister went back to College Park, she would get there 6 hours later. I had made it through the weekend and my sister as always was so fantastic.

November came and we had a relay meet at Youngstown again, this time I swam the 400 Fly relay, and the 800 IM relay, we did ok in both 10th and 9th respectively. Paul's, sprint relay was third overall and the fastest from our conference, he was really doing well, and Thai Cung swam very well also.

Two days of practice and a trip back to Arbutus, the practice before I was to go home, I was swimming butterfly, in one lane and hooked my shoulder with one of our swimmers in the next lane. It did not hurt as much this time as the last time I did this, but I knew something was up. I called my mom and said can you get me in to see Dr. Ormond on Friday. An hour later, he will try to fit you in, but you will have to sit and wait until he can see you between the appointments he already has. He asked if it is as bad as the first time, I said I don't think so but want to make sure.

That night I told both Paul and Julia, my shoulder was bothering me, and was hoping I was just over cautious. Joanna filed an athletic injury report for me with the athletic department, this was not going to be a fun week.

The next morning, I drove back to Arbutus to be with my family for Thanksgiving, I had been invited to Julia's family but not ready for that scene at least not yet. I made it home by noon before Thanksgiving and my sister Angela had already come back from College Park. My dad had taken the day off and was with my mom finishing buying groceries, with all three children at the house for the weekend, she had to stock-up. She had purchased a fresh turkey for the day.

Thanksgiving went well until after dinner my mom how is your tutor and you getting along. I know she knows something is up, oh crap. I simply stated, we are doing well I will be almost as good as Angela in grades this semester.

She then told me she had seen Miriam coming home from college, she was graduating with a journalism degree from Georgetown in the Spring. Mom, you know that she broke it off from me like 3 years ago, and I am not interested anymore. Your tutor, is more interesting than Miriam? Angela showed me a picture of you two, she looks like she is straight form Haifa, so should I tell your father that he should not worry about you socially.

Mom, please just tell him, I am working on my grades and with swimming, I don't go out much these days.

Angela horned in, I bet not. I gave her a look that she realized she had gone over the edge and stopped any further comments.

Doctor's office Friday:

Well John, I am looking at your shoulder, I am getting an emergency MRI can you wait here they can do it downstairs? You are going to be fit in, so plan all day here before I can get results. 1 MRI and 5 hours of waiting later, Dr Ormond came into the room.

John you are lucky, nothing looks torn badly, a small tear in 1 muscle, but I think if you can stay out of the pool for 2 to 3 weeks, you will be fine. I knew I could not stay out of the pool, so Dr, what if I try to go through this? You will be in pain, and not sure you will be very effective, but if you had to you could work the same exercises you did before and hopefully it will repair. I would recommend that you refrain from butterfly for a while.

Screwed, this is going to be impossible, I swim fly. I called Paul to ask his opinion. As team captain, I will see about you only doing 1 arm fly in workouts for three weeks, but you know Coach Edwards will get the reports so this will be interesting.

Sunday morning, I drove back to AB, knowing this was going to be a lost season. While I might be able to get through the season, no way would I have the results that Coach Edwards is going to want. Julia was elated with the news, great then if you quit swimming, you and I can have more time together.

Julia did not understand, I wanted to prove I was as good as all the others, she was not in sports, she had run some track in high school but gave that up a long time ago.

Joanna had an idea of what it was about.

Monday practice was not much fun. I was restricted to 1 arm swim and kicking. My practice took about 30 minutes and then to the trainer's table. Same thing the rest of the week. The swim meet that weekend against WV Wesleyan, I traveled with the team but not allowed to compete. Unless you have competed, the depression of being injured is not just that you are not competing, is that you see others doing what you know you can do when your healthy, and you can't do anything. (Frustrating) The team managed to win, and Paul as usual took first place in his events. We were still a pretty good team, I had to remember I was mostly a depth person on this team and never would be a star.

Two more weeks until school ends anyway and no meets until we return from winter break, four weeks to heal. School work was as easy as I thought it would be so in the meantime, I managed my first 4.0.

I called my parents, and even my dad was happy for me. A later call to Angela, and she was busy with her finals. She called me back, your tutor has done well for you. Julia and I celebrated our twin 4.0's with a dinner and a more passionate resolution.

On the 20th of December I went back to Arbutus, for semester break. Julia went back home. I was due back to AB, for swim practice, Julia would be home until the 19th of January, so we were going to be away from each other for almost four weeks.

Back home was odd with James starting his recruiting, he and dad were busy with looking at schools and where they could get some offers. Angela came home literally right before Christmas, and for the first time that I could remember we all went over to

Grandmother Peter's house. We had not done holiday gift exchange in a long-time, and I would not mind her great cooking. My mom has great qualities, cooking is not one of

them, she tries and with Angela's help we get through Thanksgiving. My Uncle Roger could not make it from his home, so it was just going to be the 6 of us, plus some friends from her neighborhood. I had never had Christmas Cookies, and someone brought a Claxton Fruit Cake, I think I was the only one that ate it though.

The 27th of December, I was back at Dr Ormond for a review of my shoulder and to see what exercises I could do. After a series of exercises, the OK, to go back to swim practice was authorized. The one thing that was going to be an issue was that I had some atrophy on the right shoulder, which meant that the strain could be right back on the injured list. He asked that I not compete until the 15th of January. The exercises that were provided were all to strengthen the one arm to make sure that

I swam in the same rotation and not irritate the shoulder again. I made calls to both Julia and Paul telling them I should be ready by the third meet back to compete. I asked Julia to have Joanna call me back to get instructions for the training staff.

New Years Eve was very quiet for me, Angela had a date, as did younger brother James. Even the parents went to a NYE party at the Synagogue. I called Julia, I wanted to be with her, but we had both decided not to push the family thing at this point. I had a happy new year wish from Paul and he told me that Joanna would wait to talk to me until we started practice on the 3rd of January. At midnight, Julia called me back and wished me a happy new year, I think she must have been where nobody could hear her, then she said I love you swimmer boy, please get back here and be with me.

With nothing to do the following weekend, I made a trip to Clarksburg to see Julia, I just could not wait anymore. I had told her mom, that I was going to do a surprise visit. She decided to do it as a surprise for Julia, since she had been moping around the last few days. I want to relate this little incident.

I parked my car, about 2 blocks away from the house. Julia's mom, was waiting for me at the back door, and let me in. The family was at the dinner table with Julia's back to me. Julia's mom said that was someone delivering a package she had ordered. I touched Julia on the shoulder and asked, is there a Julia here in a disguised voice.

Julia said sure, and turned around, she started screaming bawling, and hit me in the shoulder all in 5 seconds. It hurt a little but the embrace we had after that made the pain go away. He parents made up the couch for me, and we spent the entire evening holding hands. We were at her parents so nothing else was going to happen. I think the approvals of her parents of the two of us was complete.

Back to practice again, we had our first swim meet on Wednesday. Joanna asked me to see the coach after practice.

Coach what's up. John, I have been told that your shoulder is getting better enough for you to start competing again. I have all the slots filled up for fly and was told not to swim you there anyway. I have one slot left for the 200 IM, so you will be in lane 6 and no other events. The training staff insists on strict adherence to what they say so you can swim until conference. Remember we need some points from you for us to have a chance to win the conference.

We swam against division 1 University of Pittsburgh at Morgantown, they had swum against WVU, the night before, so this helped them justify the trip by swimming 2 meets. I would love to tell you I did well, my time as no better than high school, and I managed to finish third, the top for AB. Our team did not do well against them losing by 40 points, a large margin in a dual meet.

On the 20th of January, school began, Julia and I spent the night at her apartment the night before. We had barely been with each other the last 4 weeks, and we really wanted to be back together. Joanna, did us a favor and went elsewhere for the night. I can tell you both of us were very tired the next morning for the first day of class.

Speaking of class, five classes all of which were doable, this could mean a second near 4.0, for the semester. Julia and I again had no classes in common so the studying we would do together would just be hand holding while we studied our individual classes.

Joanna asked that we study at the sofa and wing chair so she could actually get some work done herself. She also reminded both of us that she expected her sorority sister to be at the spring formal in April, so she could show the couple off that was never at parties. She scolded us that we better not break-up like last year, it was so odd having Julia out with someone else. Then looking at the two of us realized that was not going to happen again. I had learned my lesson; Julia was looking out for me not trying to simply push me where I did not want to go. I had no interest in any other girl, although I will admit we had some very attractive swimmers on the Women's team. If I had, Joanna had warned them all off on me and to treat me like an older brother. The other guys on the team though it was weird the women would talk to me and hardly spoke to them, it was simple, it was talking to a big brother, nothing else. I did get some hugs when they swam well, which Joanna did not prevent. The lovely brunette was always there so no misbehaving was ever going to happen.

My swimming was getting better, but truthfully my right shoulder still did not feel right. I did not get to swim the 200 fly the last five meets before the conference, and never swam the 400 IM, when we had a distance meet, I got to do the spring 100 fly that day and that was it. Strict guidelines.

The conference meet was scheduled for late February and Paul, as captain presented our events for the meet. Due to my shoulder injury, I had to swim 400 IM, and 100 fly. Since the 200 IM and the 100 fly were day 2 they had decided I had more of a chance here. Last day because I could not swim 200 fly, they sent me to the 1650 free basically a throw away slot. Apparently Coach Edwards was pissed as he knew I was not going to score many points at the conference.

If you remember the 400 IM, was the wild card from high school, but without a single meet to do this I was given a seed time that placed me somewhere about 20th in the preliminaries. I did not do bad, I was able to make the consolation finals, lane 1, next to last. In the finals unfortunately my shoulder started to hurt and ended up just as I started 15th overall. I accounted for only 2 points I think they were expecting more. On day 2, I swam the 100 fly, and again barely made the consolation final, worse than previous year times, and ended up dead last that night in the consolations. Even Paul ended up only third in the event. On the last day, my 1650 free was not nearly good enough to make the top 16, so for the meet I had contributed only three points and my shoulder was still killing me. Our team finished third, way behind Findlay and Ashland, we had been favored to be a push for the championship but almost nobody did well.

Nobody knew if it was the taper we did or what, but we simply did not swim up to what was expected.

Coach Edwards Office, 3 days after conference:

Please close the door John, I have something to discuss with you: John, after three years on the team, I do not feel that AB can afford to continue your scholarship, you will still get the 25% academic money, but we feel that if you choose to come back we need the money for your scholarship for some faster incoming freshmen, we are thus ending your athletic scholarship at the end of the year. If you choose to transfer to another school, I will understand it. I would shake your hand and wish you luck going forward, but truthfully, I did not think after your freshman year that we should have continued your scholarship. I think you would better served also if you went to a community with more Jewish students, I think you will be happier, and we won't have to worry about accommodating your holidays going forward. No other swimmer got days off to go to church, so you can see my point here. Again, if you choose to come back, you will have your academic money, but you are unlikely to get in any meets next year, we have 7 to 8 strong swimmers coming in. I am thinking at best, you can help Joanna out in getting logistics worked out but don't expect more than an occasional time in the water next year.

I was totally stunned and could not say anything, I just left his office quietly and knew, the bastard finally got rid of me. That bastard! He even threw in the Jewish thing; I am so pissed and don't know what to do.

When I got back to my apartment, I was in tears and Paul asked what was wrong, I looked like I just heard my parent had died. Paul, I was basically dismissed from the AB swim team this afternoon. Coach Edwards said he was pulling my scholarship to award to the incoming freshmen. Man, I wish I had just red shirted, (injured and extend eligibility) this entire year, I knew I should have simply gone back to rehab and finished.

Paul put his arm around me, damn what have you decided to do? Well one of the odd things is if you came back, we all know that you would have won the Academic Athlete award next year.

I waited to go over to Julia and Joanna's apartment, Julia had a late afternoon class and would not have been there earlier. When I repeated what had happened this afternoon, Joanna asked does he know that you tried to swim through an injury all season?

Joanna, what you don't know about Coach Edwards is that he is a devout antisemitic person, and unless I had finished probably top 6, he was not going to renew my scholarship anyway. She did not understand, remember when I asked for Yom Kippur off, he was still pissed that I took the time off, I think this was just a way for him to get me off the team.

Julia hugged me and said at least we will have a lot of time together now that you have time off. I responded Julia, I have to find the extra ten thousand dollars somehow or probably transfer and go home.

Julia convinced me to have a call with my parents that night to ask for them to help me finish next year, she would be on the call with me to help me not break-down.

15 minutes later:

Hi mom and dad, I need to tell you that after this semester, Coach Edwards has pulled my athletic part of my scholarship. In order for me to finish up here, I will need to pay $10,000 or borrow that much to finish school next year. The alternate would be to go to UMBC but lose a full-year probably and it will cost 12,000, to complete my degree. I am calling tonight to see what you think, and what is the best way to go here. Julia spoke up, John is doing well in his classes and looks like if he keeps this up his grades, he will graduate magna Cum Laude.

Then they told me to call them back later in the evening at 9 PM, I called back. Mom and dad were on the phone, we both looked at what was happening up there, we think it would be better if you came home, but we can understand that you would rather just finish up there. Julia responded, I will offer any service John needs as a tutor and waive the fees that I would have received from the athletic department. Finally, they stated, we will agree to fund the additional funds, we had this in your education funds, so just consider this done.

So at least I could come back and finish my education, Julia hugged me and kissed me, just one more year up here and you can go to College Park, for your graduate degree. I gave her a kiss and decided to come back to my apartment, needed some time for my own to feel what to do.

I was able to go home for spring break 2 days after the meeting with Coach Edwards, while I was going to miss being away from Julia for a week, I needed to be away from the team for a while. While home, I went to College Park and had ice cream with Angela. Angela always the wise baby sister was the person I looked for guidance.

Her advice was very useful, John you need to finish your college at AB for 2 reasons. First, I would love to see you here in Maryland, but family is the second reason, do you want to add another year to your college time. The first reason is you are so deeply in love with Julia, I don't think you will do anything well away from her for weeks at a time. So big brother fight the system, finish college and come back to MD with Julia. Our parents will love her, and remember you are not just about swimming, you happen to swim.

I also sought advice from my grandfather, the retired Rabbi. John, here is what I will tell you about having to deal with antisemite behavior, just be in front of them and overcome them. If you have a chance to be the academic athlete just by staying on the team, then do it, don't worry about results, just being there every day is a way to fight them. Can you imagine if he has to introduce you to the distinguished alumni, it will kill him?

With the advice from my family, I came back to AB to put my emphasis on education for my final year, try to stay on the team and not care about what happened in the water. It would be the first time in my life that academics would rule. Oh yeah, my love for Julia might have something to do with the next step.

I got back to AB, Sunday night about 9 PM. When I got to the apartment, Paul was there with a few other swimmers and the lovely brunette. In the apartment was the 2 divers Brad and Colt, Jeff Kissinger, Thai, Paul and Joanna.

Paul spoke for the group. We know that Coach Just screwed you over for your scholarship. We also want you to know we have been told if you continue what you have been doing in class you will be the academic athlete for AB. You are also going to be an academic all-American; a second all-conference academic is also probable. We are asking you to stay on the team next year, we know that you won't have the role you expected, but we want you to stay. Yes, and we also know that Julia would be very upset if you would leave Alderson Broadus.

Thanks for the intervention, I had spoken to my grandfather and sister and came up with the same solution. With my parents help I am going to finish school here and when he has to introduce me, I know what I am going to say about being able to persevere with a coach that has a serious antisemitic attitude. Yes, I am an athlete and Jewish, it is time to expose this man for what he is, simply an asshole.

Julia joined the fun at the apartment, everyone in the room could see the bond between us and the hug and kiss we gave was the first time the team had seen us together like that. Julia said so it is time for getting better both mentally and physically. Now it is time for you to heal so that next year you come back and can practice and be in Coach Edwards face just by being in practice. Frank Pompano wants you back, he would love to see you win the academic athlete, apparently, he is not a Coach Edwards favorite, tired of hearing his rhetoric about only Christians etc. In this room look what you have, we have an array of people that he hates, time to turn the table on him. We look like the future here not his fundamentalist world.

Paul said to the group, remember if I am captain he can only do so much. John let's finish this together and with the lovely brunette as team manger we can handle the crap from Coach Edwards.

Tuesday Coach Edwards Office:

John what have you decided regarding your senior year? Do you need a reference from me for another school?

After talking to my parents, my Rabbi, and friends I have decided to complete my senior year at AB. According to Frank Pompano, I have done nothing wrong either academically or in the water, so he supports me being a member of the team next year with or without the scholarship money. I know that you hate Jews and think we are the issue, but if you want to see the issue then you need to look in a mirror because you are the issue and not me. With the support of the athletic director, I will finish my senior year as a member of the AB swim team, whether you put me in the pool or not, I am aiming to win the academic athlete award. I am starting today to do rehab on the shoulder and will be doing a special training that Coach Brian at NBAC developed for me.

His response was look, I don't hate Jews, just don't think they are athletes. Jesus was from Jewish parents, so of course I can't hate all Jews. I just think you would be better with your fellow Jews in Baltimore than here, especially dating our girls.

I simply said I will be here every day, and when they introduce the 4-year academic athlete, that will be my award and you will have to live with the first AB swimmer to win this award was the Jew you tried to throw off the team.

Son, I don't hate you just don't think you are an athlete, nor your fellow Jews, you can practice with the team, the AD has your back on that, but I decide who is going to be in the pool in the meets, and rest assured, I am not interested in you being a part of this team going forward.

I left his office knowing where I stood, I was not going to get his support, or any other coaching so it is all about survival and overcoming.

For the rest of the spring semester, I simply did the rehab training I had done 4-years before to rebuild the shoulder. Since I was no longer invited to the varsity time reserved, I swam the evenings by myself, always by myself. This time though, I had an army of supporters wishing me the best every day.

One more event I had to participate in was the spring formal with Julia. This time Joanna was going to do this right, she got a limo, and then booked Paul and me a time to get custom fitted tuxedos. I want you swimmer boys on our arms to look right for the night. Julia would not let me see her dress until the night of the event. She hid it in Joanna's room.

On the night of the event, we were told to have fresh haircuts because a couple might be awarded an award from the sisters of the sorority. I had been doing a lot of lifting, and the tuxedo fitting was very difficult, to get around my 44 inch around the chest and 31-inch waist, they had to take piece one from two matching suits. Paul took 2 minutes the damn skinny tall guy had like no problems whatsoever. My tuxedo barely was ready in time for the event.

Julia was incredibly dressed, she had a powder blue dress on, hair done and make-up flawless. The lovely brunette, at nearly 6 feet with her heels on had a gorgeous low cut peach colored dress. Paul was in awe of his date, apparently, they were now getting friendly, not like Julia and me but they appeared to get along away from the pool. The night was so nice and at 10:PM, they did the announcements. When they got to couple of the year, they announce that Julia and John are our couple of the year. Julia accepted for us, and then made me come up to the stage. With a full kiss in front of everyone, Julia held my hand and made her speech. I want everyone to know the name of John Peters tonight, we started out as tutor and student now John is getting all A's and obviously you can see we are a couple. Sandra, the president of the sorority yelled, it is about time we finally get you two out together. She said to me John, I see by your holding Julia's hand so tightly that you two are really a couple. I have been told that the swim team used to have a cute pet name for you, Jewish Monk. They thought you never went out or dated, what they did not know was that our Julia had captured your heart entirely. So please put on the robes of a monk and get next to your lady.

The picture in the school paper merely said Julia and the Monk, couple of the year. I knew the lovely brunette was behind this, and it had to piss-off Coach Edwards.

Later that night, Julia and I were very romantic, and we did not leave bed until 9:AM the next morning for some coffee. Joanna, just smiled at us, and said good morning, Julia and the Monk.

Two weeks later my junior year ended, it was a terrible and great year. While I was alone in my practices, I had friends and people who really supported me. My love of my life and family supporting me for the first time, I felt included.

My grades came in as a 4.0, as did Julia's. I guess you can be active and keep good grades. I was invited to join a couple of academic societies, I had to laugh given my history around school. I gladly accepted.

I left AB for home the last week of May. I stayed as long as I could knowing I would be away from Julia for almost 3 months. I had one required trip to renew my apartment contract and would find a way to see Julia then.

My summer was set, going back home as an assistant manager of the pool and head coach for a summer team of my own. Julia was at AB, she needs 2 courses to catch-up so she could graduate with me next year. She had a part-time job at a local WAWA, a gas station and food restaurant, she was a cashier when she needed to. No late nights though, she did not feel comfortable working with the limited staff at night.

Because I was coaching, I could not go to NBAC for practice, so I had my rehab training I did in the evening after my shift was done with the team. I went over to CCC to lift 3 times per week.

On July 1, James signed a National Letter of Intent to play baseball at Lehigh in PA. Low division 1, with a great academic history, my parents were so happy. His partial scholarship made that school possible for the family. Because we would have three students in college at the same time, he also received $12,500, in reduced tuition from the college based on family need.

I met up with Paul Julia and Joanna, at AB the last week of June to sign for our apartment. I spent the night with Julia, and then went back home. It was so hard to go home, I wanted to stay but needed to get back for coaching practice and then meets.

My team did fairly well, they went 4-1 and tied for the division win. We won the division meet and placed 6 swimmers at the county championships. The swim team president asked if I could come back the following year, I could not make a commitment yet, but would let him know early enough that he could recruit if I could not come back.

After the season my family rented a house in Ocean City, I guess they wanted one more weekend with all of the children together. My sister was out almost every night at Secrets, I was not so enthusiastic but went with her mostly to keep the guys from getting too close. That was not an easy thing to do, she is a very attractive girl.

I left for AB at the end of August things were really better at home, James was getting ready for his senior year, Angela was a junior at UM College Park, and I was getting ready to enter the weird senior year as an outcast loved by the team but not by my coach. My parents were eager that I finish this year and get back to MD to attend Maryland MBA program at College Park, I suspect my mother knew that someone else may be coming with me.

My malibu, was still operating well enough to get another year in it, James had a gift of a six-year-old Impala when he got his letter of intent, so he was a happy camper.

My year would begin with 5 more classes all in my major except for political science class to finish my requirements out. Looked fairly easy, Julia had decided to take the same class as me in political science, so we had an excuse to be on campus together and studying at the library. I no longer had to hide this from the swim team, I was not going to be a part of that team, just a glorified team manager.

Because the men's team was over 20 swimmers and divers and the women's team had only 13 swimmers, and odd practice times were being organized. 17 swimmers would practice with the head coach, the lower 3 of us would take one lane when the women swam. Because I was an assistant to Joanna, I was responsible for making sure that every piece of equipment was ready for the men's practices, kick boards, pull buoys etc. Joanna was responsible for logistics and was mostly away from the pool organizing our trips, budgets and schedules. The freshman only knew that I used to be a swimmer on the team and due to injury, I was doing workouts with the assistant coach later. They were told it was unlikely that I would swim this season, but the athletic department wanted to let me finish out my senior year as part of the team. (In other words, pity the guy). A few of them wanted to give me a lot of crap, but Paul told them to leave me alone or feel the wrath of the upperclassmen.

The assistant coach got to train me, James Arnett, who had an injury, and due to his class schedule Anthony Villani. I truthfully had a weird experience having recovered from my injuries; I knew that I was posting times better than I ever had but I was just on the edge of this team.

When the rest of the team had time trials I was not invited to participate, James Arnett was able to swim a couple of shorter events, but you could tell he was really suffering. The assistant coach decided to see what I could do so over a 2-day period, I swam 500 free, 1650 free, 100 fly, 200 fly, and both the 200 and 400 IM. Bruce Farley was our assistant coach, had swam at WVU and was establishing himself as a coach. He looked at my times in the 2 fly events and said I should not tell this to you, but you are good enough to be our third swimmer in each event, and in the IM's, you look like to be second.

You know that does not mean anything; I am unlikely to swim anything other than a relay meet when nobody else wants to swim it. Or maybe if someone has a test and can't go to the meet.

Keep positive you never know what can happen.

If Coach Edwards dies is the only way I am getting to do more than that.

While swimming was on the outskirts other things came to my rescue. Julia and I had a fantastic relationship and for the first time we could openly hold hands in public without the team impact. The women's team liked Julia, and they saw me dominating in the scrubs practice, as we called it. I joined student government elected as a senior representative. I had twice a month meeting for other areas so my life without worrying about the team thing was assured.

The first relay meet, the events were posted, and I was not in any of them. Joanna told me I did not need to go with the team to Pittsburgh and to enjoy the apartment with Julia. We had a great weekend together went to Valley Falls to see them before it goes too cold to walk around. We were getting pretty inseparable, and Joanna was pretty much ok with me being there almost any night.

The second relay meet was just before Thanksgiving break again in Youngstown. I was listed in the 800 IM relay, I guess they were short on swimmers. That was the only event I swam that day, so there was no room for me reserved like the other swimmers, so I took a couple of pillows and a blanket and slept in the closet of Paul's room. I still had to make sure that anyone wanting kick board etc, got that before I warmed up. I swam well enough that my split was better than one other swimmer, I think the freshmen, were really surprised. We ended well enough to qualify for the finals later that night. In the finals I had the second-best swim from our team, and no comment from Coach Edwards, just a lanyard whip by Coach Farley.

I spent a week back at Arbutus for Thanksgiving. It was cool to see my parents and it was actually a pretty pleasant time. My dad's mom, (Grandmother Peters) was not doing well but we picked her up from her assisted living home and she was glad to escape the boring life there. It was good to be with them, and really wanted to be in West Virginia with Julia, but that would be later.

Before I left, my mother said to me, I want to meet Julia before you 2 graduate, she has been fantastic for you. I also know from Angela, that you and she are going public with your dating, I am not going to tell your dad, he will not understand why you kept it quiet. If you 2 get married, I don't care what religion you are, you will always be my first and she must be a great person to have captured your heart so intensely.

I had three weeks back including finals, Julia and I studied Political Science together but the nerd couple as some called us, were doing well in school. I was lucky because of my grades I only had 2 finals to take Julia had 4.

The team had a dual meet against Fairmont State at Fairmont on a Saturday, I was invited to stay at AB. I really did not care, rather be on campus now than travel with team to hand out towels etc. Joanna had that handled, so I could finish my studies and be ready for finals. The team beat Fairmont easily, they only had ten swimmers, a couple of rock stars but with the talent we had nobody was going to take AB easy this year.

AB cancelled the Homecoming event that had been an annual dance, Julia's sorority had an event but not formal dresses, this was a casual event with alumni. We attended an "Abba" tribute band that the school brought to campus, but nothing for Julia to dress up for.

Right before the semester ended, I was notified by e-mail my grades were 4.0, Julia was still waiting for her West Virginia history class, but it looked good for the nerd couple to both get a 4.0. I told Frank Pompano about my grades, he just said keep it up young man, you have really grown up these last 4 years. He told me that he approved of my relationship with Julia, he said you 2 are the talk of the campus. The nerd couple is what they call you studying all the time while holding hands all the time. I could not be prouder that you and she are so close. I am sending the University of Maryland a recommendation for your graduate school application, I hope this helps you deserve any scholarship they give you, what a turnaround in your grades.

So, with that my first semester of my senior year was concluded. I stayed around for a few days after to help Julia go home and spent a night in Clarksburg, before leaving for the break. Julia's mother gave me a hug like I was her own son at this point. She just told me we can't wait for you two to be married, when are you going to bring Julia home to Maryland. I told her that was going to be weird with the Rabbi and all but that it would be time shortly. I intend to propose to your daughter sometime early after we get back with you and your husbands' permission.

She hugged me and said you already have our permission; I can't imagine her being this happy with anyone else. If you have children, you can figure out what religion you want to follow, or maybe find a way to follow both. I know Julia has applied to George Washington and American Law School, so obviously the two of you want to be together the DC area.

I drove home the following day; this was going to be a drama filled last semester.

I went home from AB, for the holiday season it was going to be interesting. When I got home, I was a day ahead of Angela. James and I were going to share a room for a couple of weeks, fortunately he was in class most of the first week and at indoor baseball practice the afternoon, so I really did not need to see him much. I thought I saw Lucy one day, but at this point I was not going to try to see her, Julia was my true love. Lucy was attending UMBC I heard and living at home.

My dad got home later from work, and when he was changed and ready for dinner I showed him my grades, and he was impressed. Damn, your tutor is really the best, mine never got me those grades. My mother then proceeded to kick my dad in the shin.

Angela came home the next afternoon, and she threw her arms around me, I am so happy to see you. James responded you don't throw your arms around me. Baby brother that is because I see you like every other weekend and all you talk about is baseball and going to college. Angela then turned to me and how are you and your tutor doing. We are doing well thanks for asking, the look I gave her probably knew not to ask any more questions.

Later that night, I went to Angela's room. I would rather not talk about Julia with James in hearing range. In regard to my tutor, we are way beyond the studying ways, and I am ready to go the to the next level. You want to live with her, and I said no, I intend to ask her to marry me when we get back to school. The next thing I knew my sister hugged me and said I am so happy for you. I want to know after you have asked her, and her reaction.

The next 10 days went very routine, I spent Christmas morning with my grandmother, she still wanted to enjoy the holiday with us even though she knew we were Jewish. I was the only one from the family that went to see her, the rest of the family said we are Jewish and don't celebrate the holiday. I just celebrated another year to see my grandmother. Later in the day, I went to see my grandfather, the rabbi was doing volunteer work at a soup kitchen, something he did every Christmas, with a few of the members of the synagogue. We hugged, and he looked at me, you are so much happier than when you left for college. I guess the time you are spending with your tutor is doing you well. I then asked him what I should do if I decided to marry Julia. He said, the two of you have already conquered many things together, religion is something you can decide later, I am just happy you found someone that makes you so happy.

The second of January, I packed my car and went back to AB, swim practice was beginning the next day. Julia was not going to be back for 2 more weeks. Paul was already at the apartment and smiled at me and said are you ready for the last semester. I just smiled at him. He then asked a question that was odd coming from him, so are you going to ask Julia to marry you? I got it Paul; you were called by the lovely brunette to get the answer. No John, it was all on me, you know it was her, and she said she is worried that you two are graduating and will go your different ways. First, I intend to be at MD College Park, and Julia has applied for Law Schools in the DC area.

Paul just asked again so have you asked her to marry you.

No Paul not yet, and with that he laughed you said not yet and not maybe.

Just tell the lovely brunette, I would rather Julia be the first person to know when I ask her and not her telling Julia to be prepared. Yes, I have every intent of asking her and believe her parents are already supporting it.

About time my friend, Julia and you are the perfect nerd couple holding hands all the time studying together. I think the entire swim team is expecting something.

Julia came back the 20th of January as school was starting the next day. It had been almost 4 weeks without me seeing her. I ran to her as she opened up the door and gave her a huge kiss, I told her I never want to be away from her for that long again.

Julia said I know what you are about to say and no this is not the time to talk about it, we just missed each other so let's not get crazy tonight. We spent the rest of the night together it was like we had never been apart. In the morning, I had to get up and leave early for morning workout, since I still had mandatory morning workouts.

The team was going away again another meet I was not swimming, and since it was an away meet, I decided to stay at AB.

That weekend I stayed away from Julia most of the weekend because I needed to figure out how I was going to propose to her. This time I talked to Joanna and said, ok, you know that this is going to happen in the next week, what are your thoughts.

Joanna then proceeded to tell me how she thinks it should go. She found a place she could talk without the entire team knowing what was going on.

First, you need to get a dozen red roses from the local flower shop. I will tell her I have car trouble and have her meet me at the locker room at the pool. I will then text her that to meet me at the team room outside the locker room. I will have the entire Women's swim team in a meeting, and you will be in the room.

She will knock on the door and ask if she can come in and to pick me up. You will come from behind the women's team with your roses, and then you will propose to her with the team watching and approving.

Joanna, what if she turns me down. I will be embarrassed, and the entire team will see it.

John, don't worry, you and I know that she may be hardheaded, but she really wants you to ask her to marry her.

On Wednesday after the practices had ended, I got dressed, went to my car and pulled out the roses that I had purchased earlier in the afternoon. I went to the team room as instructed and the entire women's team was already in the room. Joanna says you know my roommate, after the quick team meeting, she will knock on the door asking if she can come in. I will be behind you with John, and then one of you will open the door. I will say Julia I'll be there in a minute, and instead of me coming out John will come out instead.

John, you know what to do after that. So, ladies are we ready to get the Jewish Monk engaged.

Julia knocked on the door, and Joanna said just a minute. One of the women opened the door and told Julia just a minute, Joanna is finishing up something. In unison, the entire team turned around and I then went in front of them.

Julia, the last few weeks told me that I never want to be separated from you again, so will you please marry me so I will never have to be away from you again. Joanna came out from the back of the room, and at the moment Julia was crying so loud that I had to ask her again.

Julia came to me and jumped in my arms, and simply said you know the answer is yes. With that we kissed passionately. The women's team all started clapping.

Julia then yelled at Joanna, ok, so you knew this before me? I did and helped John plan this there was no way I was letting my best friends to do this without me. Paul then entered the room and asked what she said to the proposal.

Joanna said what did you think your roommate was doing while you were away swimming. How was that for planning. Of course, she said yes.

The women then yelled nerd nerd nerd. Ha ha, the nerd couple were now officially engaged. Joanna hugged the two of us. Paul patted me on the back and said should I let the men's team know. Paul you won't have to the entire women' s team was part of it. I'm sure it will get leaked out and besides who on the men's team would I talk to, most of them barely know I am on the team.

Last weekend in January came and the weather was freezing, so one night I said to Julia can I stay tonight it is 3 below zero and not sure my car will start tonight. Of course, you can stay my love was her answer. I had finished studying for the night and asked Julia if she was finished, she kissed me and said I was waiting for you to finish.

We went back to her room and while the weather may have been freezing outside, the two of us spent the night creating heat. I think we made love for what felt like hours I'm not sure how long it was, and I know that we were very passionate that night.

2 Weeks Before Championships:

Julia and I became so close that nobody saw one of us without the other except when we were in our respective classes. I had clothes over at her apartment and spent many nights over there. My classes were pretty easy and took my GMAT's in January. Julia took her LSAT's for law school the same weekend.

As far as practice with the team nothing changed, I basically worked out on my own with a coach in the women's time after the men's practice and served as a set-up manager for the men's team. I got in a couple of meets where we were dominating and nobody really wanted to swim or a star swimmer just did not need the competition, but other than that Coach Edwards had completely cut me off from the team as he intended.

As a senior, I have not had much of a season, I only actually got to swim in about 4 meets at all this year. I think they let me swim in a relay at the Youngstown Invitation and swam against the old WVIAC team of Wheeling and Salem Universities. I also swam the tri-meet against Franciscan. The studs that Coach Edwards has recruited are taking all the slots that I used to swim funny thing they are barely faster than my times. I remember when we swam Marshall University 2 years ago, and I upset two of the 200 flyers, and coach only says, thought you should have won this event.

Interestingly we finished first and second in the event in our upset of Marshall. I guess he gave them a scholarship so he must swim them, hell he took my scholarship away hoping I would go away. Everyone knew now that our coach was uncomfortable around people that were not Christian, so I should have expected anything less from him.

I remember the night that Paul and others came to my room and said, look I know that you could leave the team today and without the scholarship you had really understand it if you quit. I do know that if you stay you have an opportunity to be the first Academic Athlete in our team's history, hell you don't want a women's basketball player to get that award. Julia came to the room before Paul had left and said you may as well swim, your load is going to be easier this year and I have class in the afternoon anyway. So, I agreed to stay on to swim, just as much to piss off Coach Edwards, as it was to get a trophy for being both an athlete and an academic athlete.

I have already told these stories before, so I guess I should get to what happened this week. I will tell you we have 1 more dual meet left in the season, and I know James Arnett was having shoulder tendinitis and had not swum a single meet in the winter semester. So, after practice coach Edwards says to me to come to his office, he needed to discuss something.

Come into the office said Coach Edwards, I need to talk to you regarding the rest of the season. I know you have not swum much this season, so I wanted to tell you we got permission to red shirt James Arnett. What that means is two things, we have 20 swimmers on the team, and I am trying to decide who will replace James on the roster for the conference meet. Barry Bowers swims the most competitive events at the conference and if we take him, he has almost no chance of scoring a point, but with you swimming 200 fly, 400 IM and either 100 fly, or 200 IM, you could possibly score a few points by making the top 16, in an event with those events being more open to a slower swimmer. The second thing if I choose you to be our 18th swimmer, will you be able to get yourself meet ready? I think you haven't swum much this season except some exhibitions, so can you swim this meet against Frostburg University as a warm-up. Paul thinks you could place in the 200 fly, I'm not so sure, so really need your commitment that you will do your best to be ready for conference. We have a chance to win the meet for the first time and really could use a possible 13th to 16th finish to get some points. James would have been close to making the finals, but I know that you probably don't have that as a possibility.

My response was simple, coach I have been close to making the finals for the last three years, I am not sure why you don't think I have a chance of scoring but I do get that I have had very little meet competition this year, but that was your choice not mine, just like pulling my scholarship I know you have had very little faith in me as a swimmer, just your opinion and have nothing to do with the real results. I have been here all year and I know if you need me, I will be ready. In practice I have been beating your prize athletes' times, but since I am your number 19 or 20 in your mind, I guess you need to decide. So yes, I feel like I will be ready and don't be surprised if I can even make a final.

Right before I was leaving for the cafeteria, Paul came to me and told me Coach did not feel he could tell you about his decision for conference as you and he really don't get along. I said as team captain I would let you know what his decision was. I thought all along that you were being blamed for our losing the conference last year and he has been holding this over your head all year. So simply said you're in as a swimmer at conference.

Later that night Julia and I were at my apartment, and she was talking about something she wanted to do in 2 weeks. I just burst out laughing, I would love to do that with you, but I think I will be very busy that weekend. Julia mocked so they want you to go to the conference meet as the towel boy. Nope with James out, I am being added to the conference meet team. I will be swimming the 100 fly, 200 fly, and the 400 IM. Julia laughed, isn't the 400 IM the event that nobody ever wants to swim, yes that's why I guess I get to swim it.

Julia said didn't you finish like 10th last year in the 400 IM, I said nope could not swim it, but I was 15th in 200 fly, not last year but yes, near the top 20 in the 100 fly. So now that coach has lost one of his pet's athletes, he wants you to go, I wonder why you want to help him out after he took away your scholarship.

I'm just a swimmer and besides, it will be just one more meet and them I'm done for swimming at AB.

After the meet, we can tell everyone that we are engaged and plan to get married this June.

Julia said yes, we can tell everyone after the meet and I am hoping to be able to get both a priest and a rabbi to do this, but we are going to have to recruit a rabbi as I don't think we have a real synagogue until you get to Morgantown, or Charleston.

I told Julia, you have been very hungry this week, I'll go out and get some groceries for us for the weekend. Right now, all I want to do is get some rest as I will soon have to try to get in meet shape in like a week and be ready to swim where nobody else wants to swim.

I just don't know how the heck I can be expected to score in the conference meet when I have almost no competition this year. I really don't want to embarrass myself or the team and end up last. Just maybe the 400 IM, swim it in practice this week, work on relaxing going out on the fly, breathe easier in the back, use the better Spanish based breaststroke, and then leave nothing in the tank for the free. If I swim the 200 fly, just got to figure out how to relax enough in the first half if the race to have something left for the last half so I don't die like I did last year. If I can do that just maybe I can get near the finals. First day of the meet coach will have to decide am I swimming the 200 IM, or the 100 fly. I know my choice is the 100 fly, 55 seconds of hell and then I am done for the day, unlikely to finish fast enough to even make the consolations. 200 IM, last I swam that was my freshman year and did I get smoked, not even the top 20.

So how do I do this the other guys have been peaking for the last 2 weeks, I must do a 3-week peak in one week while I am getting in meet shape in just one meet. All the while making sure that I don't peak before the meet 5 days later. In the old days they tried going totally protein for a while then all carbohydrates the week of the meet. Well, that was a program that took 4 weeks to do, let's try this in 12 days, (6 and 6), hell it is worth a try. I can get sugar very easily at the cafeteria but for decent protein will buy some red meat, and some sausages for this weekend.

I better go to the Kroger tonight, because I have no time to waste. At least Julia will be happy I can cook these all myself.

This is going to be a long night, I need a plan to find some speed and endurance, just don't know what I can do to gain speed and endurance in one week, this is just an insane request of my body. Better yet, should I really care about this just so coach can finally win a conference title, reality is that if these freshman swim well they won't need any points from me. But damn, wouldn't it be great to finish my career as both the academic athlete and somehow get an all-conference swim in.

Just how do you do it, when everyone else has been prepping for months, I have just been practicing and studying. I have never made the top 8 even when I was being prepared and trained all season. But damn, that would be a great way to end it, Julia will be so proud, and the team will really celebrate something we have never done.

Julia let's go to Kroger now, we have some food to buy, and want to make sure we have enough because you really went through our fridge this week.

(Julia here, I should also get a home pregnancy test, I am already 2 weeks late and never happened before) That will be great graduate and then get married and then have a baby, all in one year. (Mrs. John Peters, John will be so great in grad school, and I would love to go get my Law Degree at the same time)

11 days Before Conference:

I did not sleep well last night, kept putting training programs and the potential races in my mind. Julia said I kicked her with both legs at the same time, I must have been swimming my butterfly events when I kicked her with a dolphin kick.

Breakfast was funny, ate a pork chop, 1 sausage patty and 1 strip of bacon. Just to not completely go crazy ate 2 pieces of toast with butter and jelly. I had a cup of coffee because I have 2 classes this morning and need to stay awake. Like always I added a banana from the cafeteria.

Practice starts at 3:30 PM, sharp, so between 1 PM and 3 PM, took a nap and got to practice just in time. Because the other swimmers were already starting a taper, I got to play another game. While they started out doing 10 times 100 of a particular stroke, I got to do 5 times 400 IM's. (IM's are 100 each of the four strokes, Butterfly, backstroke, breaststroke and then Freestyle)

Yes, I heard them laughing because they were done, and heard, hey the old man is trying to get back in shape. Ha ha, I still can keep up with all of you and I guarantee no academic awards for any of you.

Now a set of 5 swims of 100 fly, the thought is to try to do each one at about the same time, and this stroke hurts like hell. Glad I have been weightlifting because this is going to hurt like hell.

Well, this was unexpected, each 100 fly was between 1:00 and 1:01, not bad about 4 seconds better than I normally do.

Last main thing in practice, I have to do 10 X 100 free, trying to stay steady and practice what it will be like with oxygen debt in the 400 IM. God this feels bad.

1000 warm down and time for dinner.

This is the same practice I will do before the meet Saturday, and the conference which will start 5 days later.

Dinner tonight: They had pork chops at the cafeteria, not very good but day 4 of the protein diet. I did get some broccoli to offset and I broke the protein by having a piece of carrot cake for dessert.

For snack, I had salted peanuts that my mom sent me from Williamsburg, VA, they went there before the holidays to see the Illumination events, and all I got was these peanuts, and an Illumination T-Shirt.

Need to study for 2 hours have a test in micro-economic theory on Wednesday. I know I need to be ready for this so I can get a 4.0, this is just not my favorite class.

Thursday before Frostburg meet:

I just got an e-mail from coach for Frostburg meet, they are doing other events meet instead of traditional. I have to swim 400 IM and 100 fly, they are not swimming the 200 IM, or the 200 fly so only 2 events Saturday. This also means my first time swimming the 200 fly will be at conference.

Our grades were posted this morning for the exam, not bad I got a 91, keeps an A possible but not much room for relaxing my last semester.

This is an easy day for classes, I only have a 1 credit music appreciation class to finish, and then that one is done for the year. Nothing like listening to music and identifying the artist and then the related style. This is what they call an Easy A.

Practice today was interesting, while all the others are ramping down the tapers, I am at the last day of the hard work. The soreness has diminished in my shoulder and now I am able to see what the 400 IM will be without muscle pain. The conference meet schedule came out and it is not as I anticipated, they changed the meet events, the 400 IM is the last event on the last day before the 400-freestyle relay. So, the worst of the worst will be my last event ever, I really would have preferred it to be the 200 fly or 100 fly. Not my choice. I suspect that Findlay has something to do with this change, they have some great swimmers in the IM, I have never beaten one of them. Day 1 is the 100 fly, and day 2 will be the 200 fly, so now the order is set, sprint, pain and then the ultimate painful experience equal to 3 days of hell.

My 400 IMs are getting better averaged 5 seconds better than Monday each time. Even Jim said to me, they better watch out the old man wants a final in his last conference and looks serious. The last 100 fly was under 59 today, not bad for that late in practice.

Last protein dinner tonight, they had roast beef at the cafeteria, at least that is what they said it was), I got another pork chop for added protein. Tonight, I got apple crisp for dessert can't wait until we switch tomorrow from protein to carbohydrates. Of course, I finished off the salted peanuts when I got home before an hour of studying for a biology class, boy what an idiot, forgot to take a mandatory class until my last semester of my senior year, I am the only senior in the class all freshman and me, I feel like I am the old man in that class.

Julia came over tonight, she said I look lean and mean. Yes, thanks honey, didn't I look good before? Ha ha. This joke was not well received. After having to clean-up for my joke we talked about places to get married in. Julia thinks she can get a church wedding in her home area near Bridgeport, but so far, she has not had much success in getting a contact for the rabbi. I told her my family is connected through my grandfather so, she is literally going to call my mother and ask her about where she can call to get a rabbi. She said her mom is so excited about our wedding, she wants to know how many from my family will come to West Virginia especially the Jewish side. I did not want to tell Julia that I have not even told my parents about our plans much less anyone else in our family. I owed a call to Angela first.

Julia, we need to call Angela. From my phone I put it on speaker mode, I called her number, and she answered. Good afternoon, Angela, you had made a request of me before I came back to school. So here it is, with that Julia interrupted, we are getting married in June, I want you as one of my bridesmaids.

The phone went silent, and then when Angela came back on, Julia of course I will be a bridesmaid. I am so happy for you, have you told our parents yet?

My answer is you told me to call you first, so that call will be coming I am not sure when.

She agreed to keep it quiet, but only for a few days, you know mom is going to read through me otherwise.

Oh crap, before Julia calls Saturday night while I am at Frostburg, I better tell my parents that we are planning in getting married in June. Mom has never met Julia in person. She does not even know that we have been dating officially and mostly living together. This call is going to be interesting:

Thursday night call to my parents: (8:30 PM)

With Julia and I on cell phone speaker mode, I placed a call to my home in Arbutus. I truthfully was hoping the call would go to voice mail unfortunately my mom picked up the phone.

Hi mom, this is your son John. Julia my tutor is here with me tonight is dad there? Mom went out and got dad on the other line and then we started the call.

We have something to tell you and not sure how you and dad are going to react. Yes, I am still on the swim team, and guess what I am swimming next weekend at the conference meet. The meet is going to be in Canton, Ohio, not sure you want to go but coach told me he was adding me to the conference lineup earlier this week. My grades are going well and looks like I am up for Academic Athlete in April. If I win it, they will ask you both to come to the banquet.

Mom then said That's great but what is that the both of you are going to tell us?

I guess I chickened out so Julia stepped up and said, good evening, well we wanted to let you know that we will want you to come to Bridgeport in June, because John and I are now engaged and getting a ring Sunday, and we are planning on getting married in June. My mom has reserved a church for a Sunday afternoon wedding, and we have a priest reserved. I was going to call you Saturday night to ask you if you can help us get a rabbi for the event, we want to have both in the ceremony.

The phone went silent for what felt like a minute, and I guess dad came into the room with mom. Dad simply said, your mom is in tears and crying. Ok, dad is she crying happy or crying because she is upset. Then mom came back on the phone.

Julia honey, all I can say is I am so happy for both of you, I saw how John has matured since you have been tutoring and I guess dating, I would be honored to be at the wedding and will talk to my father about getting a rabbi for the wedding. I know my father is retired, but he does occasional funerals, memorial services, and has performed a wedding or two in the last year that I know of. Would you let me ask him if he would perform the wedding, he uses a cane now to walk, but would you consider a conservative rabbi even though we are now reform.

Now Julia starts crying, and says to my mom, that would be fantastic. John says your father is very strict and only allowed you to get married after your husband converted to Judaism. Do you think that is a possibility that he will consent to do it?

Julia honey, I will get it done, and I know he will because he will want to be at his grandson's wedding. He does not travel on the sabbath, so we would have to come up Thursday before the wedding, and we can meet your parents. I am so happy for the both of you, and you can tell John, I knew that both of you were dating for the last 2 years at least. You can't keep that enthusiasm for a girl and not have your mother know that he was in a serious relationship with her son. So, John I am so happy for the both of you and cannot wait to be there in June. But if you are going to Grad school and she wants to go to Law school, have you all figured that out yet?

Julia said, I will try to get into a law school in the same town as John goes to Grad school. Since John will be at Maryland Business School in College Park, I will move to the DC area and try to get into a local law school.

Honey, I think I have some connections at American University, so let me know and I can help you get in. When will you be taking your LSAT's?

Julia's response: I already took then and expect results next month, but as you know I started school a semester late, so I am trying to graduate in 7 semesters instead of 8, so it is possible that I may have to wait a year.

Mom said I am so excited for the both of you and don't worry about a mixed marriage between a catholic and a Jewish boy. I can help you get in to law school, don't worry about it. How are you parents about the wedding.

Julia simply said, my family loves John and I really think they were wondering when we were going to tell them we wanted to get married. John and I are in love and both of us wanted to get our next steps secure before we got married. So, it was me who told John to not ask me to get married because we needed to get through school first.

I am worried that some of our family will not want to go to the wedding, they are Sicilian and guess they will be upset because I am not marrying another Sicilian.

(Julia here) Just glad she did not ask if I was pregnant, because I would have had to say maybe. I guess I will know after I take the test Saturday as I am now like three weeks late.

Good night mom and dad, I must get to bed soon, need some sleep here and we really wanted to let you know.

I simply said to Julia, well that went well, I know it is because you were the confident one and said this to my mom and not me asking. I think my mom and you are somewhat alike, when you set your mind to something you will make it happen.

I am going to bed, you going to stay tonight or are you going to your apartment. Julia said she was going to her apartment, not sure why but she looked tired when I thought she would be happy. Julia just gave me a kiss and went out of the apartment. I have no idea what that is about, but I am sure I will find out.

Friday – 1 Day Before Frostburg Meet

We will leave after practice tonight; we are swimming at 11:00 on Saturday morning and going over the mountains. For anyone that knows anything about Frostburg, it is properly named, and nothing to do but that's the way with some of these small-town schools, AB is not a lot better, but when you live here you know where to go. Frostburg is one of the worst teams in the conference, so I guess they were opened to doing the alternative events.

I am so lucky no classes today, so I am going to go to the pool early this afternoon and do a private practice, the rest of the team is just doing a warm-up, so coach says it is ok for me to do my own practice. Truthfully, I think he did not really care what I did so basically, I am on my own to get ready for the meet and he probably is really glad that I am not with his prize puppies.

So how do you do an easy workout to be ready for a meet? I think I will do a 400 warm- up just to loosen up, mostly freestyle. I will do 5 100's of fly, on a 2-minute increment, and then a few 200 IM's, and then another 400 to cool down.

I checked with Frank this afternoon regarding the student athlete award, he said you know I can't comment on that award to you, and that being said you may want to give your parents the information of when and where the banquet is just in case. The award will be announced on March 15th. (Funny the same day as the Ides of March, Et Tu Brute, I really hope not)

Since the team did their practice later and then went to the cafeteria, I had to join up with them when they were getting ready to leave for Frostburg. Because the women were also going, we had a bus that took most of the team, the trainers and supplies followed in a passenger van. I guess I was late because when I got to the bus, all the seats were already taken, so coach says for me to go get in the van because he did not want to order another vehicle. I decided to take my own car and drive better than being cramped for several hours. Joanna, our glorious manager, asked if she could go in my car, so I added her stuff and proceeded to go to Frostburg.

In the car, Joanna asked me why I had stayed on the team given that the coach had told everyone that if I had performed well the team would have won the conference last year. She said he has told this to all the athletic department, and they were the ones that had agreed to pull your scholarship.

I simply said, I was so close to graduation I was not going to transfer schools, and my parents could afford the other 50%, that the department did not honor for my senior year. So why did I swim, basically it was to win the Athletic athlete award and make sure no other swimmer was going to receive it this year. I know at least one is close and one women's basketball player is close. I then proceeded to tell her Frank has told me that I should be prepared to have my parents here for the Athletic banquet.

Time goes by, and then Joanna asks, OK, so I get that you are staying on the team to get athletic award, so this is something personal, when are you going to get married to my sorority sister. You and Julia are as close of a couple as I have ever known and nobody new until this year that you two had been dating since the end of your freshman year. Heck, she even had another guy go with her to our formal, what was that all about.

Ok Joanna, you have me, we shortly broke up my sophomore year, I thought she was being too pushy getting me to study and I got pissed off. After about 2 weeks, I realized I had been an ass an apologized to her for being such a jerk. Unfortunately, the formal was the next weekend, and I was not going to upset her plans so yes, she went to the formal with someone else and I was not happy about it. We just got engaged as you know, and we are not formally telling anyone other than our parents until after the conference meet. We are going to Kay Jeweler on Sunday to pick out a ring, my mom has sent a couple of rubies she had from some older jewelry to add to the design and reduce the cost. The next thing I know I am getting a big hug from Joanna, and she said I just knew you 2 were destined for each other. Julia will be the best partner you could ever have, she is smart, dedicated, and I can see in her eyes every time you are together that you are madly in love with her.

All I could say who else would have me. Joanna laughed, you could have asked about 50 of the local women and they would have married you on the spot to get out of West Virginia. So, you are saying Julia wanted to date me just to get out of West Virginia, and Joanna laughed no, and I bet it is going to be interesting wedding is it going to be a catholic wedding or a civil wedding. I told her the plan is for both a Catholic and Jewish ceremony in June, and I suspect you are going to be asked to be in the wedding. Since you planned the engagement event. I think I will let Julia tell me who she is having in her side, I am going to ask Paul to be my Best Man.

The rest of the trip went by fast, and we got to stay at a Holiday Inn Express in Frostburg. My roommate was our team captain Paul. I wondered why he had done that I had been relegated to the training staff all year. I heard Paul said seniors only room for the last meet, so I actually got to stay with the team for my last dual meet. Paul just said are you ready to take on the 2 events tomorrow, I saw how fast you were going, and you may surprise a few people tomorrow. I just laughed; hey I am a slow old man that apparently choked away our conference title last year. Paul sure, does anybody but me know that you had a pulled hamstring along with the shoulder injury, and could not fully swim without a lot of pain last year, much less the shoulder. I said nope but I was able to finish my events. I will never give coach the truth he wanted me out anyway, he still does not feel comfortable with non-Christians. I guess he is just not used to people outside his Midwest life.

Saturday Before Conference: Frostburg Meet day.

Unlike a lot of swimmers who cannot eat the day of a swim meet, I have no problem eating a hearty meal. For breakfast at the cafeteria, I had a bagel with butter and jelly, bacon, and a banana, plus some cheerios. The other swimmers ate very lightly, except for the divers, they always seem to eat very well.

The facility at Frostburg is a pretty nice pool, the facility has the ability to be either 25 yards or meters, plus it has both a 1 meter and 3-meter diving boards. The 400 IM today will be the event the last event before the 1-meter dive and the 100 fly will be the first event after the dive. I will definitely ask the divers to take their time so I can recover from one and be ready for the next. Since this is a warm-up match for the conference, we are swimming as many as 6 guys in each event, the women, will be after the 400 IM, and they only have 1 heat. That at least will give me some extra time. The 100 fly, I am the first of the two heats so anything I gained by the women and the fast men, will be lost.

Warm-up went well and I felt really good here, I did one 50 fly and was already hitting a low 12 second in practice, good sign for the meet.

After the relays and the 1650 freestyle, substituted for the 1000, AB was already up by a considerable margin. Paul is swimming the 200 freestyles today and we are both swimming the 100 fly. Then came the 50 free and then my heat for the 400 IM. Since coach has me as the 6th swimmer from our team, I will be assigned the garbage lane 6 of the slow heat.

The swim went a lot better than I could have expected, I was first in the heat after both butterfly, and backstroke by over 6 seconds, extended the lead to about three body lengths after breaststroke, and finished the race first in my heat by three seconds. I guess not really ready for the conference meet yet, but I imagine this really pissed off the coach, I just waxed 2 of his swimmers. In the fast heat, 2 of our team finished ahead of me one by 5 seconds and one by 2.2 seconds, so not bad for the old man of the team.

Paul slapped me on the back, not bad old man, third is not bad overall. Joanna throws me a towel and says can I call Julia, and I tell her no way, not sure I even want her to come to Canton next week. Joanna says you don't think that time will be good enough to get at least into the consolations, I looked at the conference times and you now have the 12th best time going into the conference championship.

My friends on the dive team seemed to know what to do, Brad and Colt, were really good at asking to repeat the announced dive, probably gave me an extra 10 minutes, but truthfully, I was really tired.

By the time we got finished with the women's diving, our men's team had pretty much finished off Frostburg, they had no wins and one second, so we had dominated. We still had the second half of the meet to go but if Paul won the 100 fly it was pretty much over.

My swim in the 100 fly was solid but nothing spectacular. I finished third in my heat and 6th overall something in the 55 high range, beating 2 of our team but Frostburg finished second and third. Paul won the heat and is now the favorite for the conference having just broken the pool record at Frostburg. I think his time was like 52 flat, about a second ahead of Frostburg's best swimmer, still I think he will do 50 flat at conference and has a chance to win it.

Since I was done for the day, just took a cool down swim and got dressed nothing else to do. I did call Julia to let her know how I had done and that I would be back later that night. She told me she was in Bridgeport with her family starting to plan the wedding, so not to expect to see me until Sunday afternoon. I had to confess I told Joanna last night that we were getting married in June. She was kind of angry, I wanted to tell her when I got back to ask her to be my Maid of Honor. You kind of spoiled the moment, John. Well, you still get to ask her yourself, although you could call on our way back tonight to my cell phone and ask her if you wanted to. Julia just said this has to be face to face since we live in the same apartment. Ok love you, see you Sunday.

The team ended up winning by like 100 points, we only lost the 3M dive and the final relay, we swam exhibition not to run up the score any more than we had to.

Here I am getting ready to drive back, and this time Paul decides he has had enough of babysitting the freshmen, so he says wait up John, I want to drive back with you. Can we stop at Fairmont, I want to get some Pepperoni Rolls, hopefully the place in the mall is still open? Well, I will need gas anyway we can stop but I thought you would want to go to Country Club Bakery, that is where you normally go. Nah, I know they are closed way before we will get there, so let's go to Colasessano's. I will get one for us to eat there, and then let's get a couple frozen for the road. Isn't coach going to be mad that we are not going with the team for dinner. Well, John, coach is short on funds for this trip and if we take Joanna, I don't think he will be upset because it will save him enough money he won't be over budget for the trip.

Joanna gratefully accepted our invitation to avoid the van or bus, and I was not sure that Julia and Joanna had already been on the phone to make sure I did not get in trouble with those young women swimmers. Like any of them wanted to be caught anywhere near me with a coach that thinks I am the closest thing to a cancer for his team. Both Paul and Joanna decided to stay in the back seat, no idea why, but that let me put snacks out on the other seat

Fortunately, we got to Fairmont by 6 PM, so we were able to get a decent dinner since we were over 21, we also got a beer that we definitely would not have been allowed to get if we had been with the rest of the swim team. I paid for Joanna's bill and mine, Paul insisted on paying his own way, but we did leave a small tip for the staff.

Ok you two come clean, what the heck is going on here. Joanna laughed; you are not the only one dating a swimmer boy. Julia knows and so do quite a few people you think I would have gone to these parties with Paul for the last 2 years. Where do you think I was when you were with Julia, I was with Paul.

We made it back to AB, about 9 PM, so it was time to crash after a long day. By the time I got back to my apartment, it was 9:30, and I realized I needed to study for a test on Monday. Well without Julia being here, I can get some studying in before I crash.

The next thing I knew it was 3 AM, and I had literally read like 6 pages, I guess I was really tired, and crawled up in the bed, and texted Julia good night. Then I thought about it I probably should wait until the morning.

(This is Julia, I am inserting a little section into John's book)

While John was away in Frostburg, I finally took a home pregnancy test, and it was definitely positive. I went to a clinic on Friday and then Saturday they called to confirm the home pregnancy test that I was pregnant about 4 weeks. I was both delighted and scared, really would have rather gone to Law school next year but we will be married, and we will find a way to make it happen. John is a really great guy, and I would not be the first woman in my family to get married 3 months pregnant.

Sunday before Conference:

I woke up this morning and no Julia here, so weird we have been together most weekends for the last semester plus. Joanna basically got the apartment to herself most weekends. Since she is a very attractive girl and a Tri-Sigma sorority, I guarantee she was not alone most weekends, I know that nobody has dated her on the swim team that I know of, I think that would have been odd. Well other than Paul I found out last night.

Enough about Joanna, today is full carbohydrate day. I ate pancakes, and a waffle at the cafeteria, did have some oatmeal. Ok, so if anyone reads this journal, our team is required to eat at the cafeteria, even though I had an apartment, I guess they want to see us on campus. So, I got to studying for the Monday test, in the morning afterwards and then we have a mandatory practice in the afternoon. Normally for others this is just a swim down after the meet, for me this is the beginning of taper day, so instead of 5 400 IM's I did three, and everything is down about 40%, makes it easy and practice took only about an hour. I swam at noon ahead of the rest of the team. Paul also is at the pool, since he mostly sprints his practice is almost nothing.

My first 400 IM was in the 4:40 range, and the second and third were not much slower. Paul yells at me; you better get faster than that if you want to be in the finals. Hey Joanna said my time at Frostburg is 12th, how much faster you think it will take to get into the finals, You know Joanna has the records, but last year the 400 IM required a 4:27, to get in to the finals.   Plus, since we have Jeff from last year's team finals, and also Cain as a freshman swimming you will definitely need to be ready to beat a 4:25. I am already thinking I will be lucky if

I can make the top 16 in the 100 fly and 200 fly. I know I can make at least consolations in the 400 IM, but nobody but Paul knows how fast I am swimming, and I am definitely not going to talk to coach to move up my qualifying time.

Julia came over the apartment and brought dinner from Bridgeport. She actually said she and her family went to the Wonder Bar in Bridgeport. She said her parents felt bad that I had no dinner on Sundays at the cafeteria, so they bought a lasagna dinner knowing I was supposed to eat pasta for dinner this week. It was really a lot better than the spaghetti I was going to make but it had sausage in it which I was not really supposed to eat. The garlic bread and salad really made it even better. Why did I get the feeling I was being set-up?

Julia starts snuggling up to me and says to me I want you to know the wedding is going very well, I am going to use my mom's wedding dress. I said didn't you tell me your mom was pregnant with your older brother when she got married. She started bursting out immediately, like mother and daughter. I said repeat that, yes, I have been under the weather the last 4 weeks, because we are going to have a child at the end of the year. I was totally caught off guard and I was very quiet for about a minute. Julia, started crying, are you upset why are you so quiet, and I simply said wow, this is going to be a hell of a year then we both will graduate, then get married, and then a baby. I am just totally overwhelmed and excited. Something we had not talked about, if we had kids what religion are we going to follow. All Julia said was we have some time for that baby, and we had a very passionate kiss.   Julia says, I want to stay here tonight, too late to go to the apartment, so I kissed her on the head and headed to take a shower.

I sat in my room and wondered how we were going to handle all of this, me going to grad school, a baby and moving. Not going to be a lot of sleeping tonight but I know that Julia is the girl for me, and somehow, we will find a way to make it happen. Now it is really time to focus on this last conference meet. Now the coach is supposedly counting on me for points when we had the last home meet, I wasn't even acknowledged with the other seniors, almost like I was a ghost. I get it coach, you don't like me, and I will say something now, the feeling is fully mutual, you son of a bitch.

You recruit someone, and they don't meet your expectations, then you find out they are a different religion that you guys in the Midwest are used to dealing with, so you make that student's life miserable. Nobody would ever accuse our coach of being a racist, his public comments are always guarded, but you can feel it. I know Brad is of mixed race and always says that coach is a closet racist, I am now thinking that it is true, because he is very careful on the outside, but finds ways to belittle both Brad and me. It would be impossible to prove but yet both of us have a feeling that we are not wanted, me explicitly and Brad very carefully excluded. I used to think it was because he was a diver, but now I wonder.

Way too late and I have too many things on my mind, let's not go down this pity party, let's try to get some sleep, it is going to be a long week, tests on Monday and Tuesday, then travel to conference on Wednesday, and the conference meet starts Thursday afternoon and end Saturday night. By this time next week, I will be done with swimming, and ready to graduate.

Clear the mind and start thinking about studying for economics test is tomorrow, and all I need is a "B" to maintain my grades. I really want to win this academic athlete award and prove that academics and athletics can happen if you try. Julia is my guide for this, although she decided when she got here to not play basketball, I know she was recruited as a walk-on for basketball and track, but she decided not to pursue it. I bet she was a really nasty point guard, 5'4" of pure mental toughness.

Truthfully, I am so excited to be a dad and Julia's husband, this swimming needs to be finished, so last week here we come.

Conference Week

Monday morning and reading one more time about the test material to be ready, test is at 10:00. Going to the cafeteria and get pancakes this morning, plus cereal. I left Julia in bed, she was sleeping and did not want to wake her up, I did leave her some crackers and ginger ale, I remember my mom saying that was the only way she could get through the morning when she was pregnant. I have no idea how I am going to tell my mom that she will be a grandmother. I think dad will be thrilled, especially if our child is catholic, he grew up that way before he converted when he and mom got married.

The test was not that bad, I know I got at least 90 on this exam, I think I made it out to be much harder than it really was. Julia says I have a habit of thinking my professors are going to give much harder tests than they do, just a little paranoid, I guess.

My plan today is to practice at 2 PM, team practices at 3 PM, they are just doing a very light workout, I am on day 2 of the taper so want to get my practice mostly in before they come in. So today I do 3 times 400 IM, rest 50% of the time it took to swim. Then I have to do 2 times a 200 fly, just to get used to the pain of the last 2 lengths. I then have 5 100 freestyles to swim as the amin portion of the practice, add a 500 warm-up and a 500 cool down, and that is all I get to do today. So easy in the fall we do up to 8000 yards, so this is going to be really easy.

I asked Joanna to time the 400 IM's, so that I can have someone tell me the times and the rest interval. The rest of the team will have the other 2 trainers and coach to tell them when to go and I really want to avoid them as they are just really doing a light workout.

So before practice I was able to get some pasta for lunch, took the vitamins that our team takes before meets. The vitamins make you pea green, so to be gross the team does not flush the toilets in the gym just to freak people out. I texted Julia to make sure she was able to get up and get to class, all I got was in class, so I did not pursue it after that.

As I said before got to the pool and started practice at 2 PM, nobody at the pool except me and Joanna. I swim the first 400 IM, and Joanna says your time is the same as in Frostburg meet, really, the next 2 Joanna calls out within 4 seconds each. Incredible, and they did not really feel that great. The 200 fly were painful as expected and really did not care about the times. The freestyle swims were good but not unexpected. By the time the team gets to the pool I am pretty much finished as they start practice at 3:30 PM. I hear the freshman yell POP's great you let us have the pool. They have no idea that shortly I will be a POP in reality. But let these guys have fun, they are coach's stooges, no grades just swim, you think any of them will even get into grad school.

Joanna and Paul get together and talk about my practice. Paul comes over to me and says, you really must want that all-conference in the 400 IM. I said that time is still about 12^{th,} and I need top 8 to be in the conference. Yes, that is a meet time, and you just did that in a practice, dude you are going to be hard to beat. I remind him that coach has already entered my entry time and I am in lane 7 of the third heat from the top. In other words, I am seeded 21st, and nobody will be there close enough to drive me to the finals. Paul just laughs, yes you are going to be clear of everyone with clear water, remember just because you are not in the fast heat does not mean they will beat you. Ok, Paul, let's not let anyone else know that I am at least likely to be top 12.

Please ask Joanna not to even discuss my practice with Coach, I don't need any conversation with him regarding. Just let him know it may be possible for me to make the consolations of the 200 fly and maybe the back end of the 400 IM. That will keep him from having any conversations with me that I would rather avoid at this time. Let's keep it a secret that I am potentially a top qualifier for the 400 IM.

As far as the other 2 events, just hoping not to make a fool of myself. I will tell you Paul, my fly feels much smoother at the 200 and the 400 IM then it does in the 100 fly. I still have one more practice.

Paul how much practice will you do today. Let's see I have 3 X 50 Free, as the primary, I will do 2 100 free's and then 2 100 fly's. with warm-up I think it will be a 45-minute practice. I envy you my practice just took a full hour, and it was painful. All Paul says, see what happens when you choose the pain events. Ha Ha. Just because you are six feet four all of us under 6 feet don't have this natural advantage. I hate to say it, but I will really miss him next year at Maryland, would never have thought I would have so easily friended this giant from Pittsburgh. Paul has been great and is a great captain for the team. Only 3 seniors on the team, we had 8 freshmen when we started, so we lost 5 out of 8 from the team and half left the University. I know that Andre went back to his home area of Tennessee and is swimming for his local college near Memphis. I think he is swimming for division III Rhodes college, no scholarship for swimming but I hear his family has been connected to that school for a long time. 2 others left school and we never heard from them again after the first year, just Juan left the team and will graduate.

All left is Paul as captain, me as the devil, and John Radford who really does not care about swimming much anymore, will be interesting to see him as a college professor someday, such a geek for computers. John is like the number 16 swimmer for us and has never made a consolation final in backstroke or the sprint freestyle nor do I think he ever really cared other than to get exercise, no scholarship on the line for him.

So much about practice and on my way to cafeteria, Joanna comes over to me, ok, Julia won't say anything, but I want to know is she pregnant? Yes, she is pregnant and no we did not know before I asked her to marry me. Next thing I know, I am getting a hug from a 5 '8" brunette hard enough to break ribs. Hey, be careful with the ribs I have a meet to swim in 3 days. Joanna says to me, Paul wants us to be mum about your practice and times, no problem, does anyone other than the 2 of us know that you are potentially going to make the finals. I just simply said, you and I know that I was 12th, never have made it to a final not even close. All Joanna said was never going to be married with a kid before, different meaning to the meet.

I had some time to kill before cafeteria was open and texted Julia to see how she was doing. Quick text back, test was easy, stomach better after the ginger ale. Then a text that simply said I Love You, was the last one before I knew she had a late afternoon class.

The cafeteria was having meat loaf dinner, and pork chops as alternative. I discovered that for the swim team they had done a pasta dish of shells and cheese sauce, so we ate that some bread and a salad. Of course, we had bread pudding for dinner. I did not ask if coach had said I was eligible, not saying I am paranoid, but I would not put it past him as he continues to blame me for the loss of the conference last year.

I got back to my apartment expecting Julia to be there but no evidence anyone had been there for a while. I texted Julia and waited for a response, she simply texted back tired tonight, brunette hugged me. Did you tell her. I texted back, tall brunette hugged me also, cat is out of the bag, sorry.

Julia texted back oh well, I guess I will deal with being pampered tonight. Joanna is making me soup and going to the Kroger to make sure I have food for the morning, apparently you must have told her about ginger ale and saltines. I can't wait until I have to tell my sorority sisters that I am getting married and having a baby this year. I wonder if they will be stunned that the book nerd is pregnant or that I had been dating that seriously.

A couple hours of study tonight, got to clear my head for schoolwork. Paul texted me that we are leaving noon Wednesday for the conference. He is making sure that they have room on the bus. I called him up just to find out if I needed to plan to drive or be with the team. Paul said seniors get the first 2 rows behind the driver. I simply said that means coach is next to you in the first one, can I possibly escape and go to the back of the bus. His reply simply, no all seniors get the front of the bus. It is a long drive to Canton; do you want to possibly be with the little puppies.

Tuesday: 2 days before conference:

I woke up late this morning, 7:30, and texted Julia that I love you, took about 20 minutes to get a response you better with what I am going through this morning. Stomach is very queasy and can barely keep down the ginger ale.

I left for the cafeteria, coach was leaving as I came in and fortunately was with a friend so no chance for a conversation. I simply said quickly good morning and passed him by. So many people eating nice little breakfasts, I am eating waffles and cereal, and fruit. I bet the ladies look at my plate and wonder how at 5"11" I can eat this much and not gain weight. They will never know how much exercise it takes to offset this.

I saw this morning that the Sigma Delta Nu had a fun event this weekend several of the brothers approached me about the event outside the cafeteria. Since I have some friends in the fraternity, they offered me the invitation to go to the event. They know I would have loved to pledge but the athletic department frowns on membership to Greek life.   I told them tell Zack, president of the Fraternity, that I will be away at the conference this weekend. Guys, said OK, we will let Zack know. One of them asked does that mean your friend Joanna will be away also. Sorry guys she is head manager so she will be with us at Canton. He just yells out, you swimmers are so lucky, do I have to try out for the team to get a date with her. Just laughed and yelled, maybe.

One class this morning for about 2 hours, made sure I texted Julia to see if she was doing any better. I got back you owe me. I think I will find a way to get her some flowers today from the Kroger, and then go over to her apartment. I was thinking about getting her a cupcake, but I think she is having enough trouble holding things down.

I went to the pool at 2 PM, unfortunately for me coach was there with a couple of sprinters, Paul was not one of them. All I heard him say was make sure you get your workout done before 5 PM, we have a team meeting to discuss the conference meet. I said OK, I will make sure I get to the team room by then.

Joanna was busy with the team, so I had to make sure that after my warm-up I did the 400 IM's on the clock, so coach said the assistant coach for the women would time me. Karen came over with a stopwatch and asked me what I was doing. I said I am swimming three timed 400 IM's, I get 100% rest time based on what my finish time was. After the first one, Karen asked me what my best time was, and I said the time I did a couple of years ago. Karen said Well you were 2 seconds behind that, let's see what you can do on the next 2. The second one was 5 seconds slower, and then the third was another 6 seconds slower. Karen asked does coach know that you are really doing well on these, I said he really does not care what I do to be honest, I am only swimming this week because James Arnett has been red shirted due to his shoulder injury. I told her that at best I am expected to do is maybe 15th and Karen simply said, if you don't make the finals with what I saw today I will be surprised. The next thing I know Karen is over to coach and having a conversation, he just laughed, so still no pressure for me to do much nor does he expect much after last year. I hope Paul does not let him know why I was not able to do much last year, nothing like a sore shoulder and a hamstring pull for someone trying to do butterfly. I don't want to blame coach but the doctor who treated me after the season simply said you have tendonitis, and you need to completely rest that shoulder for at least 8 weeks.

Well so much for that part of practice completed the rest of the practice just as Paul was getting in. Karen just talked to me, did you beat your Frostburg time this afternoon by 5 seconds, I said that is what she said, so I guess it must be true. Paul said, damn, your time now has you right on the cuff of the finals, you ready for that mentally. Truthfully Paul, I have a lot of other things on my mind like wedding, grad school, and a couple of other items. Joanna overheard and yes, the other items should be your primary thoughts tonight. I got it Joanna, getting flowers before I go home and taking them over to your apartment. Joanna says I want to be there, because tears are going to flow.

Really Joanna, don't make anything out of this and again I get a hug from the attractive brunette. Paul says to me do you and Joanna have something going on that I should know about and all I could say is that is very laughable.

Since, I had an hour to kill, I got a bouquet of flowers at the Kroger, and got back in time for the team meeting in the training room.

Coach began by saying, it is very seldom that a team has a chance to win a conference title, and this is our opportunity to win the first for AB. I want you all to be ready for the meet, we will be leaving at noon, and I expect everyone here no later than 11:45, I don't want to be chasing swimmers as we have a long drive to the hotel. You will have a choice either workout lightly before we go, or we have a 30-minute time slot at 9 PM. Divers, you will be diving at Canton, so you can get used to the boards and site conditions. We are taking one bus for the men and one for the ladies, so guys you need to behave, Joanna and the trainers will be following us with a college car. I would like to bring Paul up to say some words.

Hey guys, three of us have been here for 4 years and we thought we would have won a conference in our time, I want to finish my career as a champion. Who else wants to win this meet? The room erupted in clapping, let's go team Paul yells.

One of the freshmen comes over to me, I guess you get to get a championship even though you will have done nothing this year. All I said was ok, thanks for doing this for me, and will you be the leading candidate in 3 years for academic athlete. Did you even get an A last semester, I don't think so? All I heard, I was just ragging on your old man, we will get the job done for you just enjoy your swims and watch our team win.

Paul comes over to me and claps me on the back so you ready to get your all- conference swim in, laughing. I just said ha ha, you know I am not good enough for that, just ask coach. Paul just went off laughing hysterically. We all left after that to go to the cafeteria as a team.

The cafeteria treated us like rock stars, we got to eat in a private room and had a pasta kick-off for the entire team. I ate quickly and left with Joanna, and then drove to her apartment.

Julia opened the door and said she had cooked a chicken for herself and had no problem with keeping dinner down. I gave her a kiss on the cheek and gave her the flowers and said this is just to make you feel a little better tonight. The next thing I know, I am getting a hug and a kiss from fiancé, and of course Joanna started to cry. After an hour, Julia said to me, you need to go to your apartment and pack for the weekend. It might help to get your laundry done also. I said I think we have a trip to Bridgeport tonight I think it is time I make it official. I have a choice of starting laundry now or at 9 PM it would take until 10:30, so let's due a quick trip to Kaye Jewelers. Now I get a hug by both my finance and the Joanna.

We got to Kaye Jewelers in Bridgeport at about 7 PM, and we meet the person at the counter. I tell them we are looking for an engagement ring, we will need to have a diamond, but I have 2 additional rubies I want in the ring, so instead of something with 3 diamonds we would like 1 diamond and I will give you the rubies that are like a ½ carrot each. Julia looks at me and starts bawling, where did you get the rubies, the package arrived from Baltimore this morning with a check and the 2 rubies. The salespersons say the price of the ring should be $4000, and we have a payment plan that we can work for you. I proceeded to do 2 things, first, let's get a discount for me bringing the 2 rubies in as opposed to you putting the 2 diamonds in, so let's get $500, off the price, and secondly, for the price you are asking the main diamond should be at least ¾ carrot. She said she had to go see the manager and 5 minutes later they said it is a deal. Ok, so I am going to put $500 down plus the rubies. The rest is monthly for the 60 months, with interest rate of 12%. (53.00) per month. We signed the deal and were told that the ring would be ready in 2 weeks' time. The clerk just looked at us and said congratulations and we kissed.

The rest of the night I dropped off Julia at her apartment and then proceeded to do laundry and pack for the upcoming meet. Paul calls me up and says so you really did it. Well dude no looking back now that your mom gave you the rubies and the check for $1000. I know and really ready for this next journey, let's get the conference meet done and then we both can move to the next chapter. I only gave them half of the grand, and that will mean I have the first 8 payments ready to go in my account.

Joanna was very emotional Paul, maybe she will be expecting you to do something like this. No way buddy, we are way behind the nerd couple, but thanks for the warning, she may be a little anxious then.

Wednesday Morning:

Woke up at 7:am, and no classes the rest of the week. Texted Julia to see how she was doing and must have been asleep because I did not get a text back. Went to the pool to do a quick workout, 300 warm-ups, a couple of 400 IM; s and then another 200 cool down. No emphasis on time, and early enough that I was there before anyone else. Breakfast at the cafeteria and then drove back to my apartment. Julia texted back about 9:am, simply said got a good night sleep, love you will I see you before you go? If you don't have class, let me come over about 10:45, and need to leave by 11:15.

Texted back, love you see you soon.

Good morning, Julia, I say to her at her apartment, she simply responds good morning future husband. I gave her a kiss and we talked about the upcoming weekend. I told her we leave this afternoon, and I would text her when we arrive in Canton, Ohio, then the meet starts on Thursday, we will have trials in the morning and consolation finals and finals in the evening. The plan is for us to finish the meet Saturday around 6 PM, and for us to be leaving and getting back here around midnight. I suspect, I will be in bed at 1 AM, and don't expect to be up until 9:00 in the morning knowing my career is done, no matter what happens I will not choose to go to Nationals in Indianapolis. Julia said, getting a little ahead of ourselves are we. I just laughed you have not been there to see my latest 400 IM times, ask Joanna about it before she leaves this morning.

Julia says, so I have a key to your apartment, can I stay there on Saturday night if that is ok with you, the laundry is easier to get to than taking it to a laundromat like I normally have to. You know a woman in my condition has to be very careful. I said sure, I won't wake you up when I get in, we can go out for lunch on Sunday somewhere. I told her I had to leave so gave her another kiss and left for school. Julia just responded you better wake me up with a kiss or I will give you a kick in the butt.

I got to the bus at 11:30, I saw Paul and asked I know as seniors we are getting the front of the bus, anyway we can camp out elsewhere. He asked why to go against the tradition, I told him I really did not want to be that close to Coach Edwards for the next 5 hours. Paul said looks like a good plan for me, I need a rest anyway, I have the 100 Fly, day one, the 100 free, day 2 and the 50 free day 3, so getting rest for the hard event is a good idea. I look at him puzzled, if your hard event is my easy event, what does that say for me. It says you are not seeded third in the event with coach pushing for a conference title. Paul says so my friend, anybody else know that you are probably now our top 400 IM swimmer. I just laugh, yes, you and Joanna and a magician if you think I am going to beat 2 of the puppies. Paul just laughed, the puppies can't handle pressure and you know it, Henry is seeded 5th, and George is seeded 11th, so they are not that far ahead of you we know Jeff is going to be in the finals. Let's just get through the bus ride and we will see what is possible. Please do not let coach know that a top 8 is possible, I don't want him coaching up the other guys that I am a threat to them. Paul said sure and then Joanna came over and said everyone is starting to board the bus, you ready for the last ride. I said do you think coach will let me on the bus home. Yes, especially after your all-conference swim Saturday. So, you too, the both of you are a pair. Paul just laughed, a lot more likely than you think, and he got punched by Joanna. After three years you guys are a couple? Joanna then punched me, so should I let him know about June then. Joanna, I am probably sure you already have, she laughed about pillow talk.

Paul and I got on a seat in the middle, followed by the divers on the other side. Hey, they let divers on the bus, yes John even us low life divers outrank the 18th swimmer though. Don't divers count as one-half of a swimmer for numbers. Yes, smart-ass only 2 dive events, but be careful, I may just swim against you the last day. Great you want to swim the 400, IM. All I heard from them was we are not that dumb, that event sucks the life out of you. Paul just laughs, John's last swim will be that monster of a swim, mine will be the 50 free. My diver friends says so who is the academic athlete, might want to rethink that award. I have not won that award yet, but apparently the rumors are all over the place.

As predicted the bus left for a 5 -hour trip at exactly noon, with the swimmers, divers, coach and an assistant for the weekend. The managers and trainers went in a separate car following the women's team bus. Paul, when did I miss that you and the brunette were dating? Paul said we have been for the last 18 months, only came public with it the last 3 months, you're not the only one that can keep a secret. (Papa)

I must have been tired, the next thing I remember we were already in Ohio, about mid- afternoon. Paul says PAPA getting a nap before the big meet. You and Joanna and the pillow talk have got to stop, no more telling either of you anything.

For anyone that has to go to Canton, Ohio, they have the Football Hall of Fame and not much else. We saw some old steel mills on the way, I guess they still do some of that in the area. Like a lot of Ohio towns with the heavy manufacturing industry in decline they have a lot of abandoned areas, and a lot less population, like 70,000. We arrived just as it was getting dark, so we were spared looking at the abandoned buildings.

Apparently, coach wanted to either be cheap or keep us away from town, so we are booked at the Holiday Inn Express near supposedly Belden Village. To keep the prices even lower 4 to a room, so 1 each in a bed and 1 in the sofa bed. Paul yells to me, you still prefer the floor to the bed, and I said sure. No problem, you can claim the floor.

Next thing I know a pillow and a blanket are being thrown at me. The closet looks big enough to sleep in, remember me after you guys get back from warm-up tonight. Aren't you coming along, nope worked out this morning that was an option you had, just tell me how ugly the starting blocks are?

Coach gave us each $20 and gave us a list of restaurants near the hotel. I wanted to go to the Taphouse but figured I would get a little killed by the others. I walked with a couple of the swimmers, (Cain and Jeremy) to the place that sold Italian Street Food. Afterwards, I texted Julia, and she said she was doing great and to have a good swim.

She also texted that your parents took a flight from BWI and are going to watch your final event this weekend. I had to look at these another 2 times before this, they have never been to a college swim meet, and they are going to be there for the last swim of my career. I texted back, how come they sent this to you and not me. I guess they wanted to support you in your last meet and surprise you at the same time. I texted back were you supposed to let me know? Emoji came back just smiling. I texted back love you, the text that came back was you better.

Paul and most of the others came back from the pool and he wanted to talk about the team winning the conference. I told him this is going to be a close meet, I think NDC, (Notre Dame College in Euclid), is going to be very much in it with us, we only beat them in the dual meet by 3 points. The old teams from the Mountain East have one or two really good swimmers that could really make a dent if they are in the right events. I really think Findlay is the team to be watched for the event, they have been a perennial top 20 nationally, and while they graduated 7 last year, they have 3 pretty good freshmen.

We got tired of thinking about it, and it was time to go to bed, mine was the closet with a towel for my neck, pillow and blanket. I only hope that they don't forget me in case I don't get up early. In the closet, I texted Julia, say good night, and she texted back love you and have a good swim. I also texted her did you know that your roommate and Paul were dating. Of course, I did, hard to believe you didn't, why did you think they both wanted to drive with you in the back seat. I must be totally clueless, and she texted back, that is one of the reasons I love you, you only have eyes for me. With a bottle of water with me and able to hear the TV, I collapsed in the closet only to hear Paul yell, so should I tell the team you are coming out of the closet. A joke like that would probably not be appreciated by the divers. Good night not trying to sneak out to see Joanna. Nope, and she is in a meeting with coach tonight, really do not need to hear about towels and practice assignments. Yes, and maybe trying to explain that you and Joanna are an item may be interesting in front of coach. At least now I know why she never was dating anyone else, how the hell did you keep this so on the QT? Paul just said we were very creative, and there is a lot of open space in West Virginia that you can go on dates without others knowing. So funny.

Conference Meet

Conference Day One

I could not start this section of the journal without stating what it is like for an athlete to win a championship. Whether it is the NBA, NFL, Stanley Cup, local little league, or a division II, swim team, athletes meet at championships trying to come back with the ultimate in their sport a championship. Sometimes athletes like Rick Dempsey for the Orioles, never a superstar have that outstanding championship and deliver a team victory when nobody saw it coming. For our team, we were pursuing a conference championship for the first time in the school history in swimming. While that may not sound like a big deal in the total of everything, I assure you that it is the ultimate high if a team wins their championship. Our guys are primed to win something that had never happened, and even though I am only likely to score in a couple of events, you are still a part of something that has never been done before. In other words, it is a high like no other the ultimate in sports.

Day One has the following events according to Joanna, 500 freestyle, 200 Back, 100 fly, 200 IM, 200 Breaststroke, and 400 Medley Relay. The events are done as trials in the morning starting at 9:00, AM and the top 16 in each event evening finals along with the relays. Men's events first then Women's events so while it does not look like it will take long the reality is you have 10 events, and it will take about 3 hours to complete. Heats are swum in an interesting manner. The top 24 are placed in the final 3 heats according to time. If you are the third best swimmer you would get the top lane in the third heat from the top. The remainder of us are done purely by time, so I was in the fourth heat lane 7, basically, 30th ranked so way out of the predicted top 16. Paul is lane 4 of the second to best heat, thus he is seeded number 2 for the overall meet.

Championship meets are really different than dual meets. Points are awarded to the top 16 swimmers and top 8 for relays. Relays count double so very important that your team finish in the top 8 so you have a chance at raising a lot of points. Because this is a team event, teams have won this event with like 7 to 8 really strong swimmers, but most of the time it is about top swimmers and having enough others to score that you pile up points. Some teams like Findlay are highly nationally ranked and they may not be tapering for the conference meet.AB had both a strong team and a lot of second swimmers that could score strategic points. I was not considered one of them so my parents will get to see me swim probably just once this morning and then I can see them after the trials because I won't be swimming the finals or consolation finals tonight that start at 7 PM.

The day started with a knock on the door at 7: am, hearing Joanna yell time to get up breakfast in 30 minutes. I did not want to get up and the next thing I hear is a boom on the closet door. Hey John, time to get out of the closet, a laughing Paul hits the closet door one more time to make sure that I open it and get up. Paul, why are you waking me up, today is 100 fly day for me, my worst event of the three, so not likely to get out of the prelims. Paul said everyone is expected at the restaurant at 7:30, get dressed you really don't want to piss off coach this morning. Really Paul, you think this coach really gives a crap what I do today. Paul just said just sit in the back of the room, get your breakfast and be counted, that way I don't have to track you down or have Joanna do it. I was the last one that got bathroom rights, so was the lucky one to smell the adverse impact of three other bathroom visits. I hit the elevator at 7:22, and was at the breakfast at 7:27, coach just said glad you could make it, you are the last one as always. (Yes coach, tell your guys to get out of the bathroom faster, and I would have been here earlier.)

As we were going through the breakfast buffet set-up for the swimmers, men going to one room and the women's team to the adjoining room. Coach Edwards closed the door and asked Joanna to make sure that all of us were in the room. Joanna confirmed all in and then proceeded to sit down across from Paul and next to me, I guess she wanted to make sure that people did not know anything was up with them, except that Joanna hit my leg first instead of Paul's when she was trying to play footsie. I just looked at her and laughed, wrong leg mam.

Coach Edwards speech, I will paraphrase, team we are at a special time. Our team has never won a conference title, whether part of the old WVIAC, or the current format, others think we will finish second, but Findlay has desires on the top 5 of the nation, they will be good but not tapered. We can and should now win this conference meet, if everyone in this room swims their best, they have all season we can make it happen.

Remember this is a meet of total points, even if you end up in the consolation finals move up a place and we get more points. For this meet think of times and points as what we have to do. I just think, wow what kind of crap are these guys hearing. While I have that line, the others are insanely happy, and start banging the tables and yelling AB AB, we are here.

Finally, everyone here should expect to be swimming twice each day, so make sure that you are ready for trials, relax afterwards, and be ready for finals tonight. Make sure you are drinking fluids during the afternoon and Joanna will be checking the rooms to make sure that everyone is not fooling around. (Does that mean Paul can't fool around with Joanna). I bet not.

As team captain, Coach Edwards then requested that Paul say some things for the team. Paul simply said, guys let's remember this weekend for the rest of our lives. This is my final shot and I want to remember this always as our time. Let's go. With that again the team starts erupting in the AB cheer, it was deafening. Paul comes back to the table gives Joanna a high five and puts his arm around me and says let's have some fun today.

Joanna then steps up and says everyone needs to be ready by 8:15 warm-ups for us are 8:45 and we only get 15 minutes. Cool downs, after your events are in diving pool section. Additional warm-ups before your event again will be done in the diving pool. I will have 20 towels for the team and you guys need to make sure I get 20 towels back. I don't want to have to pay for any towels, so if you can't find yours then find one from somewhere else. Divers today is 1 meter dive after the swimmers' trials are over so you can hang out until noon when we get back, we will pick you up. Now let's go. With that Paul did something unexpected he gave Joanna a kiss on the cheek, I wonder how the rest of the team is going to react to that? I texted Julia, letting her know I was ok, and I would contact her later tonight after the meet.

At the pool we simply change and get ready for warm-ups, Paul was in his element as team captain, I just got into the pool and slumped into lane 2. Nobody from the team is talking to me, they are not expecting me to score so why bother, it has been this way all season as the other type of goat you are on the outside, a couple of seniors and upperclassmen only. I proceed to swim 500 yards of freestyle and then do a couple of sprint fly with Joanna timing all of us in lane 1. Another 100 yards and then done for warm-up. Pick myself out of the pool and go over to the corner of our team area, get my sweats on and then proceed to scope out a place to nap for the next hour.

The announcer then comes on and states for everyone to please rise for the playing of our national anthem. Standing up, I see my parents for the first time in my college career, my mom starts waiving to me, I hardly recognize her as she has auburn hair instead of the blonde I am used to, I guess she wanted to hide the gray and hard to do with Dark blonde hair. While we are now reformed Jewish, they still do not travel on Friday and Saturday, so they have never been to a meet. They call all the time but never been to a meet in person, I wonder if Julia had something to do with them being here.

The announcements were to start to get to the clerk of course for swimmers in the first 2 events, and welcome to the conference meet and to Canton, Ohio.

What follows is my accounting of the first day activities. First the trials and then the finals tonight.

Event 1: 500 Free Trials

Swimming for AB is Freshmen Kevin Ganey, Josh Snow and George Smythe, upper classmen swimming is Kevin Johnson. This event takes forever, after 30 minutes trials are over, with Kevin Ganey and Josh in the finals, and Kevin Johnson finishing 12th, so he will be swimming the consolations. George missed his last flip turn and had to go backwards and restart, that cost him a place in the consolations.

Event 3: 200 Back Trials

Swimming for AB is Freshmen Bob Pearson, with upper classman Jeremy Latimer. Bob appeared to be going through the trials knowing he would make the finals but barely made it in lane 1 of the finals, Jeremey hung on to make 15th to have a place in the consolations. Jeremy was seeded 20th so that could add 2 points to our possibility.

Event 5: 100 Fly Trials:

As I have said earlier Paul was one of the favorites in this event, Freshman Tom Leonard was expected to be a factor here, Thai Cung is a sprinter, so coach had to give him a third event, so he is swimming the 100 fly, and redshirt freshman Cain Paretti, is seeded in top heat lane 7, so barely top 16. My warm-up felt great this morning and my sprint 25 was 0.25 seconds faster than any time in my career.

Thai swam the heat in front of me and while he beat his seed time by a second typical sprinter, he faded in the last 25 yards and finished probably out of the consolations.

Now it was my turn, the announcer stated the names and lane assignments. I dipped to the pool put water on my head and then put a cap on my head to eliminate aby friction from the water. Get on the blocks and wait for the starter, take your marks and then a horn starts the event. I know I had a great start in the fly and when I looked around at the fifty, noticed that the lanes I could see were behind me, since I am more of a distance swimmer knew I could hold my times for the last 50 pretty well. I hit the wall and saw my time was 54.01 0.5 seconds faster than any other year, but still probably only well enough to finish just outside the top 16. I did notice that I had won the heat and by almost a half second, nice swim anyway. I jumped in to the warm-down pool and Joanna comes over to me and says nice swim, just maybe you are going to have to swim again tonight.

Heat 3; and while Tom did well enough to guarantee him a place in the consolations only 4 swimmers ahead of me, so I sit 5th so far with the top 16 to go. Well, that would at least put me around the top 20.

Paul swam well under 51.5 for the first time winning his heat and putting him likely in the finals as he would need all eight beat him in the next heat to make it. Another 5 swimmers times ahead of me, so I am now sitting 10th with an outside chance of making the top 16.

Heat 1 was amazing the swimmer from Findlay, swam 50.99, so he will be seeded first in the final tonight. Paul will be seeded right next to him as second-best time. Cain failed to do very well finishing in over a 55, so he is outside of me, and if my math is right I needed at least one other swimmer to be behind me to get in to the consolation finals. Joanna comes over to me, I don't know if you figured this out yet, but you are number 16, you made the consolations by .02 seconds beating a Fairmont swimmer that should have beaten you based on the past results. I tell her damn; I was really hoping to spend the afternoon with my parents I had not been with them in a few months.

Event 7: 200 IM

We had a lot of swimmers for the 200 IM, we had 4 swimmers with only Freshman John Ritter near the top, with Dick Wynne another Freshman finishing 13th to make the consolations. Cain barely made it as the 16th finisher, I think the 100 fly took something out of him. Jeff Kissinger, who was supposed to be a challenger for the top 8, was disqualified for an illegal backstroke turn, they said he took an extra stroke while on his stomach so that will cost the team a lot of points.

Event 9: 200 Breast

John Ritter was swimming 2 events today and you could see the impact on him, favored to be a top swimmer he finished 8th and barely made the finals. The same thing for freshman Dick Wynne who missed the finals and was seeded 11th. Our other swimmers Tony Villani, and Kissinger failed to make the top 16. They are listed a C final which won't give points and because of the combined meet the are not actually even going to swim the C finals.

Event 11: 400 Medley Relay

Swimming is a very weird sport the IM, swim is butterfly, back, breast and then free, but the team medley relay is back breast fly and free. With Paul swimming the fly leg, AB was able to finish second to Findlay, very close and will swim next to each other in the final tonight.

The divers were there, and I heard Brad yell Joanna just told me that you made top 16, I said really so how about you finish top 3 this afternoon in the prelims. Brad yelled we are looking for both Colt and I to make the finals tonight, see you afterwards.

Well, we were done after that and had the potential to have the same number of points as Findlay. WV Wesleyan and Fairmont State each had a few finalists but very little second swimmers for points so unlikely to do much more than third or fourth.

Joanna said I texted Julia and told her you made the consolations already I hope you don't mind. Joanna, some day you are going to let me tell her things before you do, she just laughed and said I will at your wedding. You can say I do before I start crying, and how will it be with you and Paul being next to each other.

My parents are waiting for me outside the natatorium after I got dressed and they said can we go out for lunch together. I say I don't think so, and then Joanna jumps in and introduces herself as team manager and Julia's roommate. Joanna says to me you want me to clear it with coach. Sure, and the next thing I know is I am in my parents' rental car and going to Applebee's for lunch. Joanna yells remember it is carbo's today, no meat, just as I was ducking into the car. I yell at her, I already have a mom here, Joanna just smiles. I did not know that Julia and Joanna had asked them to be here for my final events, apparently my fiancé can be quite forceful when she wants something.

At Applebee's the conversation got to Julia and I showed mom a recent picture of us hiking in the mountains. Mom said she looks very pretty like an Israeli woman. Mom, her family is from Sicily they tend to look great like tanned year-round and she definitely is very pretty and smart. My mom asks, will she call me mom or Sharon. Well while you are here, she may call you another term, and that is. Mom you will be a grandmother later this year also. Wait just a minute, Julia is pregnant is that why you are getting married. Truthfully, we did not know until last week, and it really would not make a difference we are in love and have been dating for almost three years. My mother just started crying, just like your dad, afraid the family would not approve so we dated secretly for almost three years. You know how hard it is going to be with you 2 going to graduate school, law school and having a baby to take care of. Well mom, I have a great couple to copy you and dad had 3 kids within 5 years of getting married and managed to make it. We will figure it out just like you guys did, and can we call you when we need some advice. I am now getting hugged by my mom, and she says you better, now I want you to make sure that Julia knows, and we approve of what is going on. Have you 2 talked about religion for the child. We had not thought that far along, but what if we make that decision later, about 8 months left before this happens.

I stepped out and texted Julia and got back so the secret is totally out, and I love you. I have the consolation finals tonight it will be late so I will let Joanna text you with the results. Ha ha is all I got back.

I went back inside and finished my pasta meal with my parents, and they dropped me off at the hotel for the team. Paul was waiting for me; did you tell your parents that you were coming out of the closet. That would have been a Brad conversation and not mine, but you know what we talked about, and Paul said that your parents are pissed because you are marrying out of the faith. Nope we talked about how we were going to make it be married and having a child by this time next year. Oh boy, and how did they take it. Surprisingly they took it quite well after all my parents had three children in the first 5 years they were married. What about the catholic thing, funny thing you ask, I forgot that my dad was catholic, his family is from some part of England, I think Wales. He was not upset, and neither will my grandmother, she will just say like father like son, like something from the other side of the tracks.

By the way John, congratulations on making the top 16, not very impressive time though 54. Something. I guess it was good enough to knock a few out that never saw that coming. I guess you will get to have a session with Coach Edwards for strategy later today. You must be kidding; I guarantee he has no playbook for me to do anything but finish last in my heat. I turned around and yelled at Paul, aren't you going to win tonight, he just said we will see.

That was at 2:30 PM, we had until 4:30 to chill, so I decided to take a nap in my closet bed. I made sure that I set my alarm. I got a text from Brad divers ended 3 and 5 we are both in finals, I just texted back great and good job, the next thing I know it is about 4:15, had to get bathing suit and stuff ready to go. Again, Paul yells, John is coming out of the closet., this is getting to be a nightmare, I should have just claimed the bathtub, and nobody would have mocked me.

Joanna drops off snacks for the swimmers and says be ready at the front door at 4:45, This time I am there at 4:35, and coach says ah, still one or two behind you your lateness must be rubbing off. No comment by me, because anything I say will just get me pissed off and I need to focus tonight, my parents have never seen me swim a conference meet so would like to finish a little better.

The warm-ups start at 5 PM, and because only 2 heats of most events, and only like 12 events, everything should be done by 7 PM, then the divers final 6 dives for events 13 and 14. Some teams do not have a diver so from 12 they got down to 8 that will dive in the finals. Even with them it will be done by 8 PM, and then off to dinner and back to the hotel to get ready for day 2.

Since there are so many less swimmers, everyone warms up together so in many lanes 10 of us so you have to be careful. I remember my freshman year I was practicing for the 200 fly, and someone from the next lane hit me in the nose, I think it is still a little crooked today. I am really making sure that I stay safe as my warm-up is only about 250 yards of freestyle stretching out. Then 2 sprint 25's timed by our trainers and coaches, times pretty good and feel is absolutely excellent. Being 16th, I am worth one point if I finish legally, every position that I move up is worth an additional point for the team. If Paul wins the event the team gets 25 points, so that would be significant. Then it drops down to 20 for second, and 17 for third, dropping down to 10 points for the last of the final heat. The more finalists you have the more the points can pile up.

Finals Night One:

The first event is the 500 free just like this morning, Kevin Johnson will swim in the consolation heat lane 6, so he is 12th overall. The final of the event has in Kevin Ganey in Lane 7[th](6th overall) and Josh Snow in Lane 2, 5th overall. Findlay swimmers are in lane 4 and 5 and they finished that way in the finals. Kevin Ganey slips in from the outside lane to finish 3rd and Kevin Ganey holds on to 5th, so the team did well. The consolations ended with Kevin Johnson moving up 1 place to 11th overall, adding 6 points to our team. In the first event first event AB is behind Findlay they had 1 also in the consolation final plus the 1, 2 finish giving them 47 points in the first event while AB receives 36 points for the event nobody else has more than 1 finisher in the finals so, still gets AB close.

Just like the morning, the next event for the meet was the 200 backstrokes, both of our guys either made the consolation final or the real final same lane as 1. Jeromy from lane 1, was able to move up from 15th to 14th, overall, for 3 points. Bob Pearson came from the end lane and after trailing most of the field at the 100, was able to rally and ended up third from the end lane. Findlay was second only so both teams with 20 points, so we continued to be behind them by 11 points going into the next event.

Our team was going to have a fairly strong 100 fly which was the next event. Tom Leonard was in lane 5, so 10th overall, I was in the consolation finals, Paul would be in lane 5 of the finals. My parents started yelling for me, damn that is embarrassing, I am out here in lane 8, the lowest rated swimmer in the event. I have a really effective start and notice that at the 25 I was ahead of lane 7, but could not see anyone else, at the midpoint of the race, I looked over and noticed that I was even with lane 6 and ahead of lane 7. After finishing the race, I looked up at the scoreboard, Tom had finished second in our heat, and I had somehow managed to beat 4 swimmers in my heat and ended up 12th overall. So just from the consolations we had already received 12 points not bad. My time of 53:01, would be the best of my career, not bad considering I would have rather swum the 200 IM, know I was as good at that event, but again coaches' choice not mine. Mom is yelling way to go John, and dad smiles giving me the high sign.

Paul was next and I yelled at him good luck old man, and he simply smiled. I know Paul and have never seen him so relaxed. From the start to the finish, Paul never looked back and won the event breaking the 50:00 second mark he had wanted to break for the last two years. The Findlay swimmer just managed to break the 50 second barrier in finish second, I wonder what he will do at nationals fully tapered but not going to diminish the victory Paul had. Paul's win was our first in the conference in 2 years. I looked over at Joanna, and she is clapping and tearing up. Paul is ecstatic and comes back to the team, and yells no excuses, AB, AB, AB he yells. Findlay had swimmers finished third and eighth, so while we received 37 points Findlay still managed to get 27, the two teams are almost deadlocked with Findlay being 1 point ahead. After each event the places are announced by the announcer so when Paul's name is called out, I put my arm around him, not bad for an old man. I know Joanna wanted to give Paul a kiss and I know for sure that she did later at the hotel, I walked in on them as they were kissing, sorry about that gang, problem is when you have 4 people to each room, you never know who was going to be there. I know that I should express that while Paul came over to congratulate me for making top 12, none of the coaches said anything to me which is fully what I expected. Edwards was hoping for me to get like 4 points, according to Joanna, for the whole meet and what was he going to say to me getting 5 points just in the first event. As you can guess he said nothing to me, just Joanna saying nice swim John.

I wish I had been swimming the 200 IM instead of the 100 fly, but I can see why I was not chosen, John Ritter, finished the preliminaries in third, and Dick finishing 13th and Cain finishing 16th, made the consolation finals. Cain would not have made it but as I said earlier, we had someone get disqualified. Findlay had one swimmer in the final's lane 5, and one as the top in consolations so they were possibly going to get 28 points, and if we swam as we were stated would have received 22 points, but that is the reason you actually compete twice each day.

In the consolation heat a rested Cain managed to win the heat from the outside lane, and Dick managed to move up one place to 12th, so we got 13 points while the Findlay swimmer in the event finished 10th. Cain really blasted his time and had he swam his time in the morning would have been 4th overall, I guess that is what happens when you swim events like he did.

In the finals, a swimmer from Ashland false started and was disqualified out of lane 1. The restart was amazing, the two lanes were tight between Findlay swimmer and West Virginia Wesleyan swimmer with the third swimmer John Ritter, sitting behind them until the last length where he put on a surge and simply touched both of them out for a surprise victory our second of the day. The three swimmers ended the event a total of .1 seconds apart, the smallest of margins. It took a review of the electronic times and hand timers to declare John victorious. Findlay third and WV Wesleyan swimmer second. As you can imagine the team exploded with the victory and because of the event win and our solid placing elsewhere, we received 38 points in the event, while Findlay did not do badly, (24 Points) we were now ahead by 13 points overall. So that was coach's babies that won the event, and you could hear the team going berserk going into the next event. This was the first time ever that AB had been in the lead of the conference, and it was like a fever.

Our next finals was the 200 breast and since our 2 best swimmers for the event were also our 2 best 200 IM's they only had about 30 minutes to cool down and get ready for the breaststroke event. Findlay had only 2 swimmers both of which were in the finals seeded 3rd and 5th, so it was likely our lead in the meet was going to be very short lived.

Dick was leading the event after the 100 but you could see the double dip had done on him and he faded in the last 25 and was passed by a Fairmont swimmer at the very end.

While I know John Ritter is a beast he is not as good of a swimmer in breaststroke as he is in the 200 IM. He was on lane 8 and it really never got close to the leaders he did manage a 6th place finish after being in the top three for the first half of the race. A swimmer from Hillsdale won the event and the Findlay swimmer close behind, the second Findlay swimmer ended up 5th overall. (Findlay received 33 points while we were able to manage only 19 points, so again Findlay was leading the meet by one point going into the relays.

The last event of each day is a relay event, for this meet the medley relay was on day 1, and it was going to be a tight race between Findlay and Alderson Broadus. As I said earlier the relay is very important because the points are double and individual event.

Paul was again swimming the fly leg, and we had new swimmers from the morning for back and breast. The race was very even until the fly leg, where Paul bettered his time from earlier in the night to just under 49 and gave our team a 2 second lead going into the last leg freestyle. I never would have had a freshman be the anchor, but Bob Weaver was fresh and ready. While the Findlay swimmer was very fast, Bob never lets the swimmer gets within a body length, and we won the event our third victory of the day. AB receives 50 points and Findlay having 40, we were done with swimming for the day 9 points ahead of Findlay.

After we were complete it was next the divers starting to warm-up. Colt asked me what place we were in, and he said no worries, Findlay has a one diver in the finals, good but the diver from NDC-LE will win the event they have a huge lead.

Our divers performed well, and Colt was even able to finish in 4th when the diver from Fairmont ahead of him had a failed dive on an inward 2, I really don't blame him inward dives are scary as hell, you actually rotate back into the diving board instead of away. I have viewed hit head with that one so understood the impact totally. We finished 3rd and 4th, with our 32 points and Findlay only getting 20 points, our lead was completed after day one at 21-point lead. I really can't imagine what it would have been like had Findlay been shaved and tapered for the event.

For people that don't follow swimming, shaved and tapered means exactly that, you shave your arms, legs, and chest to get a better feel of the water. Well at least that was the old days, with the new bathing suits, most guys have the legs covered with a suit, so it is like shave your chest, shave your feet and arms. I forgot, a whole bunch of them shave their heads, it can be a real ugly site. The taper is that you build up really hard swim practices and it causes the muscles to be totally sore, and then you reduce the workouts by the time the conference happens your body is rested and the strength from the hard work has enhanced the muscles, performance goes insane. That was how I was discovered in high school, the state meets and with as magical finalist in 2 events, all of a sudden college wanted to recruit me. Oh well wish I had done them earlier may have been able to stay closer to home at a D1 school, but that nothing I can do about that now. I remember It has been 4 years since.

By the time the diving was finished it was 8 PM, our team has reservations for dinner at Applebees at 8:30 PM, they have a room for us and a pasta buffet for us. I hear that Fairmont and a couple of other teams came to the restaurant, but they got to order off of the menu. I guess that is what happens when you have a team of 10 versus a team of 20. Truthfully, the meal was fine just getting really tired of pasta meals. I can't wait until I get back from this and I am going to get meat and more meat at the cafeteria. Maybe buy a steak on Sunday and Julia and I can make a steak dinner, I will even eat a salad.

Joanna came over to the table where Paul and I were eating and asked if she could eat with us. I just started laughing so you don't want to eat with the freshman, she just told me to said quit being an asshole, otherwise I may text Julia that you have your eyes on one of the women swimmers. And she also said, besides I am the last one that gets to go through the buffet line, everyone else was at a table so the open spot is the only one I can sit at besides sitting with the coaches. I don't blame you for not wanting to sit with the old people. Paul just laughs wait a minute; didn't you call me an old man after I won the fly. Yes, I did.

Joanna sat down besides Paul and asked me if I had texted Julia about finishing 12th and I said I hadn't I assumed you had already done so. Joanna, well I thought about it, but you need to do it, it is nearly 9:00 and she is probably wondering when you are going to text her. Truthfully, I will give her a call after we get back to the hotel, I didn't do anything special, your friend over here is the hero of the day. She just smiled at me, and I noticed that each only had 1 hand above the table, so I know what was really going on. John was that you parents rooting for you from the stands, and I said yes. I don't remember them ever seeing you swim before, and I had to admit that they never had been to any of my swim meets. Joanna, do I have you or Julia to thank for them being here this weekend. Well let's just say her soon to be in-laws were convinced to come here. I was on the call for coaching.

We got back to the hotel, and each of us had a candy bar with our team logo on it in the rooms, except mine. It was in the closet, so much for this coming out of the closet thing I had enough. I went down to the lobby to call Julia and let her know what was going on and saw Coach Edwards talking to the assistant coach Bruce Farley, all he did was nod so I was spared another discussion with him. At 9:45, I finally got in touch with Julia, she had been at the library studying, and she asked how the day went. Well, you know from your roommate that I made the consolations which was as much as I could have hoped for. My parents took me out to lunch and then we had the finals and I moved up 4 places, to 12th. I did my best time in the 4 years here, and by now you already know that Paul won the event. How did you know that I already knew, simple, Joanna and Paul were holding hands at dinner tonight and I just caught them kissing at my hotel room, I expected that she would have texted you? Julia simply said, you know her well and she is my closest friend. Julia how are you doing, and all she said is we are doing fine. I am so glad that this will be over in 2 days, can we get a steak dinner on Sunday? I am so over eating any more pasta. Well, that could be a problem, my mother is coming up on Sunday and wants to have dinner with us and as you know she loves to cook pasta. Can you at least ask her to bring some hot Italian sausage, I need protein, I think?

"Julia how is school going? I have a test on Friday so need to get off the phone soon and get to studying.

By the way did I forget to tell you that we are in first place, the divers did well as did one of the Freshman, we also won the medley relay, so we have mostly done well. Thank God that Findlay is not tapered, they are not doing as well as I would have expected.

I have to move the coaches are coming towards me to get to the elevator and I really don't want to hear anything from either one.

In the background I hear from assistant coach Bruce, nice swim John while coach Edwards just smiled and went to the elevator.

Wow Julia, I just got a piece of a compliment. I heard her laughing and see the coaches even noticed.

Let's not get into that discussion, so glad that this will be over shortly. I love you Julia and can't wait until Sunday to see you. Julia just said, you better we are waiting for you to come back and if you get back before midnight I want to come over and stay the night. John, I miss you and without Joanna, I am kind of lonely here.

I will let you know if we are going to be home before midnight or you can just have your roommate contact you, not like she won't anyway. Finally, I said let me get out of here and to the hotel room. I will call you Friday night after swimming.

I will be swimming the 200 fly on Friday; I have been told I am seeded in the top heats so that will be different.

"Good night, Julia."

When I get back to the room Paul asked so how you are love birds doing. I simply said, "not as nice as you two."

Paul just laughed; "oh I forgot you saw us earlier."

"Yes, old man, I saw you and the lovely brunette lip locked."

So, John, you can now go to the closet so in the morning I can kid you about coming out of the closet again. "

"Paul, I need to study for a test next week, so you will see a light in the room I need about an hour of study before I go to bed."

Paul said to me "I thought you already won that award; you only have 6 weeks of school left give it a break." Enjoy the 200 fly on Friday, I get to swim for about 20 seconds and go rest.

Now you must rub it in. God, I must be stupid to swim the 200 fly.

Paul replied, "Well, if you didn't swim it, you probably would have been left off the team, and then we would have lost your 5 little points."

Good night, Paul,

And with that off to my closet to lie down and study. One day down two to go. A little bit happy that it is ending and in tears that it will end. I just want to get home and be with Julia, can't wait until I see her.

Conference Day 2

With a knock on the closet door, the second day of conference starts. Again, Paul yells at me to come out of the closet and that we need to be at breakfast at 7:30 AM. Today's events will be the 200 Free, 100 back, 50 Free, 200 Fly, and 100 Breaststroke. The relay today is the 800 free relay, and then divers will do the 3-meter dive to complete the day.

The lovely brunette came to our room, no kissing of Paul this time, and let us know our daily schedule. Breakfast downstairs at 7:30 to 08:30. Be at the bus by 8:45, (make sure I am there no later than 8:35, to avoid listening to coach Edwards and then leaving for the pool and arrive at 09:00. Our warm-ups are 10 minutes each team, and the meet starts at 10:00. I forget that while the men swim the odd numbers the women swim the even numbers, that creates more time to get rest but, in most cases, less women's heats so not quite the same. I know for sure Paul went outside the room and suspect stole a kiss from Joanna.

Our room fights for bathroom rights and this time I am second, want to make sure that I am on-time for the breakfast no desire to be the Coaches whipping boy. After doing my business, I arrived at the breakfast area by 07:15, and luckily no comments for the coaching staff. I am early enough that there are like 4 swimmers and no coaches at the breakfast line, in fact they were just starting to put out the breakfast buffet. After grabbing oatmeal, fruit cup, and some bacon and toast, sat down at a table in the private room far away from the front so did not want to be eyeball range of the coaches.

By 7:30 everyone was down and by 7:40 even the lovely Brunette had food and of course came back to the rear table and sat with me. She could not sit with Paul as he was with the coaches in the front of the room. She just smacks me in the back of the head and said you ready for another swim today.

I said sure, by the way you have any idea where I am seeded, and after she looks in the book tells me lane 2 of the third to the best heat. You are seeded like 13th overall, so coach has you rated finishing 15th in this event good for 2 points. This is the event coach thinks I should do better, basically he knows I flatten out and can somehow normally stay with others who die. Good to know he expects me to back-up 2 positions.

Coach Edwards stood up and asked everyone in the room for attention. Good morning and welcome to day 2 of conference. Thanks to the team and our divers last night we are in first place after day 1. We have a 21-point lead and have won three events yesterday. You know what that means, nothing unless we do well the next 2 days. Guys today we have to keep the pressure on Findlay, they may be not as tapered as we are, but they are a very good team and never forget we have never beaten them in a conference meet. We need to think beyond our first places, it is all about multiple swimmers and scoring a lot of points at this point, for those not rated fast enough to make the finals, then make it to the consolation finals, and then gain positions each point for us is one the Findlay can't get. We know that WV Wesleyan has a chance to win a couple of events and that even Frostburg has a strong swimmer or two, but this is our chance to win, it is our time to win, so are we ready to take this event?

With that the team again erupts in cheers, yelling AB, AB, AB.

Coach Edwards asked Joanna to come up and tell everyone the schedule today and as the lovely brunette was talking, I could see Paul focusing on her, and not what she said. Joanna, always the professional simply told us be at the bus by 8:45 and warm-up etc. Then she talked about the afternoon and then evening schedules, and finally about divers' times, 20 minutes after preliminaries this morning completed would be when the diving trials starts, with warm-ups expected around noon. Finals for the dive would follow the 800 free relay tonight and would conclude the evening events. Joanna concluded with and let's kick butt.

Finally, Paul was called up to the front of the room, and with a smile as he passed Joanna. Good morning, guys, if you are not psyched up for today, you must have ice water in your veins. We have an opportunity that no other team in our school's history has had a chance to do. Last year we came close so this year, we need all the points we can get. Look at the back there and you see an example in John Peters. John was not rated to make the consolation finals but somehow managed not only to make the consolations but then proceeded to move up to 12th place, getting 5 points that will add to our possibility of winning. Paul just pointed to me, and only he is clapping, the rest of the team looked uninterested as it was only a 12th place finish.

Paul then talked about we had three conference champions last night 2 individual events and a relay. You know how many other champions we have had at conference championships before last night. (3) We are here to create history this week, a new chapter for Alderson Broadus, remember this weekend the rest of your lives.

The team starts banging on the tables and walls, yelling AB,AB and AB.

Coach Edwards then came up and asked everyone to finish breakfast, be ready to go to the pool, and remember to stay hydrated as the pool will have a full deck of swimmers and will be hot. So, team let's get going, day 2 has begun.

On our way-out Paul says to me, "I thought I needed to call you out for your efforts last night, 5 points from nowhere covered others that did not do as well. I wanted them to understand points can come from everyone here."

Well Paul, that one hit a manure bomb, I guess the rest of the team still thinks of me as a failure.

Then something unexpected came about, Coach Edwards came to me and said, "hope you can do that result again today, we really need you to get another 5 points tonight."

"All I could say is sure coach."

Paul then came over to me and said, "see even coach is with you.

I said, "Paul was that you or the assistant coach that told him to say something." "Paul simply said you probably will never know which one of us."

We just lined up for the bus, I went to the back of the bus and no comments from the coaches o team about being one of the last to get on the bus. 15 minutes later we were at the pool.

When I got out of the bus, Joanna came over to me and said, is it true your nickname for me is the lovely brunette? Yes, I said OK you caught me. She said not sure I like that comment you know I am going to get a degree in marketing Cum Laude. Rather than say anything, I just leaned over and gave her a kiss and said don't tell my fiancé about my infatuation with you. Never mind, I am sure you 2 have already talked this morning.

Joanna gave me a hug, and said "you know I am lovely, and yes; I have talked to Julia this morning. Please text her this morning to let her know you are ok."

All I could say is thanks for the reminder, Mom, remember my real Mom will be here today, not sure she will be at finals if I get top 16 today, she will probably insist on going to services tonight, assuming a congregation exists out here.

I simply texted Julia, the lovely brunette and I talked this morning. To clarify, I love you and good luck with your test today.

A response came back, love you 2, kick ass.

My response back, kick ass, what would your catholic mother say to that? She would say, go John Peters, and be nice to my daughter, the text wrote.

My Dad was waiting for me as we got to the pool. "I have convinced your mother to not go to synagogue this evening if you make the finals tonight." Oh, crap Dad, I guess I really need to do well this morning. He simply said "I know you will you have my athletic genes. He just clapped me on the back, and said go get them, and with a tear in my eye, ran to catch up to the team and get ready for warm-ups. I heard him say, we are proud of you. Nothing like motivation from your family."

(While in the Olympics they do sprint events for the Back, Breast and Fly, they do not do this for college conference meets)

Warm-up felt very good after a typical 500 free and some easy fly, I did a couple of 50's and they were matched times. Both were 30 flats, which meant I was going to be able to break a minute, and then hold on. Finished up with a couple hundred yards and then got out.

Joanna asked if I wanted any sprints and said to her not with this event coming up. 200 Fly today no sprints required.

One of the members of the girl's team, (Michelle Lee) came over to me and said John, congratulations last night, not bad. If that was your weak event, how are you going to do today, I said I would like to make top 10. Michelle also said way to go PAPA, and all I said was who told you, was it the lovely brunette manager? You know she loves you and your fiancé. Next thing I know is I am getting a hug and a kiss, and she said have fun or I will tell Julia you let me kiss her. Laughing, that was the first kiss I have ever received from a member of the Women's team, and Michelle said, we never had a chance after you met Julia. Good luck today, John. You also Michelle and kick ass apparently my fiancé thinks that is something good to say.

At 9:55, the announcer asked for everyone to stand for the pledge of allegiance and the national anthem. Now good luck everyone, please report for the first event today, men's and Women's 200 free.

Day 2 Preliminaries:

Event 15: 200 Freestyle Kevin Johnson and Josh Snow were in the third to best heat of the seeded heats, Josh in lane 5, and KJ in lane 6.

In the next heat was Bob Weaver seeded in lane 6. In the fast heat was Kevin Ganey, KG in lane 3, meaning it would be close for him to make the finals. Findlay had the best swimmer in lane 4 of the final heat and lane 5 of the heat prior meaning they were likely to have 2 swimmers in top 4 or 5.

That was the seeding and not the results. Josh won his heat and KJ finished third with an outside chance of making the final. Bob Weaver also finished third, in the next heat and the Findlay swimmer ended up second. In the final heat, Findlay swimmer dominated, with our KG, finishing second overall.

For the event, AB ended up with 2 in the Consolations, seeded 10 and 12, while in the finals we also had 2, KG in lane 5, with Findlay swimmers in lane 4 and 3. Our final swimmer in the finals is Josh seeded 5th overall, in lane 2. If everyone swam as they were seeded for the evening Findlay 44 points and AB 45, so while Findlay had strong swimmers, AB could counter with depth.

Event 17: Our 100-backstroke team again consists of Jeremy and Bob Pearson. Bob was in lane 4 of the second to best heat, meaning he was seeded 5th overall. Jeremy, was in the third to fastest lane 6, meaning he was the 12th. Bob was his heat winner and as seeded ended up third in the finals. Jeremy had a decent swim and ended up 11th for the consolation finals. Just like AB, Findlay has 2 swimmers, one is seeded number 2 for the finals and one more in the consolations seeded 10th. Potential based on seeds are 27 for Findlay, and 23 points for AB. But that is just the preliminaries and not the results.

Looking at our first 2 events, Findlay would cut slightly into our lead, again we will be waiting for the real swimming.

Event 19: 50 Freestyle This event has 8 heats, so a lot of swimmers and some quality even from West Virginia Wesleyan, Notre Dame college, Fairmont and Frostburg. Thai Cung was in the third seeded heat 15th seed in lane 2. Our captain Paul, was seeded as the number 3 seed and was Bob Weaver doing his double for the day, was in the second to fast heat lane 4. Findlay had the top swimmer in the second to top heat or second overall, and another in lane 7 of the final heat.

After the swims, Bob Weaver and Paul were in the final heat lanes 5 and 6 respectively, Bob really did well and is second seed. Thai made the consolations and will be in lane 7, or like 15th overall. Findlay has one swimmer again in the final and consolation final, so AB should be able to gains some points for the first time.

I guess I have never explained the lane assignments, so here is how they go: Lane 4 fastest

Lane 5 Second

Lane 3 third

Lane 6 fourth

Lane 2 fifth

Lane 7 sixth

Lane 1 seventh Lane 8 last or eighth.

Those are your assignments and rarely do the results mirror the way they are seeded, so I write these, and finals will be so different.

Event 21: 200 Fly

The event is really grueling a lot of teams only bring in 1 swimmer for this event teams with depth can really clean-up here. So only 4 heats here 30 swimmers, of which 16 make the consolations or finals. George Smythe was in the heat just before the last 3 heats and finished 17th overall, or just 1 outside the consolations. I was in lane 7 of the final heat, Cain Peretti, was the same lane in heat 2, and Tom Leonard was lane 3 of the final heat with me.

Cain swam faster than his seed time and still managed to be at risk for not making the final as a couple of unseeded swimmers did well. Ended up 15th overall.

In our heat, I knew that I had to swim very consistently. I knew I went out fairly slowly as I could only see lanes 6 and 8 next to me and both were ahead of me at the fifty. I swam an easy second 50 and was now ahead of lane 8 and just about equal to lane 6, could not see Tom and the leaders ahead of us. At the 150 I had finally cleared lane 6 and could only see that the three middle lanes were quite a bit ahead of me. When I finished, I was 4th in my heat and 13th overall, just as my seed would have said. Tom Leonard proceeded to be third in the heat and 6th overall for the finals. I have no idea if he eased up or not, I was still about 5 seconds behind the top 3 in the pool. Findlay again has a top 3 swimmer and one that just missed the finals finishing overall 9th.

The first seed finisher was one of the few swimmers from Davis and Elkins, just shows that even a small team like them who can only field one relay and has 7 swimmers can have a really outstanding swimmer. Again, Findlay could yield 25 points while based on our seedings, we would be lucky to get 18. Findlay could gain 7 points but through the first 4 events again we are very competitive with Findlay.

After I finished the race, had to cool down near the divers, and Brad clapped me on the back and said, "old man you did pretty well this morning."

"I just responded one more event left after tonight and done. I also yelled at him you guys better do well."

Joanna, came over to me and asked, can I tell Julia you made the consolations or do you want to do it.

"Joanna, you can do it, I am going to try to have some time with my parents before we leave for the hotel."

"She said I can tell coach you want to support the divers and I can get you in the van later that comes back about 4 PM, you just won't have much time before mandatory meeting coach is calling."

"Thanks Joanna."

My Dad yelled good going; I don't remember you ever swimming that event in high school. I yelled back; I was not that stupid then. He just started laughing. Hey Dad, I am going to come up to the stands and see you and Mom while our divers are competing. Joanna has squared it with coach let's just enjoy some time together while the divers compete. I want to support Brad anyway; we are friends even though he is a diver. Is he the one you told us about that came out after his sophomore year, yes, he is? Really great person, some on the team did not like him after he came out, but we joked and still are really great friends. I have met his current partner; they are really nice people. Second diver is a nice guy also, he is a sophomore and I think whatever Brad tells him he does it. May be why he is fairly close to Brad in competition, they challenge each other.

Event 23: 100 Breaststroke

AB has a lot of swimmers here as does the conference, 7 heats in all. Tony Villani was in one of the early heats and while he improved on his seed time by 2 seconds was not a real candidate to make the consolations. Jeff Kissinger was in the second to final heat in lane 3, swam slightly slower than his seed time and ended up 15th in the trials.

John Ritter and Dick Wynne were in the final heat in lanes 5 and 6, and both made the finals, 3rd and 5th seeded. Findlay had the best swimmer in the meet here and placed another in the top spot of the consolations. If the seeds went as finished Findlay would get 33 Points, while AB would get 32 points, basically a wash. Again, that was the seeds and not the evening results.

Event 25: 800 Free Relay Great thing here the conference only allowed one team per school, so only 2 heats. With our team placing 4 of the top 16, we knew we were likely to be top of the heap, and we were holding Paul back for the finals tonight. Findlay still managed to finish in second place, hoping that means we will get 50 points, opens up the events for tonight. The one thing you have to worry about in the trials of a relay is to make sure you don't false start either in the beginning or between racers, and our team made sure they were clear and were really slow, I think they gave away a couple of seconds, but they had it to cover.

After the women's team finished the same relay preliminaries were done for the day. Just before 2 in the afternoon, diving began, the rest of the swim team went back to the hotel and I went up to see my parents for a while before they took a nap before finals tonight.

Event 27: Divers started warming up during the relays and competition started for men and women. You can't have the three-meter dive event going because they really need to concentrate on the finish a blown dive here really hurts. As a kid I used to play at NBAC on the board and did a belly flop, it took 2 days for my stomach to feel better.

I kept one eye on the divers while my parents and I talked about the upcoming graduation and then a month later coming back for the wedding which looks like it will be in Bridgeport. Grandpa has agreed to be our rabbi for the wedding, but he insists on meeting Julia prior to the wedding, so trying to figure out how to get them together, thinking graduation weekend fits, now that he is retired maybe we can get him here on Friday before sundown and go home Sunday after the graduation ceremony. We are trying to find a hotel where he can walk to the restaurant we are looking at.

Mom and Dad left for the hotel and at 3:30, the smaller van picked up the three divers from AB and me and took us back to the hotel. The third diver was our women's team, and she was in first place and very talkative this afternoon. (Karen Swift) How did a diver get a name Swift I will never know; they are never swift. I just chilled. Texted Julia to say I would be swimming again tonight and wishing her that she feels well, just chit chat type things.

We hit some traffic and I barely got back hung up my trials suit to dry and hung up my team sweats in time for the team meeting in the hallway. Coach Edwards looked at me, trying to be late again, Joanna stepped in and said he was supporting the divers and we had a traffic delay. That seemed to ease the mood. Coach Edwards asked the divers what place they were in, and Brad said same as yesterday, with the Findlay diver currently in second. Well that still gives us a potential 10 points more than Findlay.

Well done guys.

At: 4:15 the entire team was together, and Coach Edwards said guys warm-ups tonight start at 5:45, meet starts at 6:30, tonight. We have a chance to put some distance between us and Findlay if you all perform well tonight. Guys are you ready for tonight, then get some rest and the bus will be her at 5:15, PM. Make sure you are on-time, we don't have time to chase you.

Joanna then yelled, I will be coming to rooms to knock on the door between 5 PM and 5:15, so be prepared to get moving. We will be giving you sandwiches, and protein bars at that time, that you can eat between 5 and the time you swim tonight. Divers you can eat at the restaurant and come later; we will make sure a van is available to you. After the finals tonight, we will have a late-night dinner and meeting. Please don't make me chase you down to make it here, you will have 15 minutes from the time we get back to the time we will meet for dinner.

With that over, I switched out my trial suit for my jammers for the evening session and went into my closet to rest for a while. I must have fallen asleep because I hear Joanna banging the door to the closet, then realized it was just her and Paul fooling around, because I heard woops sorry about that. It was 4:55, I could have had at least another 10 minutes of sleep. I quickly texted Julia, that we were getting ready to get started for the evening.

Julia texted back, top ten honey. I thought, wow Joanna has already told her about the goal for the night.

I quickly got my gear together and was there by 5:10, and the assistant coach just smiled and said good you are one of the early ones this time.

I got to sit in the back of the bus, letting all the swimmers out before I left to go to the pool. I had no intention of talking to Coach Edwards, but he said to me, we may need a top 10 tonight, John, as I was leaving the bus.

I just thought 7 points for 10^{th,} and you were hoping I would get 5 for the weekend. Sure, coach no problem. Time to smile and nod 1 more day after tonight.

Joanna and Paul were trying their best so others would not see them eying each other. I just passed by and said Hey lovebirds no fooling around. Remember what they said in "Rocky", broads ruin your legs. At that the lovely brunette, stuck her tongue out at me, you are such a poop.

I may be a poop, but you were a tattle tale today, I know I can make top ten tonight, but you did not have to tell everyone.

I am so proud of you overcoming this year and doing well, I just had to share, and Julia agrees. BTW, have you told the men's swim team that you are getting married in June.

My response, only to the few I choose to, so please don't let that cat out of the bag also. Especially to the coach, God only knows how much he would give me grief regarding since Julia is Christian. Nobody else needs to know that we are also having a baby, so keep it mum please.

Joanna simply replied to you can count on me. I had serious doubts about that.

Warm-Ups

The same thing as Thursday, a lot less people in the pool so they do a 30-minute warm- up for everyone. I chose to simply loosen-up no sprints. I saw Paul doing a few timed sprints, but again he is swimming for like 22 seconds totally unless they need him for the relay tonight.

Finals:

At 5:55 PM, we heard the request to clear the pool which meant all swimmers out so they can get ready for the events of the evening. The order of events will be the same as the morning with the exception, that the final 8 divers, will complete 3 dives in the finals before the 800 Free Relay, it allows the divers to get some exposure and at the same time some of the swimmers need rest before the relays.

Our dedicated trainer, Justin Leonard came over to the team and prepared us for the evening. First, I want you to know that I am here for any of you that need some attention. Second, I want you all to know I am proud of you men, and it is time for AB to come home with a championship. The school deserves it and all of you here tonight will always remember this weekend the rest of your life. We may win more championships, and you will never forget the first one, nor will the school. Now go out there and kick ass. (Again, those words) A minute later he came to me, can your shoulder handle this much stress the 200 fly is a tough event? I wish you had let me tell the coach last year that you truly were injured and should have been nowhere near a pool. I still think a surgery would have been a better solution that 8 months of rehab and lifting to restrengthen the shoulder.

My response was simple, one more weekend I think it can handle it. The lack of meets this year actually was required to let it heal from last year. I haven't had a tingling feeling in my fingers in over 8 months.

Justin says sarcastically, I guess Joanna's roommate has helped you with back massages. By the way congratulations Papa, good luck the rest of the weekend.

Wow, Joanna, you need to really only tell things to the right people. AB up by 21 points going into the finals tonight.

Event 15: 200 Freestyle – In the consolation finals, Kevin was chasing the Frostburg swimmer for all 8 lengths and started coming from behind just to be touched out at the wall, finishing 19th overall, just .1 second behind the winner. I was amazed that Frostburg had held this guy out when we swam them, damn he was fast. To our surprise came Bob Weaver right behind him and was touched out by a swimmer from Notre Dame of Ohio. AB finished pretty much as predicted and 12 points in our column. In the finals, it was never really close, the Findlay swimmer, who had once swum for Michigan State, was dominant so it came down a race for second, Kevin Ganey, who likes the distance events came back in the final 50 and touched out Findlay's second swimmer. Findlay swimmer set a conference record and pool record in the effort. Josh managed to move up to 4th overall after chasing the top three for the first 150, he hung on for the 4th place finish. Findlay received 42 points and AB without 4 swimmers managed to pick up a total of 47 points, so our lead stands at 26 points, getting better.

Event 17: 100 Backstroke - With both Findlay and AB having 2 swimmers in the evening events, it was going to be place that meant what would happen. In the consolations, Justin, got off to a lousy start trailing the field, sprinted past a few others in the second half of the race and ended up 12th. The Findlay swimmer just missed winning the heat, and so ended up 10th overall. In the finals, the Findlay swimmer was outpaced by the Davis and Elkins swimmer, a really fast swimmer from Eastern Europe, and not sure how he ended up here. He also broke the conference record and pool record. The Findlay swimmer was away back still ended up second. Bob Pearson finished fourth overall never really contended for the top 3 slots but was better than anyone else in the pool. Findlay managed to achieve Findlay 27 points AB only 20, lead down to 19 points.

As soon as this event was over, I went to the pool to loosen up for the 200 fly, a lot of stretching and about 4 lengths of one-arm butterfly, then out of the pool so I could see the men's next event:

Event 19: 50 Free – Yes, I yelled let's go captain from the warm-up pool, Paul just smiled and pumped his fist in the air. If anyone has never watched the 50 free it is a blink of the eye, even in the 25-yard pools, most races are decided in hundredths of a second. Thai swam the consolations and while he swam his quickest race, he still finished 14th overall 3rd from last in the consolations. The Findlay swimmer was barely second in the heat .003, behind the swimmer from Fairmont State. With our team looking for an upset with Paul and Bob on the finals, the race was over in what felt like 2 seconds but was really about 20, with the Findlay swimmer beating Paul by just .05, seconds and Bob Weaver managing to close in at the wall in fourth, .002, behind 3rd.

With the win, Findlay receives 32 points for 10th and first. AB, 38 points so the lead was up to 25 points, or a first-place finish in an individual event.

Joanna was in tears as her boyfriend did really well and she yelled way to go Paul. I think she may have given away her relationship in that moment. She then pats me on the butt and says go make the roommates proud tonight. Go win your heat and shut-up everyone.

The women's heats were so close that a conference in the official's room was held delaying the meet. Apparently, the place judge declared a swimmer from Notre Dame the winner, but the Malone swimmer's time was .001 second on the clock slower. After 10 minutes, the announcer came on. We just received the results and in an unusual turn of events the .001, difference is not enough to declare a winner for the Women's 50 free, so both swimmers will be placed as the winners, so no second-place award for the event will be shown. I was just glad for the extra time to stretch for this hard event.

I just smiled at her, I have this one and want you are free to text Julia, this is going to be a different year.

My Mom and dad are waving at me, and I heard dad yell make us proud.

Unlike the morning swim, as the gun went off so did my feet, and noticed that at the turn for the 50, I was just behind the 2 inside lanes, so standing third in my heat, Cain Paretti is already a body length behind me. I was feeling a good rhythm tonight, and noticed at the 100 fly, I could not see anyone ahead of me, so I knew it was going to be good, the third 50 felt just like the second and without pain, I looked over and saw the leader just turning when I turned so virtually a tie at this point. All the rehab and I knew that the death of the last 50 would probably be coming, but through the 7th length, no pain, and then underwater for what seemed like eternity, came up and heard my teammates screaming every time I came out of the water. As the colors on the lane ropes ended in the last red colors, I was dead, but somehow found strength of my kick to keep going and finished as hard as I could with both arms and legs. At the wall I looked up and saw heat champion, lane 2. I had just done the best time of my career, and very close to the varsity record. Cain finished as was expected 15th overall. Findlay swimmer ended up 12th, so we have done better than expected with 10 points for the race as opposed to Findlay getting 5 for a 12th place finish.

The finals were amazing to watch, with 2 Eastern European swimmers finish 1 and 2 both beating the former conference record Findlay swimmer still managed a third-place finish with Tom ending up 6th. With our results in the consolation and the finals both teams managed 22 points, the lead was unchanged took us 3 swimmers to do it but the points are the same.

I had to cool down after that event, and when I left the diving area could see my parents hugging each other. My Dad yelled way to go and had a fist pump.

Joanna and Paul ran over to me, and we had a group hug. Joanna said she had already called Julia; you did way too well for me to just text her. No way anyone was expecting you to win the consolation heat and overall, your time was 6th best.

Justin our trainer came over and said to me I guess you made the right decision in doing rehab.

I just replied I did what you told me I had to do, and it really paid off.

Even Tom said to me way to go Old Man, maybe we will get to swim this one again at nationals.

Joanna laughed, "did I forget to tell you that you made the National Qualifying time." "Yes you did."

Even Coach Edwards patted me on the back and said nice swim, knew you had it in you. (Can I have my scholarship money back)

Event 23; 200 Breast – I had to get notes from Joanna for this event, I was late getting back due to warm-down and glad handing a few swimmers. The coach from WV Wesleyan came over to me and gave me a high five, nice way to finish your career.

Here is what I got from Joanna: Jeff Kissinger swam well but did not move up from his 15th position in the consolation heat, Findlay swimmer won the heat. In the finals, Findlay swimmer dominated and won the race but did not break pool or conference record. Our swimmers ended up 4th and 5th, second from our side of the conference.

Findlay scored 33 points to AB 30 points cutting into the lead of our team. Our lead now stood at 22 points, with only the 800 relay and diving to go on day 2:

Event 27: Men's diving finals. As I said previously, they decided to go out of order so teams could warm-up and get ready for the 800-freestyle relay. In the meantime, I got to watch Brad do well again and finish top 3 and Colt just barely behind him in 4th. The Findlay diver managed a second-place finish. Brad did a great last dive and we thought he would move up to second but was 0.25 points behind second place finisher.

Findlay gained 20 points and AB with 2 finalists received 32 points increasing our lead to 34 points getting close to a big lead.

I forgot to say, Karen Swift, from the Women's team won the first event ever for AB Women's swimming. She qualified for nationals and probably will be there with the coach and her only in Indianapolis. She did a fantastic 21/2 off the 3-meter and landed it with all 9's. I grabbed her around the shoulders and just said so proud of you.

She said look who's talking, have you called Julia yet.

I answered, the lovely brunette has done that for me already. You know Joanna, she is tight with Julia, I said how about you.

Karen laughed; I think Colt would like to take me out for a date. Yes, I think he would like to marry you if he could. Karen said no way, but his puppy eyes after she won and the hug, he gave her was a giveaway. (I already knew they had gone to a movie together and hung out together, everyone else thought it was a diver thing, Joanna had told me they were dating I just did not believe it.)

Event 25: 800 Free Relay

With the results AB had in the finals tonight in the 200, we thought we would be a strong team, and when coach decided to put Paul in to lead-off the race, we knew this was going to be interesting. The 800 free relay has 4 swimmers each swimming 200 freestyle. The event started off badly for Ursuline, the lead swimmer false started, and the team was disqualified. Paul had swum about 10 yards before the second gun and rope stopped him.

Because lane 1 was now empty, and the swimmers had started already, the race was delayed 2 minutes to get everyone back in place. Having you best sprinter lead off was a rare chance for our team to get a body length lead after Paul's swim. Coach decided to put our 2nd best after Paul, and Kevin did well, and we led by over 2 body lengths over Hillsdale second and Findlay best swimmers yet to come. It looked like a rematch of the consolation finals with the third swimmers and our lead over Hillsdale went down to about 1.5 body lengths and 2 over Findlay. All pressure on Josh Snow to anchor the relay, I would never have chosen a distance swimmer to anchor a relay much less a

freshman, but I don't get to make those decisions. After a slow start which saw the Findlay swimmer get within a body length at the 100, Josh showed why he is a really great distance swimmer and proceeded to outlast Findlay by half a body length, over

Findlay with Hillsdale finishing a distant third. With that the men's portion of the evening was concluded. Paul had his second conference championship with the relay win. Our team now led by 44 points, if we did just as predict we would end up winning the championship.

Time to get dressed fast and then get to a local Italian restaurant that was staying open for the combined AB swim teams for dinner. I saw my parents briefly right before we left the facility. Mom said to me that she was proud of me helping our team with that great swim. She also asked is there something between the manager and your team captain. I had to tell her, yes, they are definitely a couple. I did not know it for a long time, but Julia is her roommate and knew it. Mom said that explains why she was on the phone right after you finished, I guess she was on the phone with Julia.

Mom, the lovely brunette, is what I call Joanna, and she will likely be maid of honor at the wedding and Paul will be my best man. I will ask James to be one of the ushers for the wedding. Julia told me three from each side, so if you really don't mind, I am going to ask Brad the diver to be the third.

She just laughed, what a lot of your friends at this wedding, Grandpa will be so happy that the team will be there, so many gentiles. That is not funny I hope he will still officiate.

I jumped on the bus, and the next thing I know, the freshmen were waiting for me, hey look it is the old man, decided to make nationals in his last weekend at Alderson Broadus. Josh just shook my hand and said welcome to the big boys' club, you nasty old man. I heard the call from Joanna to your girlfriend, is it true you are getting married in the summer? I simply said yes, and he said, well Joanna says you 2 are insanely tight and that your lady really helped turn around your academic career. I nodded yes.

Marianne, a freshman swimmer on the women's team, said, well if you need some help Josh, let me help you on your academics.

I laughed, "that was how it started for me Josh, be very careful of what academic help you get."

The look I got from Marianne could have melted the steel on the bus. Josh is a good- looking guy at 6' 2", blue eyes, and sandy brown hair. Marianne apparently had her eyes on hm for a while.

I sat down at the rear of the bus surrounded by the freshman swimmers for the 10- minute ride to the restaurant.

At the restaurant, the place was closed except for our team. Coach Edwards stood up and said, we have a buffet tonight, eat well and enjoy being in first place for the men and women first time in top 3. For this night only, seniors get in the line first, so with Paul leading I got my pasta and bread and salad. While I had some time waiting for others to get dinner, I took out my cell phone and texted Julia about the swim tonight.

Julia, had a crazy fast swim tonight, won the heat, qualified for nationals so may have another meet in Indianapolis in 2 weeks. The text came back with a smiley face. Then another, aren't you done after tomorrow? My text back was can I swim at nationals, pretty please. The answer back was we will have to have that talk; I don't want you away for a whole week.

After we all had been through the buffet line and sat down, then Coach Edwards came over and boasted so this is what first place feels like. Remember everyone we have a lead, but we have not won yet, everyone here has to perform for 1 more day. We have received some champions today congratulations to the 800 free relay and to our very own Karen Swift, first AB diver to win a conference event. I want to have Paul come up and talk to you but first we have to hear from our great manager Joanna on the events for Saturday.

Joanna stood up, (she was not sitting near Paul for a reason, people were starting to guess what was going on) Good evening, well for the swimmers you have another day of trials and finals. For you divers, you are all now assistant managers because you are done for the weekend. Ok, swimmers, early morning, as trials are odd on Saturday.

The 1650 will be swum with all but the fast heat swimming in the trial in the morning. All other events will be after that, so we have an unusual morning. 1650 swimmers your warm-up is between 7:30 and 8:00, so divers help me get them up and out with breakfast sandwiches. Others your warm-ups will be at 10:00, and then meets starts at 10:30. Swimmers you have breakfast on your own, $10.00, limit so don't get greedy.

Trials over at 2 PM, and then we get lunch and a break, finals will start at 5 PM tonight and expected to finish by 7:30 PM. Normally we would be on the road but this year we may have to stay around for some hardware, so we are assuming that we will be on the bus at 8:30 PM and go directly back to Philippi by 12:30 PM. Let's win this championship.

Paul stood up afterwards and said welcome to first place. Hey divers' thanks for the support and enjoy the rest of the weekend, I know Joanna will work you well. To the women's team, this will be you next year, we were third last year and with the new troops we are a force, this will be you by next year. Let's have a good evening, no partying, because we have one more day and for us seniors our last time at the conference. Everyone let's get rest and be ready for our last day.

The room erupted in the AB cheer again, and this time the lovely brunette and Paul were close to each other.

Coach Edwards told everyone to be quiet. Remember we have a lead and we have not won the championship yet.

With that we all went back to the hotel, where I got to go back to my closet bedroom. Simply texted Julia, goodnight, and one more day. I did not receive a text right away, then it came back yeah, we will be waiting at the apartment.

I did hear a conversation between Paul and Joanna, well a little conversation and a lot more kissing from outside in the hallway. How they expected the team not to suspect something is beyond me. I know coach had to have an idea that something was going on between them.

When Paul got back to the room, I just told him broads weaken legs. His response was "smart ass."

So tired I remember hearing the TV go on and was asleep in like 5 minutes, it had been a long day. All I could think of the 400 IM is left, the hardest swimming event in history and it will be the last one of my swim career. I am seeded 12th so not that much pressure on me.

Conference Final Day Saturday

With a knock on the door again, the lovely brunette came into our room. Ok gentlemen, this is a change from our previous days. First, we will not be coming back to the rooms we have here so make sure that you pack your bags and make sure the divers have them so we can store them in the vans. Next trials are a little different today, the distance swimmers will be leaving at 7:00, for warm-up and then the races. For the rest of the swimmers, you have to 9:00 before we leave so today will be breakfast on your own, no organized team breakfast. So, everyone please get moving, Kevin you have the 1650 this morning, so haul ass now.

Kevin Johnson groaned, I guess I get the damn breakfast shakes, see you guys at the pool I have the 1650 this morning. The rest of us went back to sleep for about an hour, or well we just kind of relaxed. I texted Julia, the last day and I get to see you tonight. Big lead, team can win this year. It was 7:00 AM, so she did not text back, I guess some people do get to sleep in on a Saturday morning.

8:00, Brad Fox knocked on the door this time. Swimmers time to haul your ass out of bed, go get breakfast at the hotel buffet, we have a special price according to Coach Edwards. I yelled, damn divers they take the fun out of everything. This time Brad responded, and you thought it was funny when I came out of the closet, does Julia know? BTW, John, I hear you have a lot of fun this morning, 400 IM, isn't that the event you have wanted to swim for 4 years, we'll let it fly baby.

I could only say yes, it is, and God why I am so stupid to swim this event.

Paul and I ate together, he asked me, you ready to swim our last day together? Put his arm around me, thanks for the 4-years together, I can't imagine how it would have been without you. How would it be if the two of us, made all-conference in our last events, you would be the academic athlete and I could up for the outstanding 4-year athlete, it would be a hell of an athletic banquet. Jeff Kissinger piped in, just follow me, and we will get you to the finals tonight. Old man, your fiancé will be so proud of you, when you bring back your all-conference notification.

Two freshman that were swimming the 1650 were at the hotel when Paul and I came down to the restaurant. Hey guys, why are you here. The final heat of the 1650 is swam at the finals later tonight, so we got to sleep in.

There were 8 heats of the 1650 this morning, 4 for the men and women each, the final 2 heats are swum tonight. With only 8 heats this morning they will average 3 per hour, so you guys get to warm-up in the diving section. They put qualifying times otherwise we would be here all-day.

I finally received a text back from Julia saying good luck today. Another text from my parents wishing me good luck in my final swim day in college. I picked-up the phone and James called and wished me a good swim. Angela was the only one that had not called this morning, I received a voice mail from her yesterday wishing her big brother a great last day of swimming. James as always was nowhere to be found, I guess he is doing something with the house to himself. Suddenly I realized after this day, no more 2-a-days, and no more sore shoulders, feet and knees. I teared up realizing this is the end of over 15 years I was known as 'Swimmer Boy', now time for a new path. The very tough 400 IM is the last and final event of my career.

When we got to the pool just before 09:30, the last two women's heats were finishing up of the 1650, so we had 40 minutes to warm-up in the diving tank, and then we had 20 minutes to warm-up in the competitive lanes. I chose a warm-up in the diving tank, and 2 sprints when the main lanes opened up. My sprint according to Joanna, were faster than I had done 2 days earlier in the 100 fly, so I was thinking this would be something special.

We heard that Kevin Johnson had finished 7th before the last heat, so worst case he was going to end up 15th, a couple of points for us. George Smythe was not as fortunate and finished outside of the top 8, so very unlikely to score. Findlay had a swimmer just ahead of Kevin, so a minimum of 14th, and a point cut into our lead. In the final heat tonight Findlay has one swimmer and we have 2, so hope we can keep the point lead.

Event 29: 100 Freestyle Finally, the 1650 was over and we were ready to go for the 100 Freestyle, Thai and Bob Weaver both swam well, and we ended up with 2 both in the consolations. Paul set a team record and finished second for trials, Findlay had 1 swimmer in the finals as the number 3 seed, and the fastest in the consolations.

Seven heats of women's 100 freestyle and we were ready for the 400 IM. I was really nervous with only 4 full heats for the most horrible event in swimming, I was in lane 6 of the third to fastest heat. Cain was in the second to fastest heat with Jeff Kissinger seeded 5th in lane 5 of the same heat.

The first heat was slow and took nearly 6 minutes to complete. By the time they cleared the pool, I could hear so many yelling for me. Paul had just finished his cooldown, and I could hear my parents yelling go John. The lovely brunette told me to make Julia proud hugged me and hit me in the bathing suit.

Adjusting my goggles, the starter asked for all swimmers on the blocks, then the beep of the start and away we went. I felt like I had never been this fast, shaved my body last night in expectation of this event to get all-conference. In the first 50 of the fly leg, I turned and noticed nobody was ahead of me. At the end of the 100 fly, I noticed nobody was ahead of me in the heat so doing much easier and better than expected.

The backstroke seemed to take forever and when I looked over the 2 center lanes had passed me. I was still feeling at ease and none of the pain I was expecting had come. With my strong breaststroke, I passed through both swimmers and nobody else on my side of the pool was even close to us, at the end of the 100 breaststroke, I held a nearly 1 body length lead over the next lane and slightly less to the fastest seeded swimmer.

Freestyle leg was never my best, but this was my last event, and nothing was left in the pool, I still held a small lead at the end of first 50 freestyle and even with lane 3 at the end of the 75, but the swimmer from WV Wesleyan nipped me at the end of the race, I had finished second in the heat by .1 seconds and held off lane 5 by another .1, crazy close. Two heats left to see if I was fast enough to make the finals tonight. 15 minutes later, Joanna and Paul came over to me and said stop your cool down, I was like what's up.

Joanna said OK, asshole, now I am calling Julia you just made the finals tonight, I was like no way I was seeded 12th, no way I beat 3 from the other heats. You will be in lane 1 tonight, you finish tonight, and you will have made it all the way back to all- conference.

Jeff Kissinger came over to me, "I told you to follow me wow you finally listened."

My parents were in the stands when the finals were announced, my dad had both thumbs up. Cain had made the consolations, so we were primed to get some points. Findlay had the top swimmer in the event and another one in the finals, we had 2 in the finals and 1 in consolation, so unless something changed, Findlay was going to gain some points.

Event 33: 400 Free Relay – Findlay and AB were in the fastest lanes of the fast heat. We had Paul leading off the relay, with Bob Weaver, Thai, and Bob Pearson, as our 4.

Paul gave us a lead of about .5 second in his 100, Thai went second, and the two teams ended neck and neck, Bob Pearson and the Findlay swimmer were head-to-head, and then the worst-case scenario happened. Only 1 thing could prevent AB from winning the conference title and that was exactly what happened. Bob Weaver left the blocks early on the exchange between him and Bob Pearson. AB was disqualified and this created a huge increase in points for Findlay. AB had a 52-point lead, and with Findlay gaining 50 right there, we were going to scramble in the finals in the afternoon if we were going to win the meet.

The coaches appealed the disqualification, after 15 minutes the appeal was denied and now, they were scrambling.

If everyone did as well as they thought possible, we still had a chance. That was what they told the team, meanwhile knowing that any failure to hold on to our places could let Findlay back in and again win the meet despite not being tapered.

For me I was just happy to make my first finals in college. I had been within 4 seconds of Jeff Kissinger's team record. My parents came over to me and let me know they had just extended their hotel and would see me tonight. My dad was on the phone getting a flight for Sunday morning instead of tonight as planned. Joanna had already called Julia with the news. I looked at my cell phone, Julia had tried to call me, and I called her back. She picked up the phone, wow, all-conference I bet Coach Edwards will be congratulating you.

Right, then I told her that it was about a 1 in 3 chance that we would win the conference after the team was disqualified in the last relay. She basically said, tough luck but not your issue, let the coaches figure it out how they are going to win. Julia, I may also be qualified to swim this event at nationals, and she responded, not unless you take me with you. I am not going to have another week away.

As always, she was the smarter voice and with that I finished getting dressed and got to the team van ready to get lunch. Joanna told me that Coach Edwards wants to meet with you after we finish lunch. He will be there with you and assistant coach Bruce will be at the meeting, do you think Paul should join the meeting. Coach Bruce said just the three of you and nobody else.

Ok, I will meet with them, where are we meeting? They are asking that you meet with them at the private banquet room, it is not being used and they said coach could use it for meeting with the swimmers for tonight. I will come to get you when they want to talk to you. I was thinking I may want to have Joanna in the meeting. Joanna then told me; you are the only one with 2 coaches everyone else is just talking to Coach Edwards.

I was not looking forward to talking to Coach Edwards, I thought that was all over. At least someone else will be in the room to keep me from simply telling him Fuck You I told you I should have been swimming this event.

Banquet Room:

Please shut the door John, Coach Edwards asked me, Coach Bruce joined us in the hall. Joanna closed the door and left immediately.

John, first I want to congratulate you on making the finals tonight. I knew when we recruited you that we could see a performance like this. It just took way too long for it to happen. I'm not going to dwell on the past because your time at AB is ending, and I know that you will be leaving us soon to go back to Maryland. I know that we have not had a good relationship over the last 4 years so I'm going to ask Coach Bruce to talk to you as the last year you have been under his coaching and not mine.

Bruce said, "John, I cannot tell you how thrilled I am to see the results you have had this weekend. I know we have been working out in our own little group, and the only people that knew you were finally recovered and ready to go was our little group of three. I told Jim Arnett and Barry about your making the finals tonight, and they were thrilled for you. BTW, Jim is scheduled to have his shoulder scoped next week, they found he had a calcium deposit. I am getting off topic, so let's talk about our team situation. As you know we will have to have a lead of 51, points going into the relay, because Findlay is going to win it and we are getting nothing as a result of the disqualification this afternoon. If everything holds true, we will need a minimum of fourth place from you if things go as expected for the team to win the conference. It may not come down to this, but with Findlay swimmers doing well today, we are up against it. Jeff is likely to be at least top 3, but we need a strong showing to get enough points out of your swim, to give us enough points to be clear of 50."

Now it was my time to talk, "Brian thank you for training me the last year and seeing me through the rehab work, the results this weekend are something I knew I could always do, but never had a chance to swim my best events shaved and tapered. So now that your championship is possibly dependent on another miracle swim, you come to me last and expect four years of being pushed aside and being told that I am not a competitor because of my religion. Something you don't know my father was Catholic and converted to marry my mother. My fiancé is Catholic, and she has no issue with whatever religion we choose, but for four years you threw this in my face. Why should I give a flying fuck about the championship?"

Brian stepped in, "because I know you want to end your career with a championship, let's find a way to get this done. As far as your relationship with Coach Edwards, he has made some mistakes, including pulling your final year scholarship. Let's find a way for us to complete the greatest miracle swim of your career, and then this year you will be married and will have this memory for the rest of your life. Coach Edwards, can you please leave the room, John and I have to map out a strategy for the race and I think you may be a distraction."

1 minute later Coach Edwards gathered his stuff and left the room. He was not very happy about being told by his assistant coach to leave but he had no other options here, he knew I would never listen to anything he said.

Ok, now that Coach Edwards has left the room let's talk strategy, you swam a race this afternoon that was fast, but you can do better. I think here is the plan. The first 50 of the fly I want you to relax and actually go slower than you did this morning, you will still be right near the lead, but we are saving energy. The next 50 will be faster and I expect you to be able to be near your 100 fly that you did earlier this weekend. Your weakest 100 is next everyone expects you to not be close to the lead but here is what you have to do. We need you to arch your back a little less and reaching further back to reduce two strokes per length, and make sure that you are taking in more air than you have this morning, where you were breathing every other stroke. For this to succeed, you need to have more in the tank than this afternoon and we are saving strokes. The third, segment is breaststroke, solid for you and I expect that nobody knows that you can beat our best in the 200, I have your times. Think of this leg as the last 100 of a 200 breaststroke, and you will be hanging out with the top 3, probably out right behind Jeff but still good enough that in lane 1 nobody can see you. Then the last 100 is freestyle, nobody knows what can happen here. The idea is to be close going in to the last 50 and borrow whatever oxygen you have left and sprint like all hell and you will make the top 4 or better. You will be redlining your oxygen, and with everything you have left your body is going to fight for you to stop, but you will overcome this and finish. If you follow this strategy, you will make all-conference and possibly top three this evening.

What a way to end your career here. I want to tell you that it is likely that I will not be here next year, it is very possible, that I will take over as the new head coach at California University of PA. No matter what I want this to be your glory night, you are going to qualify for the nationals in 2 weeks, and I want to be there to see you make a shot at All-American.

We gave each other a high five, I thanked him for believing in me when nobody else did.

I looked up and said shit this is possible; the time would make the Nationals and be close to taking Jeff's varsity record off the books.

Coach Bruce said, not only is this possible, but you will also be favored to place at Nationals if you can do this. Don't just think of all-conference, you can make All- American with this strategy.

I shook my head and simply said, " shit this is unreal, nobody wanted me on the team I have been an outcast and now with one swim left you all are talking to me like this is 4 years ago."

Coach Bruce simply said, this is your time, after this go marry your Julia, and have this championship for your old age to remember. You and she will always remember when you were the difference that caused Alderson Broadus to win our first conference championship. Your story from rags to championships will be something that I will always remember as a coach, thanks for being so coachable.

I was left in the room and started to cry, four years and now it is all on my shoulders. I called Julia immediately and she picked up the phone in the apartment. I explained what was going on and she simply said, make us proud and come home tonight. I teared up again, I love you and want to spend the rest of my life with you. I came out of the room; Paul saw me in tears and put his arm around me.

Paul said, "Let's end this on a great night John with our championship and a national ranking for both of us. We both came as young swimmers, and both met our dream mates, Joanna and Julia. Let's finish this off and we will be here 50 years from now calling each other about that day we won the championship."

With that done, all was set. One more swim to go. Then life with Julia and our soon to be born child.

I saw my parents and explained the situation, that I was in the last heat with our team championship depending on Jeff and my results. My dad put in baseball terms, so it is the bottom of the ninth, bases loaded, two outs, and you have a 3-2 count. The championship comes down to you and them. He came over to hug me and said one more swim John take that pitch out of the park. I started to bawl like a baby. My mother and father were also crying, it was a scene.

Joanna came over to me, and said it is time John, let's get on the van to go to the pool, warm-ups in 30 minutes. Joanna gave me a hug; I am so proud of you and can't wait to be at your wedding. Let's all finish this together. I had forgotten that this was also Joanna's last day as team manager, she had done such a fantastic job nobody could have done a job like her. The whole team respected her; I did something that I probably should never have done.

I gave her a kiss on the cheek and said to her thanks for letting me share your apartment. You have been an amazing team manager; nobody could have done better than you have. You will always be my unofficial second sister; I may have to explain how my second sister has a nice southern accent, but you have been as close to me as my sister Angela.

Wiping tears from her eyes, now let's go and finish this the right way. Get into the damn van. Awaiting her in the van was a dozen red roses. The card said from the team, thanks for everything. With that we were on our 15-minute ride to the pool. Joanna started to cry heavily while the team started chanting Joanna, Joanna, thank you for everything.

When we got out of the van, Paul pulled Joanna aside and gave her a full kiss on the mouth in front of the entire swim team. All I could hear from the team, it's about time, the women's team started clapping. The monk and now the captain have been secretly dating roommates. Any other guys on the team need tutoring, there must be something in the tutoring that works well. The entire team started laughing.

I got a text from Angela, she said good luck big brother, looking forward to being in your wedding in June.

I texted back please be prepared to be in the wedding as a bridesmaid, you trained me well with the ladies. Tonight, I am going to prove to everyone, I always had it in me.

Off to the pool for the last time, since I was not a part of the 18 core swimmers most of the year, I did not receive the current sweats for the team. I put on the sweats from my freshman year, a slightly different color and different writing than the rest of the team. Paul yelled; you will need to borrow a current sweat suit for the awards ceremony later tonight. Now off to the pool to do a warm-up for the last time. I decided that I did not need a long warm-up just did some stretching lengths and a couple of sprints.

The announcer welcomed everyone to the championship final evening. Then the national anthem was played. Finally, would the last heats of the 1650, please report to the clerk of course it's time for the meet to begin. At that point every team started doing a college cheer, AB was no different. That lasted about 5 minutes.

Event 27: 1650 Freestyle:

While our guys had done well in the 500, they were both in the back of the finals most of the way. We thought Josh was doing well finishing 4th in the heat, but from the earlier heats one of the swimmers had moved him to 5th overall. Kevin Ganey also did not do as well as thought and ended up 8ith overall. Findlay swimmers were first and 14th, even though we had more swimmers they received 28 points while we were at 25. The lead had shrunk to now 49 points, which meant that our team was most likely to end second unless something happened. So here we go, this is going to be a tough night, we need to come back in the last 2 events and make sure we had a 51-point lead before the relay. The tiebreaker for the championship was individual winners in swimming, Findlay had the tiebreaker on us.

Event 29: 100 Freestyle First up was the consolation heat with both Bob Weaver and Thai in the heat. Thai had barely made it, but Bob was next to the Findlay swimmer in the center lanes. Then another worst-case scenario, Bob false started and was disqualified from the event. Thai finished last as was expected, and the Findlay swimmer ended up first in the consolations. Our lead had shrunk even more.

Next up was the finals with Paul in lane 5 and Findlay top sprinter in the lane 4. Joanna was a nervous wreck getting ready to watch Paul. She kept yelling for him, she need not worry. Paul got off the blocks like a rocket, at the first turn he had a lead of about 2 feet and at the 50 he was leading by half-body length. The Findlay swimmer was not done yet and at the 75 he was at Paul's shoulder and closing. The last 25 was epic, and when we looked up at the finish, Paul had won by .03 seconds, almost impossible to detect. Joanna went crazy as did the entire team, but the damage had been done in the earlier heat. Findlay received 28 points and with only our 15th place finish, AB only received 27 points, the lead was down to 48 points going into our event.

This night was not going well, and Coach Edwards was pacing the floor with coach Bruce trying to calculate. The meet was slowed as they announced the results of the 1650 freestyle for men and women. Two minutes later they did the same for the 100 freestyle. Paul was announced as conference champion, the team erupted in yells for the captain who had won 2 individual events and 1 relay, likely the MVP of the conference meet. The damage though was now official when they announced only 15 swimmers with results.

Coach Bruce then came to me and said the team was going to need second and third in this event to offset the Findlay finalists. I jumped in the diving pool and swam a couple of lengths to get rid of my nerves. I gave him my book I had been writing in and asked him to write down the race for me. He agreed:

This is coach Bruce as John calls me: John asked me to write in his book what happened in the 400 IM, he wanted it from someone else to write-up his final event.

I need to explain the 400 IM that John is about to swim. It is by far the hardest event in swimming. Four different strokes, four different breathing patterns. Each 100 is a different specialty that a swimmer must get through and still be competitive even in the strokes they don't do well. This is the ultimate stress on a swimmer's body. At the end of the race swimmers have been known to have this condition some call it fighting red. It is said that with many getting pulse over 200, that swimmers swear they can taste their own blood in their mouth.

The consolation heat went as expected Cain Peretti, ended up overall 15th, good for him but as a team we were now tied with 50-point lead going into the finals. Findlay has swimmers in lanes 2, and 4. AB swimmers Jeff in lane 3 and John in lane 1. Unless AB disrupted this order, we knew the conference would go to Findlay. They would get 38 points to our 28, so we need a real change of results. AB needed somehow to move to second and third to have a chance and with John having never been here before nobody was expecting that our team could win. I patted John on the back and sent him to the starting line.

Each of the eight lanes were introduced John being first as he was in lane 1. Jeff Kissinger our record holder was in lane 3 and had done his best time in the trials in the morning.

With all 8 swimmers on the blocks, starter stated on your mark, and then the beeper of the electronic starting gun. John led all of the swimmers into the pool and by the time they came up from under water he had a half body length lead with Jeff holding second. John was doing as I asked him to reduce the number of strokes and at the 25 still led all swimmers, I'm sure he could see he was ahead when he turned. John was obviously the best butterflyer in the 400 IM, and not only led at the 50 but had started to increase his lead over the entire heat. At the completion of the fly John was ahead by a full body length and Jeff was between the two Findlay swimmers. I'm not sure that the fastest Findlay swimmer was even aware that he was ahead of him. Next came the 100 backstroke and John was using the strokes we had asked him to do longer and leaner. At the midpoint of the backstroke AB was running 1 and 2, with John's lead down to a half a body length over Jeff. At the end of the backstroke, Jeff and John literally hit the wall together. The fastest Findlay swimmer was a body length behind both of them, but his strength was supposedly next in breaststroke. John, with his physical strength stretched out the underwater portion of the turn forcing the

Findlay swimmer to increase his pace to catch-up to both swimmers, at the half-way point of the 100 breaststroke, John maintained a half body length lead and the Findlay swimmer was using more energy than was expected. Jeff was in third holding off the second Findlay swimmer.

At the touch of the final leg of breaststroke John now has a ¼ body length lead over the top swimmer from Findlay with Jeff and the second Findlay swimmer just about even.

At this point I have to tell you the entire team of AB both men and women were jumping and screaming for John and Jeff. John's parents were up in the stands and his mom was yelling Go John Go, loud enough that everyone heard it. Paul was next to the lane yelling at John every time he came up to breath. I looked at John's splits they were insanely fast, like top 12 in the country fast for Division 2. The Findlay swimmer knew that Jeff was the best freestyler in the 400 IM I'm sure but neither was doing much to gain on John, they were busy looking at each other, the first length ended with John maintaining his lead. The second Findlay swimmer now was going to be fourth at best he was off the pace of the other three swimmers. Paul was getting hoarse as John did a flip turn at the midpoint still a half body length ahead of the Findlay swimmer. It appeared that John's shoulder was starting to bother him as he started using a strong- arm weak arm combination in his freestyle, instead of a normal equal strength stroke, giving up some speed, Jeff and the Findlay swimmer were now a half-body length behind John as they hit the last flip turn, John came out still in the lead and you could definitely see something was off as the other 2 swimmers' pace was faster than John's, but John hit the perfect flip turn to give himself more space for the last 25 yards of his career. At this point, the entire team was yelling at John every time he breathed. Jeff and the Findlay swimmer finally saw John and they seemed to find a way to start catching him as his stroke was really starting to catch John his lack of experience looked like he may give up the lead and then with only 5 yards, it looked like he found a gear to stay with the fast-approaching swimmers, and saw him breakout in a kick like he was a sprinter that seemed to offset the loss of one arm. We saw the end of the race coming with three swimmers almost aligned as one. John appeared to have been behind but took one less stroke and reached for the wall. Everyone in the entire natatorium looked at the scoreboard because we could not see who had actually won the race.

Then it flashed a 1 for lane 1, John had won the race with the Findlay swimmer. 08, behind and Jeff another .05. in third. The final Findlay swimmer was beaten by a swimmer from Davis and Elkins so with the results assured all took our eyes off the pool.

Paul and Joanna start screaming we won we won, and even Coach Edwards was jumping up and down. We had a lead of 59 points and no matter what Findlay did in the relay, we had won the title.

Then our eyes went back to the pool, we noticed that John was at the end of the pool still hitting the end time after time, like he still thought he was swimming. We all realized something was seriously wrong. Trainers from several teams and I ran to the pool, when we got there, we could see John was definitely out of it, we were able to stop his arms from repeating the freestyle stroke. The trainers got John out and immediately started doing mouth-to-mouth as it appeared John had stopped breathing. They continued to do this as the ambulance crew on standby came running in with a complete crash kit. John's heart was no longer beating, and they had to shock him twice and finally his heart started back up again, but he was still not breathing on his own, so they hooked him up so they could get oxygen flow to John.

I looked up at the stands and could see John's mother collapsing in the arms of his father. She was sobbing so loud that with the silence elsewhere we all could hear it.

The ambulance crew got John stable, we all were sobbing as we knew this was not going to be a good ending, they rushed him to the nearest hospital.

Joanna ran with the ambulance crew, and she went with John to the hospital. We could see John's parents rushing to follow the ambulance to the hospital.

The announcer for the meet said that we wish our best to John Peters and announced he had just set the conference record in the 400 IM. I looked and he was now top ten of the country based on times. While they announced it nobody really cared, all we could see was swimmers crying from every team at the pool.

Ten minutes later, the announcer stated we will start the meet again in 10 minutes. The place was eerie dead silent. The relay race was swum, and nobody cheered, it was like the entire place had gone dead. The last relays were swum and while you heard some cheering it was so muted that it sounded like a hollow chamber with a couple people yelling, just like an airport after midnight.

With the swimming completed awards were to be announced. Paul Cunningham was announced as outstanding swimmer, and AB was handed our very first team title. John was announced as most improved swimmer in the conference for his all-conference win. Nobody cheered the awards; it was like the energy had left the building. Coach Edwards was announced as 'Coach of the Year', his first.

The team dressed quickly, got in the vans and went to the hospital. Nobody could say anything, and Paul had his head in his hands, sobbing so hard that the entire van felt for him. I agreed to stay with the seniors and Jeff Kissinger at the hospital, the rest of the team with Coach Edwards was leaving for AB, as we had lost our hotel earlier in the day.

When we got to the hospital, Joanna was shaking her head, this is not good, and she ran to Paul both of them crying again. We stayed as long as the hospital would allow, they helped us out and set-up some rooms for our swimmer stay somewhere overnight.

At 7 PM, Joanna and Paul were given a quiet area to call Julia. That was the last that we ever saw John again. John never recovered from his injuries, and we were told the next afternoon, that John had succumbed to his brain aneurism. The 10 of us left, simply cried for what seemed to be an hour. Julia was with John, somehow, she had made it to the hospital in the middle of the night.

His parents called his sister Angela sometime during the evening, she was at the airport when she got the news that John had passed away. I was told the airline assisted her and drove with her back to College Park.

The few of us at the hospital were given rooms in a local motel that had heard of the events and donated us three rooms for the night. All but Paul and Joanna went back the next morning to AB, I don't think a word was spoken except for Brad who had done his podcast for the school. We were all heartbroken. Paul and Joanna sat together as we dropped them off at the hospital, they had a lot of traveling to do over the next week.

The Aftermath

Saturday 7 PM:

J oanna called her friends from sorority at AB, Michelle Span, and Linda Crew, to get them to drive over to Julia and Joanna's apartment. Michelle answered the phone and after the request from Joanna, she asked what was up. I have horrible news for Julia, and she needs to get to Canton as soon as possible. Can you or Linda be with her and drive with her to Canton. Once you get with Julia, I will call you again. Ok Joanna, on my way, and both Linda and I can get to Canton if we need to and come back Monday.

7:20, Joanna and Julia's apartment. Hi Michelle and Linda, what's up. We were asked by Joanna to come over and be with you, she is calling in a couple of minutes.

Joanna proceeded to call at 7:25, PM. Julia, please answer the phone. Good evening what's up Joanna, are the guys on the way back. Julia, I have some horrendous news regarding John, and need you to listen and be ready to come to Canton. Julia was hysterically crying, what's wrong with John.

Julia honey, John had the greatest swim I have ever watched as a swimmer and won the conference title tonight. When we went to see him, all we could see is John was very white and looked totally out of it. The trainers immediately started CPR, and we got his heart fully started again, he is having a really hard time breathing. He is at the emergency room, and we expect surgery a little later tonight, it appears he may have had a brain aneurism, on the last length of freestyle.

Julia was hysterically crying and asked, how bad is it, Joanna? Joanna only could say you need to come to Canton as soon as possible, I don't know how to tell you, but he is in a very bad way. You need to come here before it is too late. John's parents are at the hospital, and it is very bad. I will text Michelle the address of Aultman Hospital and get here as soon as possible.

Julia, Michelle, and Linda were ready to go in Linda's car by 7:50, PM, and got to the hospital in Canton, just about 2: AM Sunday.

Julia ran to the hospital emergency room and asked for John Peters. The nurse said John Peters is here, and his parents are with him now. Are you a relative, because he is being sent to Intensive Care Unit? Julia started crying I am his fiancé; I need to see him. The nurse said since you are not related, I can't send you back to see him. The only other person with him is the assistant coach from AB. Just then, Sharon Peters came out hearing the commotion. Sharon just hugged Julia and said to her the John you know may be gone. What do you mean may be gone!

Julia, we are testing John for brainwave activity right now, John may already be pretty much brain dead. Julia crying excessively, where is he, I need to see him.

Sharon held her hand, and said he looks ok, but he has not responded to anything we are doing.

Julia ran to John's bed, she held his hand and it was still warm. Sharon, he feels warm to me, yes, he is breathing with the respirator and his heart is beating. We are awaiting the results to see how much damage there was to the rest of the brain.

At 3; AM, the EEG came in and the doctor monitoring, said I am sorry to tell you the John you know has already left us, no conscious thought, nothing going on except the section of the brain that is responsible for his heart. No hope of a recovery damage throughout was viewed.

With the pronouncement Julia started sobbing, damn it I knew John should have quit last year.

Later Sunday:

This is Brad Fox; I am coming to you via the Alderson Broadus Podcast. Today I come to you with great and horrendous news. As a diver on the AB swim team, I wanted to let you know that for the first time in our school's history we are the champions of the combined conference in swimming. Our male swimmers and divers have defeated Findlay by 9 points for the championships. Several swimmers including our beloved captain Paul Cunningham will be competing in the national division 2 championships in Indianapolis next month. Your reporter just barely qualified in the one-meter dive, so we will continue this podcast through the rest of the season.

While many of the swimmers will be going to the nationals, one conference champion who qualified for nationals in his final race will not be coming with us.

At the end of the 400 IM, John Peters, my friend, completed the most courageous swim I have ever viewed, from outside of the top 24 ratings most of the year, he won the conference championship, which gave us enough points with our own Jeff Kissinger third-place finish also, that we won the championship even though our relay team had been disqualified earlier in the day.

John Peters apparently had a brain aneurysm on the last length of the 400 IM. We just got back from the hospital where his parents and fiancé, fellow AB student Julia Ferrara, were together for the first time. The paramedics were able to get John's heart pumping after the race thanks to the heroic efforts of several team trainers. At the hospital in Canton, it was discovered that after they ran an EEG it showed very little brain activity. John had lost most brain function and while his heart was functioning with little support, he was breathing only due to the respirator he was on. Crying on air but this is my friend.

At 12:15 this afternoon, it was decided between his parents and fiancé, that they would not continue the treatment as John had no hope of recovery. At 12:30 they turned off the respirator, and while it took nearly 15 minutes for his heart to stop, we noticed that he appeared to mouth the words" I Love you Julia", as she held his hand and his lifeless body. By 1 PM, this afternoon, our friend John Peters left this world, Assistant coach Bruce and some team members are nearby at the hospital parking lot with our team trophy all but one of our team will return tonight.

We will be starting a fundraiser for John and Julia, so we can help pay the costs of flying John's body back to Baltimore. He will be buried as soon as possible, with his Jewish tradition. Funeral services are scheduled for Tuesday afternoon in Baltimore, MD. His grandfather will be performing the service. We are trying to help defer the costs that are estimated to be 25,000. Joanna and Paul will be driving to Baltimore along with Julia.

The service will be available for students at the gym, we are working to get this streamed to the gym. Please contribute whatever you can to help the family defer the costs of the funeral.

I would like to continue this podcast, but I need a minute, as John was a friend of mine. I'm sorry but I need time to cry, I will miss him and his friendship, when I announced I was gay John put his arm around me and simply said to me, does this mean you won't hug me anymore. We laughed, and he said because Julia may be jealous.

So, for this podcast, Brad Fox, signing off, John Peters, I will miss you.

Tuesday Noon:

Baltimore, MD – Pikesville Tuesday afternoon.

This is a service to mourn the passing of my grandson, John Peters, for those joining from Phillipi, WV, my name is Rabbi Goldbaum, and this service will be held as a Jewish ceremony. The one thing that his mother Sharon asked for was to have the following prayer read in Hebrew, as John was an adult in our religion.

Sharon, then came to the bema, and said the following. Today, we mourn my son John, he was a great child very independent, and was ready to take his place in life only to have this sudden death. He was taken from us way too young, and 7 months before he would have become a father for the first time.

for those that don't know Hebrew we have an English version of this prayer ready for you that makes it possible.

Yisgadal v'yiskadash sh'mei rabbaw (Amen)	May His great Name grow exalted and sanctified (Amen.)
B'allmaw dee v'raw chir'usei v'yamlich malchusei,b'chayeichon, uv'yomeichon,	in the world that He created as He willed. May He give reign to His kingship in your lifetimes and in your days,
uv'chayei d'chol beis yisroel, ba'agawlaw u'vizman kawriv, v'imru: Amen.	and in the lifetimes of the entire Family of Israel, swiftly and soon. Now respond:
(Cong: Amen. Y'hei sh'mei rabbaw m'vawrach l'allam u'l'allmei allmayaw)	Amen. (Cong Amen. May His great Name be blessed forever and ever.)
Y'hei sh'mei rabbaw m'vawrach l'allam u'l'allmei allmayaw.	May His great Name be blessed forever and ever.
Yis'bawrach, v'yishtabach, v'yispaw'ar, v'yisromam, v'yis'nasei,	Blessed, praised, glorified, exalted, extolled,
v'yis'hadar, v'yis'aleh, v'yis'halawl sh'mei d'kudshaw b'rich hu	mighty, upraised, and lauded be the Name of the Holy One, Blessed is
(Cong. b'rich hu). L'aylaw min kol birchawsaw v'shirawsaw,	He (Cong. Blessed is He) beyond any blessing and song,
tush'b'chawsaw v'nechemawsaw, da'ami'rawn b'all'maw, v'imru: Amein	praise and consolation that are uttered in the world. Now respond:
Y'hei shlawmaw rabbaw min sh'mayaw,v'chayim	Amen. May there be abundant peace from Heaven, and life
awleinu v'al kol yisroel, v'imru: Amein Oseh shawlom bim'ro'mawv, hu	upon us and upon all Israel. Now respond: Amen.
ya'aseh shawlom, awleinu v'al kol yisroel v'imru: Amein	He Who makes peace in His heights, may He make peace, upon us and upon all Israel. Now respond: Amen.

Rabbi Goldbaum went on to introduce John's family and then introduced Paul Cunningham and Joanna as his true best friends. Paul, please do not feel guilty about John's death, he loved swimming and you were his best friend. Joanna, please continue to be the strength behind the scenes as John stated to the family. I see you two holding hands, so I guess you are also a couple besides John's friends. I want to recognize Angela Peters she wants to be the first to talk today.

Good afternoon, I am here to talk about my big brother, I am going to miss him like crazy. John was known to most of you from AB as a swimmer, but he was the greatest big brother one could have. I am going to miss him every minute of the day, whenever I needed to talk, he was here for me, I know that I would not be ready to become a doctor without him. You know him as a swimmer, but he was a great person, a fantastic student once he met his Julia, and fiercely independent. I would like to say more today, but I can only relate how he treated me, and it was always with respect, even when I had manipulated him in to dating one girl his senior year of high school. He forgave me and all the others that had abandoned him so many times in his life.

Rabbi Goldbaum, then stood back in the bema again. It is seldom that I have a Roman Catholic speak within our synagogue except for Thanksgiving joint services, I call on John's fiancé Julia to come to the bema.

Julia, wearing black dress and vale, came to the bema. For those here with us this afternoon, we say farewell to John Peters, my true love. John will always be my love, I saw him at school and instantly fell in love with him, with his hazel eyes, funny humor, and zest for life, we fell madly in love and were very seldom separated the last 2 years. John is my great love, and we were to be married in about 3 months, and about 5 months later we would have been parents together. I know he would have been a great dad; I just look at the example his parents have been, and I know he would have been a father with love and pride and no matter what religion our child would have been, we would have loved and carried on our family traditions.

At that point Rabbi Goldbaum came over and hugged Julia. He then announced, a private burial will be held shortly (Moses Montefiore Woodmoor Hebrew Cemetery, driving instructions for the family and a few friends will be provided.) To my grandson, you chose wisely, and I will miss you, no parent should have to bury their child especially both parents and grandparents.

With that the service was concluded. The family then proceeded to leave the sanctuary and the service was concluded to AB feed. Julia, Paul, and Joanna were the second car behind the Hearst and with hands held went to the site of the burial. When they all arrived, the body was lowered into the ground, per tradition with only the close family and the three close friends John Peters was buried. Even James had come to the burial, I wish I had been closer to you big brother.

The Sports Banquet

This is Paul Cunningham, I am captain of the AB, (Alderson Broadus), swim team and wanted to finish John's journal of his time as a swimmer at AB. Julia found the journal John was keeping, and we wanted his family to see it completed. Tonight, was the sports banquet, for all the teams and the awards to include best athlete, academic athlete, and other awards and announcements. Coach Edwards was there to accept the award for the Coach of the year, funny because the guy that gave him the victory, was probably not even supposed to be at the conference meet. Had James Arnett, not been injured, I am sure that John would not even made the travelling squad. I am getting ahead of myself, but I wanted to make sure that this evening was posted as the final chapter because it was a weird night tonight.

The master of ceremonies was Frank Pompano, and the evening events were meals, then a speech by Mary Lou Retton, as the keynote speaker, and then the awards, (Coach of the year, student athlete, and then Athlete of the year). I had been told earlier this week that this year was going to be mostly an all-swimming event, and that I was athlete of the year for winning 2 individual events at conference, the 100 free and 100, fly, but again I am going off topic. I asked that we change the order so that student athlete would be last, as I knew John with his academic efforts the last 2 plus years with Julia, should have won this award. I am telling you this because we had something planned for the event and it went way crazy.

Mary Lou Retton talked about her Olympic experience and what it had taken to leave West Virginia to exceed in her sport. Typical dinner motivational talk that lasted about almost 45 minutes.

Coach Edwards then accepted his award as coach of the year, his award was presented by another coach, Basketball coach Kirk Lancini, described how they had recruited Coach Edwards from being an assistant with a Big Ten school and promised him a great life in a small town. Coach Edwards now is in his eighth year at AB this was the first conference tournament win, and our first swimming championship in fifty years, when we were in the old WVIAC. The New Mountain East Conference does not have a real core of teams, so we won the Great Midwest Athletic Conference and Mountain East Conference combined event, same city as Football Hall of Fame, Canton, Ohio.

Coach's speech talks about the efforts of our team and managing expectations. The speech was about 15 minutes how when he got here, he only had 7 swimmers his first year and now he had a large team of 20. Not a single word about the magical swim by John

My award came next, with my parents in attendance I accepted the award from AD Frank Pompano, first swimmer ever to win this award. I guess winning 2 events at conference and finishing 8th in the Nation in the 100 fly impressed a lot of people that give the awards out. My speech centered on my 4 years and the team and personal accomplishments. It was odd that Coach Edwards did not present the award, maybe because he had announced this morning that he had accepted the coaching position at East Carolina University, just shows that he was already past this little school and town we were just a steppingstone to his career. I don't think they have announced his replacement, but his puppies will be nervous as to who will be the next head coach and if they will keep scholarships, but I am off the subject. I hope Coach Bruce will get the head coaching job, but then again, he says he wants to start somewhere new, away from the awful events.

My speech also talked about growing up in Pittsburgh, and then falling in love with the small town in Philippi. My parents then came up for pictures. I was thrilled and was glad that soon I would accept a position with Amazon. My girlfriend Joanna Harrison felt uncomfortable being in the pictures, but it was great for her to be at the banquet. She is very beautiful, I guess she wanted me to be in the spotlight and not her.

Then came the Award for Academic Athlete and we all knew something was up when it was announced that the award this year will be awarded to 2 individuals. Annette Frankel, a point guard on the women's basketball team, was announced as one of the 2 participants, and she was allowed to present her speech and let everyone know she was soon going to Graduate school at Marshall University. Her speech talked about the opportunity that the school had provided her and the school's opportunities for an African American female student.

Frank then asked Julia to come up to the podium. I knew at that point, John should have won except that he did not technically finish his senior year of school, his sudden demise ended that hope.

So, I am going to create the scene as best as I can as we all were both emotional and busy.

Frank as I said earlier asked Julia to come up to the podium, she was expecting something in honor of John as they had just got engaged on just before Valentine's Day. Julia, thank you for accepting our invitation for being with us tonight, John technically had the highest GPA for a 4-year athlete by a slim margin but because he would not have graduated, he normally would not have qualified for the award, so AB has awarded John a BS degree in Business Magna Cum Laude. The degree is being mailed to his parents in Baltimore, as will a copy of the plaque you are about to receive.

Julia, before we present you with this plaque, I wanted to let you know that the University has been doing some work on your behalf. The ring that John had made only 2 payments out of 60 is considered paid in full by Kay Jewelers. I am here to provide you with that ring tonight. The local outlet asked what to do in this case with corporate, the school stepped in with the local store and we were able to get this present for you.

Kay has stated that they will forgive any additional payments for the ring, and it is now yours to keep. Now for the presentation of the plaque, Julia, please accept the Academic Athlete Award for this year, John Peters 3.54, not bad considering he had a 2.5+ his first semester of his Freshman Year. Pictures were taken, with Annette and Julia, plus Frank, I will bet it will be in the local papers shortly.

Julia's speech was incredible given that she was not told she had to give one or what the award John was getting.

I will paraphrase, so thanks you so much for John's award and letting me keep the ring, Frank. I can't believe the boy I met almost 4 years ago would go from a C student his first semester to 4.0's the last two years. I know he had a hard time staying swimming especially after Coach Edwards pulled his scholarship for his senior year and he had to take on student loans and assistance from his parents to complete his senior year. I only wish that John was here to accept the award, his miracle swim not only were the critical points for the team to win the conference, but he showed you could be in a demanding sport and do well academically and socially. While I am here, I wanted to let everyone here today know that John and I were going to get married in 2 months and I am expecting our child late this year. Prior to the conference meet, I found out I was pregnant with his son. Excuse me for a moment, I am sorry for the tears, but I loved John and he will never get to know his son. For those wondering about how John and I coming from really different worlds could meet and fall in love, I think I owe it to his mother who taught this son to respect everyone, hard to believe I am a Sicilian Roman Catholic and his is Jewish, but we fell in deep love and our love seemed to make him concentrate on his career after school, so grades became very important.

Frank, then came over and hugged a crying, Julia. Frank announces, Julia, not only is Kay Jewelers doing your ring, but that have agreed to fund a $20,000, per year scholarship for a swimmer each year. The name of the scholarship is the John Peters Memorial scholarship.

So, everyone expected that to be the end of the night, and then Frank stated as many of you know we are planning on a new Natatorium. The team came into the room with a banner that stated John Peters Natatorium, One Last Swim. Even Coach Edwards puppies were holding the pennant. The entire room erupts in clapping, Julia is in tears, and you could hear John's parents sobbing from the line we had to them.

The Athletic Director, says Coach Edwards you have the request what do you say regarding naming the new Natatorium.

Coach Edwards response to this request was not what we expected. Everyone in attendance thought Coach Edwards would agree. All he said was Frank, while I know John lost his life while finishing his race for us, he seriously was not that great of an athlete for his four years, I can't in good faith honor the new facility with the name of an athlete that simply won one event in our conference championship. I know without that swim we may have not won the conference but really one swim does not warrant a new facility with his name on it.

The place erupted in boos, and truthfully the team wanted to punch our coach out. Julia interceded and said to the crowd, John was way to humble for this award, and coach we all knew what you thought of John for four years, good luck in your next job. I only wish that John was here to accept the award, and he died for that trophy in the corner, and he will never know his son as a result. Thank you to the swim team for thinking of honoring John this way.

Frank then abruptly ended the awards banquet; it was an insane scene with the banner and people arguing with coach right after he won the award. I suspect he will get some press but not the press he wanted.

That is the final story for John's Journal. I only hope I was able to convey the night properly.

I knew John could have quit the team the last year, and a few of us upper classmen asked him to stay despite coach taking away his scholarship money. I wish now that we didn't do it, was the trophy worth it. I miss my friend, and I feel guilty because I was the leader to keep him here, I knew a healthy John would do great, which he did, I would rather have lost the championship and had my friend and go to his wedding. I should not have to bury my 22-year-old friend with everything to look forward to.

Opening Ceremony

The Natatorium Opening Ceremony:

This is Julia Ferrara, it is now slightly over three years since the great and awful event that cost John his life. I saw this journal John had done and decided that this story needed to be finalized: He wanted our children to know what drove him to compete and so they would have a record of what he had done and why he had done it. Well, I am completing this for our son, who I named John Peters Ferrara. I know in his faith he could not be named after a living person and since he was no longer alive, I wanted my true love to always be a reminder in his name. I found out I was pregnant with Little John about 2 weeks before the funeral and right before the conference meet. I had been feeling awful and found out I was pregnant with Little John who was born roughly 7 months later. I know that it has been over three years since John has passed but not a day goes by that I don't think about how our life would have been as a married couple. I chose not to go to DC for Law School, instead I am starting this Fall at West Virginia University Law School in Morgantown. I will be teaching also, so I get childcare through the University money for us to live and Little John will be able to see his grandparents who said they will come by and teach to Little John about his father and be a part of our lives. My parents are only about 90 minutes away, I am sure some weekends we will go to see them. I have not even thought about dating, and friends say it is time for me to do so, but I have John with me every day through our son.

After John made the miracle swim, that won AB the title, and ultimately ended his life, I know the swim team wanted to name the new natatorium as the John Peters Natatorium. The banner they showed at the Athletic awards banquet was kept in the old pool locker room for the last three years and now that we are opening the new pool it will be retired. While coach Edwards, used the championship to leave AB and go to East Carolina as the head coach, he still had poisoned the naming committee so we did not get "The John Peters Natatorium", but the name that this site will be known by and revealed today how the community really felt about our miracle title.

So here is what happened earlier today, with Little John and me in attendance, Frank Pompano as the chief of the Alumni Association, as master of ceremony.

Good afternoon, I am Frank Pompano, today we are proud to announce a partnership between our town and our college to house a unified Natatorium. It has been five years in planning and construction, and we are here today to finally open this facility. The pool will be a state of the art 8-lane 25-meter pool with separate diving tank with 1, 3- meter boards and a 5-meter platform. This pool can be converted to 25-yards for college swim meets, with that adjustable bulkhead. Alderson Broadus will own about 50% of the time and will house both the Men's and Women's practice facilities, weight rooms, and with a large score board we hope to attract regional meets for swimmers from PA, Ohio, and WV and western VA. We also are hoping to be the home of the conference championships for the Mountain East and whatever combination of other conferences will be a part of the meet. This was funded with funds from the community, the college, Federal matching funds and a $1 million grant from the West Virginia Legislature. We also have a party area, and we will start hosting events, like conferences for companies and fun things like birthday parties. We will be hiring a company over the next few weeks to market the space to others for events.

While a lot of us would like to have a different name for the facility, I call on Julia and her son to come to the front of the crowd and be with me to cut the ribbon. With many of the swimmers and recent alumni from AB behind us, Little John and I came to the front of the crowd.

The sound of the clapping and standing ovation was really too much for both of us. Little John was crying from the noise, and I was in tears in the memory of the man that John had become: His best friend and now fiancé Joanna were here to come back.

Paul was asked to say a few words right before we did the ribbon cutting and he simply said. Today we open the new natatorium that a lot of us here would have liked to have been swimming in here when we attended. We are also here to provide closure to our friend John Peters, who we buried 3 days after our conference victory. John, you will always be in our hearts, and we look forward to seeing your son John grow up.

I am going to introduce our lead diver at the time, Brad Fox who is here with his partner James for the opening of this event.

Good morning, everyone, mayor, and state officials and friends and family. John Peters was a great friend of mine, and while others shied away from me because I was a diver, my friend John Peters was always encouraging the divers to do well. I really think he could have done our dives almost as well as Colt over there, but again John was our friend and was always encouraging. I want to say hello to Little John, and let you know that your father was a really great person and I know you won't remember this day, we are recording it so your mother can explain to you why your dad is not with us anymore. I miss my friend John and wish he was here today. Oh well, I dedicate this new pool and facility to our friend and fellow swimmer.

I simply said to the community enjoy this facility and let you all know we love our community, and this is a great place to be. A White Oak is being planted on the other side of the parking lot to represent John's Maryland roots. With tears in my eyes, I look up to the sky and say I wish you were here to see it.

Julia and Little John please cut the ribbon together on the new facility and with that statement, we opened the new facility with the name nobody really wanted.

"Welcome to One Last Swim Natatorium"

I want to thank everyone who has helped Little John and I get through the last three years. Little John starts water babies swim lessons next week. I think he may be the only one with 18 young men and numerous young ladies helping him learn to swim. He will never swim one event though. Everyone please celebrate and look at the pictures of John that will be in the front hallway.

With that I turned and saw John's parents and his sister Angela in the background, they were crying as they saw Little John and said he is the spitting image. Angela came over to me, hugged me, and said I know John chose wisely, I will stay in both of your lives.

She picked up Little John in her arms, she hugged him very tightly. I am your Aunt Angela, and I will always be in your life. My younger brother James should have been here, but he is still at Lehigh and is away at a baseball game.

Julia if you need any medical information, let me know, I am about to complete my final year of medical school.

The ceremony was ended and a few of the team stayed around to see us. I simply wish I had John here. I still miss him every morning.

www.ingramcontent.com/pod-product-compliance
Lightning Source LLC
Chambersburg PA
CBHW051146120626
46547CB00012B/957